THE RELEVANCE OF APOCALYPTIC

THE RELEVANCE
OF APOCALYPTIC

A Study of Jewish and Christian
Apocalypses from Daniel
to the Revelation

by

H. H. ROWLEY

the Attic Press, Inc.
GREENWOOD, S. C.

First published 1944
Second edition 1947
Reprinted 1950, 1952, 1955, and 1960
New and Revised edition 1963
Reprinted 1980

Library of Congress catalog card number: 64-12221
ISBN: 0-87921-061-3

TO THE REVEREND PROFESSOR
THEODORE H. ROBINSON
LITT.D., D.D., D.TH.

MY FORMER CHIEF
AND ENDURING FRIEND
THIS VOLUME IS INSCRIBED
IN GRATEFUL RECOGNITION OF
ALL I OWE HIM

Contents

vi

Notes

Preface

THE FOUR chapters of this book consist of four lectures delivered at the Vacation Term for Biblical Study held at St. Hilda's College, Oxford, in the summer of 1942. They are published substantially as delivered, save that some sections of the third lecture had to be omitted for lack of time, and in the other lectures a measure of compression was dictated by the same necessity. I am conscious of the inadequacy of the survey of the literature, but I know of no way to combine adequacy with the necessary brevity, and to expand now to the point of adequacy would be to write a large work, which would bear scant resemblance to the lectures delivered. They are published in the hope that they may be of service to a wider circle of readers in days when apocalyptic commands much interest.

In times of crisis there is always a revival of interest in apocalyptic, and confident prophecies are made on the basis of some of the writings here treated. Two disciplines serve to expose the folly of this approach. The first is the study of the history of the interpretation of these works, with its dismal unfolding of the long series of false prophecies to which this approach has invariably led. The other is the study of the canonical writings of the apocalyptic order in relation to the non-canonical writings of the same order. In the present lectures this latter study is briefly undertaken. It should suffice to show that in the circles that produced these writings little importance was attached to those details on which the schemes of the interpreters are commonly built. For there is the greatest variety in the conception of the order of the expected events that should mark the end of the age. Sometimes there is attention to detail in order to point the first readers to the contemporary circumstances of their day, but at other times the details are formal and schematic, or designed to fill in the picture. Nor is it merely that the separate works differ from one another. Within a single work we continually find a variety of detail that has led to theories of composite authorship, instead of to the recognition that the author has no desire to pin himself down to details. In the Book of Revelation the triple series of woes, while successive in the vision, must almost certainly be interpreted as parallel, yet cannot possibly be parallel in detail. For the author wished rather to emphasize that he anticipated a time of great tribulation than to indicate the precise order and character of the elements of that tribulation.

It is when we realize this that we are able to appreciate the real worth of these writings. Instead of that meticulous attention to detail that has led astray successive generations of interpreters, we are able to concentrate on the broad features of the hope of these writers, and on the spiritual principles that underlay their work. We are able to realize that a truly prophetic purpose inspired them. For it was of the essence of Biblical prophecy to use prediction not primarily for the sake of unfolding the future, but for the bringing home of the message of God to the men who first received it. And the apocalyptists are able to speak to us just because they spoke primarily to their own contemporaries. Their purpose was essentially practical, to proclaim a great hope to men and to call them to a great loyalty and watchfulness. Instead, therefore, of casting aside these works in an age of tribulation that drives others with false presuppositions to them, we are able to find them speak a relevant word to us just because they spoke a relevant word to men in like days.

My indebtedness to others who have worked in the field of apocalyptic, and especially to R. H. Charles, who was by far the most energetic of British workers here, will be apparent throughout. I have not slavishly followed my predecessors, however, but have endeavoured to reach an independent judgement on all that is of importance for my argument. On other matters I have been content to indicate variety of view.

In the field of the New Testament, which is not my *Fach*, but which my subject compels me to enter, I must confess the diffidence with which I treat of disputed matters. Here, as elsewhere, I have not concealed the disagreements, but have referred the reader to the works of those who can offer him guidance which he may prefer to follow. I have kept the footnotes to a minimum, and so have but inadequately acknowledged my indebtedness there. In the Bibliography at the end of the volume I offer some amends, and include a large number of works to which little or no reference is made in the body of the work, but from which I have derived help. I am well aware of the scantiness of the Bibliography in so far as it concerns the Old Testament writings dealt with, and I have no doubt that many of my readers will observe a like inadequacy in so far as it concerns the New Testament. It is my hope that in the less familiar field of the non-canonical apocalypses it may be more useful, though it makes no claim to be more than selective here. To one or two works I have been unable to gain access, and my only knowledge of them is from reviews. I have included reference to them in the Bibliography in the hope that in happier days they may be accessible to readers who wish to pursue their examination of some of the matters dealt with.

H. H. ROWLEY

UNIVERSITY COLLEGE OF NORTH WALES,
BANGOR
March 1943

Preface to Second Edition

I HAVE TAKEN advantage of this new edition to make a number of corrections and additions, and to deal with some points raised by my reviewers. Most of the additional matter has gone into the footnotes, where it will not get in the way of the general reader. In one matter—the question of the date of Slavonic Enoch—I have modified the view taken in the

earlier edition, though I have not taken the logically consequent step of eliminating the section that deals with it from
the book. Otherwise I adhere to the positions of the first
edition.

H. H. ROWLEY

MANCHESTER UNIVERSITY
July 1946

Preface to Third Edition

SINCE THE second edition of this book was published there
has been much renewed attention to the works here dealt
with, due in no small measure to the finding of the Dead Sea
Scrolls. A section on the Qumran Scrolls has been added,
and I have tried to keep this on the scale of the rest of the
book. This has not been easy, as several thousands of books
and articles on the Scrolls have been issued, and it would be
easy to be drawn farther and farther into the maze of the
literature on this subject. A separate section on the Scrolls
has been added to the Bibliography, but again, to give a full
bibliography would destroy the balance of this work, and I
can only tender my apologies to all whose works I have not
included. The titles I have included are those of publications
I have actually drawn on in preparing this volume.

Naturally I have taken the opportunity to make some use
of recent publications in the other sections of my study, and
have added references to some older works of which I made
no use in preparing the original edition. Here, once more,
completeness has not been my aim, since that would change
the whole character of the book.

H. H. ROWLEY

MANCHESTER
October 1962

CHAPTER ONE

The Rise of Apocalyptic

THE APOCALYPTIC writings of Judaism and of the Christian Church have in modern times commanded much attention from scholars, and many books have been devoted to their study, but they are still far too little read outside the ranks of scholars. In the case of some of the non-canonical works, their relative inaccessibility is perhaps a sufficient excuse for this,[1] but in the case of the great apocalypses of the Old and New Testaments, Daniel and the Book of Revelation, no such excuses can hold. So far as Daniel is concerned, the stories of the first half of the book are well known, but too often merely as stories, and it is with some relief that many learn that modern scholarship has demonstrated several historical errors in the Book of Daniel, so that their refusal to find anything more than stories in these chapters appears to rest on something more respectable than mere scepticism. The visions of the second half of the book are found to be less entertaining, and are therefore ignored. So far as the Book of Revelation is concerned, a few passages are familiar and treasured, but merely as isolated gems, unrelated to the context of the whole, and the rest of the book is treated as something bizarre and alien to our outlook, a historical curiosity of interest for the understanding of the mentality of the early Church, but serving little other purpose in the Canon of the New Testament.

It is true that there are some who adopt a different attitude to these books. They rather elevate them to the highest place in the Bible, and devote to them a minute study beyond any they give to what most Christians regard as the more

[1] The S.P.C.K. has rendered invaluable service by publishing most of the texts in inexpensive translations in the series "Translations of Early Documents".

spiritual parts of the Bible. They believe that the events of our day, and of the future that lies before us, are irrevocably set forth in these books, so that they hold the key of the ages. It has always seemed to me curious that these "students of prophecy", as they are often called, are firmly persuaded that by the exercise of their ingenuity they can break the seal which is on these books, and lay bare their secrets. For on their view they are compelled to believe that God Himself decreed that the Book of Daniel should be sealed till the time of the end (Dan. xii. 9). The belief that they can break the seal is therefore a belief that they can defeat the purpose of God! The student of the history of interpretation is well aware that all down the Christian centuries the same approach has been known, and claims as confident as any of our day have had their falsity and futility as relentlessly demonstrated by events as their modern counterparts will be.[1]

One thing these two attitudes to the canonical apocalyptic books have in common. It is the tacit assumption that these books as wholes are spiritually negligible. The refusal to study them as wholes can never discover the profound and enduring spiritual principles on which they are based, while the obsession with the equation of the words of Scripture with the events of our day converts the books into intricate puzzles for the ingenious, instead of spiritual messages to harassed souls.

It is the thesis of these lectures that both attitudes are here wrong. The stories of Daniel are more than stories. They are divine messages, addressed indeed to the age in which they were composed, but addressed also to every age. The visions of Daniel and of the Book of Revelation merit attention not alone to the details of their form but also to the great spiritual principles which they everywhere assume. They are true with a deeper truth than historical or prophetical inerrancy. They are spiritually true, and if we miss that spiritual truth, however fully we may understand the ap-

[1] In my "Darius the Mede and the Four World Empires of the Book of Daniel", 1935 (reprinted 1959), I have reviewed the history of interpretation of certain parts of Daniel.

proach of modern scholarship to these books, or however eagerly we may impose upon them the pattern of the events of our day, we miss their treasures.

The roots of apocalyptic lie far behind the composition of the books which belong to this class.[1] They are certainly complex, and any attempt to analyse them is likely to give the appearance of over-simplification. Yet some analysis is necessary to the understanding of apocalyptic. For it is essentially the re-adaptation of the ideas and aspirations of earlier days to a new situation. When once it had come into being, indeed, it found imitators who copied it for its own sake, until it became the vogue in some circles. But it was created in an hour of desperate need, not in any self-conscious desire to set a fashion, but in eager desire to minister to the need.

That apocalyptic is the child of prophecy, yet diverse from prophecy, can hardly be disputed.[2] An earlier generation emphasized the predictive element in prophecy, and the relation between prophecy and apocalyptic, in which the predictive element is particularly prominent, appeared beyond question. In modern times the prophets have been seen rather in the background of their own age as preachers of righteousness and godliness, and the link with the apocalyptists has seemed less close. For the traditional view of the apocalyptists has seen in their works a message to ages other than their own, and even modern study has emphasized their moral and spiritual message far less than in the case of the prophets. Both the predictive element in prophecy and the moral and spiritual element in apocalyptic need to be emphasized.

There are, of course, certain obvious differences of form between the prophets and the apocalyptists. The prophetic books consist largely of brief oracles, sometimes set in a

[1] Cf. J. Bloch, "On the Apocalyptic in Judaism", 1952, p. 23: "There was no sudden transition whatever from prophecy to apocalyptic."
[2] On the rise of apocalyptic cf. O. Plöger, "Theokratie und Eschatologie", 1959, pp. 37 ff. T. F. Glasson ("Greek Influence in Jewish Eschatology", 1961) argues for much direct Greek influence on the apocalyptic and pseudepigraphical Jewish literature. On the relations between prophecy and apocalyptic cf. B. Vawter, in *Catholic Biblical Quarterly*, xxii, 1960, pp. 33 ff.

biographical or autobiographical framework, but often with no indication of the precise situation to which they were addressed, or the events that called them forth. The oracles themselves are usually in poetic form. The apocalyptic books are in prose, with occasional poetic snatches, and they are more continuous in their view of history. They review long periods of time, and are fond of dividing them into ages, each marked by its own spirit and character, and they are less concerned with a single situation and its immediate outcome. Moreover, apocalyptic commonly has an esoteric character. Its message is represented as something to be kept from general knowledge, and to be handed down in secret. Thus Daniel is told to shut up the vision (Dan. viii. 26), or it is said to be sealed till the time of the end (Dan. xii. 9). Similarly, Enoch declares his revelation to be not for his own generation, but for a far-off generation to come (1 En. i. 2); in the Slavonic Book of Enoch the writings are committed to the care of Michael until the last age (2 En. xxxiii. 10 f.); in the Ezra apocalypse the seer is told to write his visions in a book and put it in a secret place (2 Esdr. xii. 37).

Yet actually both prophets and apocalyptists were men who spoke to their own generation, and who spoke because they felt a divine urge within them. The form and content of their message varied from age to age, according to the circumstances and conditions of their day. But it was ever the conscious delivery to men of what was believed to be God's word to them. The pretence of a long secret transmission was an inevitable corollary of the pseudonymity of apocalyptic, which we shall consider below, and it is improbable that it deceived anyone, or was intended to.

When prophecy first comes prominently before us in the Old Testament, in the days of the founding of the monarchy, it is both political and religious. It seeks to revive the flame of political unity that the alien oppressor may be driven out, and it seeks also to kindle anew the flame of loyalty to the national God. It is not to be supposed that this was any exploiting of religion for political ends. It was rather the clear recognition that the distinctiveness of Israel's religion could be preserved only in political independence. That was true in that age, and often in other ages. Again and again in Israel's history we find this recognition, so that wherever we find a strong move for independence we find evidence of a revival or reformation of the national religion, and wherever we find evidence of religious revival and reform, with the exception of a single period, to which we shall return in a moment, we find also evidence of political revival.

Thus, when Gideon raised the standard of revolt against Midian, the first thing he did was to break down the local Baal altar, and call men afresh to exclusive loyalty to the national God (Judges vi. 25). In the days of the foundation of the monarchy, as has been said, the revolt against the Philistine domination had at its heart the prophetic passion for Yahweh. When the house of Ahab was overthrown the Rechabite zealots, as well as the prophets, supported the revolution (2 Kings x. 15 ff.), because the Tyrian alliance had not alone brought in a spirit that offended the free sentiment of Israel, but had also menaced the religious loyalty of Israel. When Hezekiah joined in the revolt against Assyria he would inevitably and necessarily throw off the marks of religious subordination which Ahaz had accepted (2 Kings xvi. 10 ff.), and it is therefore not surprising that we read of a religious reform which he carried through (2 Kings xviii. 4 ff.). Doubt is sometimes cast on this reform,[1] and it is rarely associated with his revolt against Assyria. Yet just as the acceptance of a foreign yoke involved religious consequences, so the throwing off of that yoke would carry religious corollaries, and would provide the occasion for a reform that might well go beyond the minimum the occasion required, and bring a larger revival and reform of the national religion.[2] Similarly, when Josiah carried through

[1] So J. Wellhausen, "Prolegomena to the History of Israel", Eng. trans., 1885, p. 25; B. Stade, "Geschichte des Volkes Israel", i, 1889, p. 607; T. K. Cheyne, "Encyclopaedia Biblica", ii, 1901, cols. 2058 f.; G. Hölscher, "Geschichte der israelitischen und jüdischen Religion", 1922, p. 99; A. Lods, "The Prophets and the Rise of Judaism", Eng. trans., 1937, pp. 115 ff.

[2] Cf. T. H. Robinson, "History of Israel", i, 1932, pp. 392 f. Cf. also H. H. Rowley, in *Bulletin of the John Rylands Library*, xliv, 1962–3, pp. 425 ff.

his great reform, though we have no account in the Old Testament of its political side, we know there must have been a political side.[1] Josiah could not have eliminated Assyrian religious practices so long as he accepted the Assyrian yoke. We know that at the time of his reform Assyria was weak, and had her hands full with the Babylonian revolt of Nabopolassar. A century earlier, when Merodach Baladan planned revolt, he sought to intrigue with Hezekiah to ensure a parallel rising in the west (2 Kings xx. 12 ff.), though in that age the Babylonian rising had been crushed before the western plans were ripe. What was more natural than that now the revolt of Nabopolassar in Babylon should be accompanied by a parallel rising in the west? It used to be thought that Josiah was pathetically loyal to his Assyrian overlord, and that when he went to Megiddo it was to oppose in the name of Assyria the hostile arms of Pharaoh Necho (2 Kings xxiii. 29). It is now known[2] that Egypt had been the ally of Assyria against the Babylonian and Median forces that brought about her downfall, so that Josiah was clearly at the time of his death the enemy of Assyria's ally,[3] though Assyria herself had by then disappeared as a state and empire. All probability points therefore to the time of his reform as the time of Josiah's revolt.

In view of this frequent association of political revival and religious awakening, it is not surprising that in the Maccabaean age the revolt against Antiochus Epiphanes should have begun in an act of religious protest, and should have had a religious character, so that when apocalyptic first

[1] Cf. H. H. Rowley, in "Studies in Old Testament Prophecy" (T. H. Robinson Festschrift), 1950, pp. 161 f.

[2] Since the publication of C. J. Gadd's "The Fall of Nineveh", 1923. The A.V. and R.V. translation of 2 Kings xxiii. 29 is therefore incorrect, and instead of reading "Pharaoh Necoh king of Egypt went up *against* the king of Assyria", it should read, "Pharaoh N. king of Egypt went up *to the help of* the king of Assyria". The ambiguous Hebrew preposition can have either meaning. R.S.V. "went up *to* the king of Assyria" does not bring the meaning out so clearly as it might.

[3] For the view that Josiah did not lead an army to oppose Pharaoh Necho, as stated in 2 Chron. xxxv. 20 ff., but was summoned to the presence of the Pharaoh and summarily executed, cf. Welch, "The Death of Josiah", in *Zeitschrift für die alttestamentliche Wissenschaft*, N.F., ii, 1925, pp. 255 ff.

comes prominently before us in the Book of Daniel it is associated with a movement which is both political and religious. We know that some who at first supported the revolt on religious grounds later withdrew their support, when they believed their religious goal had been reached, and suspected that religious loyalty was being exploited for other ends (1 Macc. vii. 13 ff.), but that only makes it the more clear that at first the rising was no less religious than political.

The one notable exception to all this is the period of Nehemiah and Ezra.[1] Here we read of a quickening of the national life, and a revival and reform of the national religion, completely unassociated with any revolt against the suzerain power, but rather under the aegis of that power. This is because the Persian Empire pursued a religious policy more enlightened than that of any other imperial power that figures in the Old Testament. When Cyrus conquered Babylon he acknowledged the Babylonian gods as his protectors, and he conciliated local sentiment by reversing the centralizing policy of Nabonidus that had so greatly offended his people, and returning to their own shrines the gods that Nabonidus had brought to Babylon.[2] Cyrus does not seem to have enforced the recognition of his own religion in Babylonia. Similarly, he is reported to have treated the religion of the Jews with respect (Ezra i. 2 ff.), while later monarchs of this empire are said to have sponsored the missions of Nehemiah (Neh. ii. 5 ff.) and Ezra (Ezra vii. 11 ff.). A

---

[1] It will be seen that I follow the view now commonly held, which places Nehemiah in the reign of Artaxerxes I and Ezra in that of Artaxerxes II. This view was first advanced by Van Hoonacker, "Néhémie et Esdras", in *Le Muséon*, ix, 1890, pp. 151 ff., 317 ff., 389 ff., "Néhémie en l'an 20 d'Artaxerxès I; Esdras en l'an 7 d'Artaxerxès II", 1892, and in subsequent articles in *Revue Biblique*, x, 1901, pp. 5 ff., 175 ff., xxxii, 1923, pp. 481 ff., xxxiii, 1924, pp. 35 ff. It was followed by Batten, "Critical and Exegetical Commentary on Ezra and Nehemiah", 1913, pp. 28 ff., Touzard in *Revue Biblique*, xxiv (N.S. xii), 1915, pp. 59 ff., and by many later writers. Cf. H. H. Rowley, "The Servant of the Lord", 1952, pp. 129 ff., and *Bulletin of the John Rylands Library*, xxvii, 1954–5, pp. 550 ff. (reprinted with modifications in "Men of God: Studies in Old Testament History and Prophecy", 1963, pp. 229 ff.).

[2] See Cyrus Cylinder, lines 26 f., 32 ff. (R. W. Rogers, "Cuneiform Parallels to the Old Testament", 1912, pp. 382 f.).

still extant papyrus from Elephantine, dating from towards the end of the fifth century B.C., informs us that the Persian authorities enjoined on the Jewish colony there the observance of the feast of unleavened bread.[1] While, therefore, it need not be doubted that Persian rule had its irksome side, as all alien rule must have, its religious toleration made possible religious reorganization without the necessity for a hopeless attempt at political revolt.

Of the significance of this for Israel and for the world little note is commonly taken. For this was the formative period of Judaism, when the writings of the prophets were collected and edited, and when the lessons of the long struggle with indigenous Baalism and imported idolatry were learned, when the forms of religion were fixed and ordered to make them the vehicle of loyalty to God, and when there grew up that deep veneration for the law that was the mark of Judaism. For all this, Persian religious toleration offered an opportunity that was lacking under pre-exilic masters.

It may be replied to what has been said that the eighth- and seventh-century prophets were consistently against revolt from Assyria, and consistently in favour of religious revival and reform. The close association of the bid for independence and the reform of religion in the days of Hezekiah and Josiah, therefore, may seem less obvious than has been suggested above. For how can the prophets have at once favoured reform and opposed revolt if these are the obverse and reverse of a single policy? It must be remembered that there were many prophets besides the canonical prophets who strenuously opposed the latter in the name of Yahweh, and whose policy was usually favoured by the court. Like the early prophets, they were devotees of the national God and ardent

[1] See A. E. Cowley, "Aramaic Papyri of the Fifth Century B.C.", 1923, pp. 62 f.; H. H. Rowley, in "Documents from Old Testament Times", ed. by D. W. Thomas, 1958, pp. 258 ff. This papyrus is frequently referred to as the Passover Papyrus. While, however, it is possible that it originally ordered the observance of the Passover, in its present broken state the word *Passover* does not appear, but a reference to leaven has survived. Cf. A. Vincent, "La religion des Judéo-Araméens d'Eléphantine", 1937, pp. 234 ff. The word *Passover* may, however, stand on an ostrakon from Elephantine, where the context is too broken to allow any certainty of the meaning. Cf. Vincent, ibid., pp. 265 ff.

lovers of political independence, eager to throw off every foreign yoke, both political and religious. The great canonical prophets of the eighth and seventh centuries were certainly interested in religious reform. But they were less interested in those elements of reform which symbolized the repudiation of foreign dominion than in other elements. They declared that the essence of religion lay less in its forms than in its spirit, and that it was vital to understand the character and will of Yahweh, and to reflect that character and will in the life of the nation. To them it was like putting the cart before the horse to rebel or make a bid for independence, without first getting right with God. And getting right with God was more than a matter of the cultus. It was a matter of revitalizing the life of the people by the abolition of injustice and oppression, and by the abstention from that debauchery and drunkenness which characterized so much of the religion of the day. None of this would involve the nation in trouble with the suzerain power, and with this the prophets would have begun. Without it no revolt could succeed; with it none would be necessary. For the interests of the nation could safely be left with God, when His will was truly honoured.

From this it will appear that while throughout prophecy was both political and religious, there was development in the method it pursued. In its earlier stages it promoted revolt against foreign dominion and internal revolution; in its later stages it provided two sharply divided schools, each of which accused the other of being false prophets. The one continued to promote military revolt, while the other steadily opposed it.

When we come to the Maccabaean age we find that the apocalyptist who wrote the Book of Daniel pilloried the oppressing king and supported the cause of the revolters. In this he might seem to be the heir of that strain in prophecy which opposed the canonical prophets. This, however, is much less than fair to him. For in his day the practices of Judaism were proscribed, and refusal to renounce its faith was itself a political offence. Moreover, while his sympathies were doubtless on the side of the revolters, he was far less interested in the military side of the revolt than in the religious loyalty in which it began. All his stories inculcate passionate loyalty at any cost, and he nowhere contemplates a victory that should be won by the strong right arm of the rebels, but only a supernatural divine intervention. It is fortitude under persecution that he encourages rather than revolt against oppression, and in this he is the forerunner of other apocalyptists. The great New Testament Apocalypse, like the Book of Daniel, writes of war being made on the saints. They but suffer, borne up by the hope of the deliverance which shall be effected for them. There is, therefore, nothing comparable here to the policies advocated by the false prophets of earlier days. Here were situations quite different from those viewed by pre-exilic prophets, and since these writers were men in the true prophetic succession, they mediated God's word to the men of their day, instead of echoing the message given to earlier generations.

In the Maccabaean age men were suffering because they refused to disobey what they and the author of Daniel believed to be the law of God. It was because of their very loyalty that they were being martyred, and the revolt began in the uprising of persecuted saints. The position was therefore wholly different from that of the great pre-exilic prophets. They were fundamentally interested in the moral and spiritual conditions of their times, and unsparingly condemned the things they saw as an offence to God and a denial of His will, calling down the punishment of God upon Israel. Their conviction that intrigue with Egypt and revolt against the Mesopotamian powers was futile did not spring from any love of the imperial overlords, but from the certainty that men who were blind to the will of God in the internal policies of their land could not be guided by that will in their foreign policies. And without that guidance there could only be disaster. But in the Maccabaean days the men who were suffering were those who strove to keep themselves pure in the eyes of God, and who were most deeply loyal to the spirit of that Judaism which had learned the prophetic lessons.

Hence, when the author of Daniel promised deliverance for the sufferers and disaster for the alien oppressors he was not placing himself outside the succession of the great prophets, but basing his different message upon principles which were fundamentally the same. To him, as to them, loyalty to God was all that really mattered, but his message was addressed to the loyal, whereas the great pre-exilic prophets were addressing those whom they condemned as disloyal.

Nor should we forget, indeed, that the pre-exilic prophets recognized the presence of a loyal element within the nation, and uttered words of hope for this Remnant, which held the seed of promise for the future. It was to survive the bitter trials that lay before the nation, and carry forward into a brighter age the torch of loyalty (Isa. iv. 2 ff., xxxvii. 31 f.). On the other hand, in the Maccabaean age there were many who did not share the ardent loyalty of those to whom the Book of Daniel brought strength and courage. But the author limited his message to the saints of the Most High, who would not eat the king's meat, or bow to his image, or heed his prohibitions.

Widely held, of course, were ideas of a great day of divine deliverance and of a Golden Age to come, and these both influenced the message of the prophets and constituted one of the sources of apocalyptic. The phrase "in that day" is repeatedly met in the Old Testament, and, like the phrase "the day of Yahweh", it frequently has in mind a divine judgement that shall mark the climax of the present age, while the phrase "the latter end of the days" denotes the horizon of the present, and the age that shall follow this.

In the popular hope the day of Yahweh was to be a day of divine deliverance of Israel, and vengeance on all her foes, but Amos, the earliest of the canonical prophets, declared that it was to be a day of darkness and not of light, a day of judgement on Israel rather than deliverance for her (Amos v. 18 ff.). It must not be forgotten, however, that Amos also looked for divine judgement on the nations that had cruelly oppressed their neighbours, and been guilty of crimes against humanity. And the prophets throughout pronounced woes on foreign nations as well as on Israel, sometimes with bitter scorn, and sometimes with eager relish. Hence, when Zephaniah thinks of the day of Yahweh as a day of universal judgement he is not propounding a wholly new idea (Zeph. i. 14 ff.), but merely gathering up into one great climax the many judgements the other prophets had foretold.

While, however, the prophets had little immediate hope to offer to men, they were not without ultimate hope. Beyond the day of Yahweh they saw on the far horizon, in the latter end of the days, a fairer world. Familiar are the passages which look forward to the days when peace should be universal, and all men should live as brothers because all should be the children of one God, whose worship should be the bond of their union (Isa. ii. 2 ff.); when even the nature of the beasts should be transformed, so that the wolf should dwell with the lamb, and the leopard lie down with the kid, because the earth should be full of the knowledge of Yahweh (Isa. xi. 6 ff.); when God should create new heavens and a new earth, in which life should be preternaturally lengthened, so that the death of the centenarian should be regarded as premature (Isa. lxv. 17 ff.).

The combination of these elements yields a picture of divine judgement on the nations, but of deliverance and vindication for the righteous Remnant, leading to the Golden Age of justice and peace and infinite bliss. That combination is characteristic of the eschatological hopes of the apocalyptic writers. There are, indeed, passages in the prophetic books where we find this combination, and especially in post-exilic prophecy do we find this gravitation towards the outlook of the apocalyptists.[1]

---

[1] Cf. G. R. Berry, "The Apocalyptic Literature of the Old Testament", in *Journal of Biblical Literature*, lxii, 1943, pp. 9–16. By a misuse of terms Berry says: "The apocalyptic passages in the Old Testament are all pseudonymous. The only complete apocalyptic book is Daniel, which professes to have been composed by Daniel, shortly after the Exile. . . . The other apocalyptic passages are all parts of the books of earlier prophets. Some of these may have been originally anonymous, and their insertion in the prophetic books may have been the work of editors" (p. 12). But this is not pseudonymity. S. B. Frost ("Old Testament Apocalyptic", 1952, pp. 144 ff.) similarly calls Isa. xxiv–xxvii "Pseudo-Isaiah". But there is no evidence that these chapters were inserted by

Thus, the author of Isa. xxiv–xxvii depicts the approaching world catastrophe, when all the earth shall be laid waste, and divine judgement be meted out to the peoples, when Yahweh shall come to reign in Zion, and His people be gathered together from the ends of the earth to find enduring peace and joy. That there is much in common with the eschatology of apocalyptic here is undeniable, and since apocalyptic is commonly confused with the eschatology of apocalyptic, this section is frequently spoken of as an apocalypse. But eschatology and apocalyptic are not coterminous in their significance, and Lindblom, in a study of these chapters,[1] has noted that many of the marks of apocalyptic are absent here, and has therefore denied them the character of apocalyptic.[2] Similarly, Skinner had earlier observed, in writing of these chapters: "The strongly-marked apocalyptic character of the ideas and imagery has impressed nearly all commentators. There has perhaps been a tendency to

their author in the Book of Isaiah, any more than Isa. xl–lxvi were inserted in their authors in that book, and no evidence that the author attached the name of Isaiah to these chapters before they were added to the book. Frost declares (p. 146) Isa. xxiv–xxvii to be "the first biblical pseudonymous work". It is scarcely to be supposed that the book of Deuteronomy is later than the middle of the third century B.C., to which date Frost assigns Isa. xxiv–xxvii (p. 143), and as Deuteronomy is manifestly pseudonymous, unless it was actually the composition of Moses (a view which it is improbable that Frost holds), it is hard to see how "Pseudo-Isaiah" can be the first pseudonymous book in the Bible.

[1] "Die Jesaja-Apokalypse (Jes. 24–27)", 1938 (*Lunds Universitets Årsskrift*, N.F., Avd. I, Bd. xxxiv, No. 3). On these chapters cf. O. Plöger, "Theokratie und Eschatologie", 1959, pp. 69 ff.

[2] Lindblom defines the marks of apocalyptic as transcendentalism, mythology, cosmological orientation, pessimistic treatment of history, dualism, division of time into periods, doctrine of two ages, playing with numbers, pseudo-ecstasy, artificial claims to inspiration, pseudonymity, mysteriousness. Some of these are rather the accidents than the essence of apocalyptic, however. Cf. H. Wheeler Robinson (in Manson's "Companion to the Bible", 1939, pp. 307 f.), who defines the marks of apocalyptic as: "(1) It is deliberately pseudonymous and not simply anonymous; . . . (2) its view of history is deterministic, following the divine appointment and culminating in some crisis which is that of the writer's own age; (3) its emphasis is thus on the future and tends more and more to become extra-mundane, in contrast with the prophetic conception of a Kingdom of God in this world (though this may be included); (4) apocalyptic is literary, not oral, and is marked by the excessive use of symbolism, the use of animal figures being especially noticeable." Cf. also E. Lohmeyer, in "Die Religion in Geschichte und Gegenwart", 2nd ed. (edited by Gunkel and Zscharnack), i, 1927, cols. 402 ff.

exaggerate this feature; if we compare the passage with a typical apocalypse, like the Book of Daniel, the differences are certainly more striking than the resemblances."[1]

Similarly, the Book of Joel looks to the approaching day of Yahweh as a day of destruction and terror, through which the children of Zion shall come to ease and plenty, to experience the outpouring upon them of the spirit of God, and to be joined by their brethren of the dispersion. Or again, Zech. ix–xiv depicts the miseries that shall precede the Messianic age, and Yahweh's defence of Jerusalem against its siege by the massed forces of the heathen, followed by the restoration of the House of David, and the acknowledgement of Yahweh as King over all the earth.

To all of these writers history was moving swiftly towards a great climax, and the birth of a new age which should belong to the faithful Remnant of Israel. From this it was but a short step to the treatment of these themes by the apocalyptists. In their hands the concept of a great world judgement was given increased prominence and definiteness, and it was placed in a setting of history. The court of judgement was about to be set up, and sentence about to be

---

[1] "The Book of the Prophet Isaiah, chapters i–xxxix" (Cambridge Bible), 1909 edition, p. 179. Cf. W. Rudolph ("Jesaja 24–27", 1933, p. 59), who observes that one can only refer to Isa. xxiv–xxvii as the "Isaiah-Apocalypse" with reserve, though sundry apocalyptic motifs may be found here. In a review of the first edition of the present book, L. H. Brockington (*Journal of Theological Studies*, xlvi, 1945, p. 76) accuses me of pressing the distinction between eschatology and apocalyptic *in order to* exclude Isa. xxiv–xxvii from my list of apocalyptic writings and give the priority to Daniel. In fact, the reader will observe that I do not press the distinction at all. On the contrary, I recognize a few lines below that only a short step separates this section from apocalyptic. Moreover, I could have no possible interest in pressing this distinction *in order to* exclude these chapters from apocalyptic. Brockington apparently supposes that the recognition of these chapters as apocalyptical would embarrass my view of the genesis of pseudonymity in apocalyptic (see below). But since these chapters are not pseudonymous, they have no bearing whatever on that view, whether they are recognized as fully apocalyptic or only closely approximating to apocalyptic. Surprisingly enough, however, Brockington goes on to tax me with failing to recognize that pseudonymity is *integral* to apocalyptic. By this canon, Isa. xxiv–xxvii must be adjudged not fully apocalyptical. How I can be blamed for excluding what Brockington himself much more sharply excludes is not clear. As for the canon, it would exclude the first half of the book of Daniel from the category of apocalyptic, and also the Book of Revelation. I am not therefore able to accept it.

executed on the great world empires, and the Golden Age was about to burst in its glory. It was no distant hope that they held out to the faithful, but one on the point of being realized, and because it was set forth in association with the recognizable past and the recognizable present, it forcefully declared that it trafficked not in the things that should some time come to pass, but in things that were right here. In this world of thought the author of Daniel moved when he described the four world empires, culminating in the Little Horn, whom his readers would have no difficulty in identifying, whose fall was to be an item in the great final judgement, to be followed by the creation of an enduring kingdom, which should be administered by the saints of the Most High. To share in the glory of that kingdom many of them that slept in the dust of the earth should awake, and they that were wise should shine as the brightness of the firmament, and they that turned many to righteousness as the stars for ever and ever (Dan. xii. 2 f.).

Moreover, while the concept of the Messiah, which figured in the prophet's dreams of the Golden Age, does not appear in the earliest apocalyptic writings, it later exercised an influence on their thought. It is important that we should distinguish clearly between the term "Messiah" and the Messianic concept.[1] In New Testament times the concept was attached to the term "Messiah", and in its Greek equivalent it passed over into Christian usage as "Christ". But in the Old Testament the concept was not attached to the term "Messiah".[2] The Hebrew word which is transliterated as "Messiah" simply means *anointed*, and is applied to reigning kings of Israel, to high priests, and even to Cyrus. There are passages in the Psalms where the term is held to refer to the ideal king of the future, but of these the interpretation is disputed. In any case, the majority of the occurrences of the term

[1] On the messianic concept in the apocalyptic literature, see J. Giblet, "L'Attente du Messie", 1954, pp. 109 ff., and P. Grelot, "La Venue du Messie", 1962, pp. 19 ff.

[2] Cf. W. O. E. Oesterley ("The Gospel Parables in the Light of Their Jewish Background", 1936, p. 24): "In the Old Testament the Messiah as a technical term does not occur."

in the Old Testament are clearly without the ideal reference. On the other hand, the passages which unmistakably refer to the ideal future leader of the kingdom do not use the term.

To the pre-exilic prophets it was natural to think of the community as headed by a king in the Golden Age, and every southern prophet would naturally think of a scion of the house of David in the kingly office. Thus Mic. v. 2 ff. declares that out of Bethlehem should arise the future ruler of Israel, destined from of old to be great unto the ends of the earth; Isa. xi. 1 ff. points to a shoot out of the stock of Jesse who should rule in righteousness and power in the age when the earth should be full of the knowledge of Yahweh, and the nature of the beasts should be transformed; in Jer. xxiii. 5 ff. the promise is given that a righteous Branch should be raised up unto David, who should execute judgement and justice in the land. In the early post-exilic period, when the High Priest became the religious head of the community, and when the religious leaders were more concerned to use the religious freedom granted them by the Persian authorities, the dreams of a Davidic leader fell into the background, though the hope would always be kept alive by the passages in the older prophetic books, which were edited and preserved in this age.

In some later works, outside the sacred Canon, particularly the Testaments of the Twelve Patriarchs, the concept of a Levitical Messiah has frequently been found, and this has been held to be a readaptation of the messianic idea due to the occupation of the throne and high priesthood by the Hasmonaean house,[1] giving rise to the substitution of a scion of the house of Levi for a scion of the house of David.[2] It

[1] Cf. E. Barker, "From Alexander to Constantine", 1956, p. 147: "As Levi had taken the place of Judah in the office of king with the establishment of the Maccabaean dynasty, so the tribe of Levi takes the place of the tribe of Judah as the source from which the new Messiah is to come."

[2] A. Schweitzer ("The Mysticism of Paul the Apostle", Eng. trans., 1931, p. 78) strangely ascribes the revival of the hope of a Davidic Messiah in the Psalms of Solomon to the Hasmonaean house. He says: "Through the Hasmonaeans the Jewish people had again become a nation ruled by kings. . . . The Hasmonaean kingdom created the conditions necessary for the reintroduction of the Davidic Messiah into eschatology." It is more usually supposed that dissatisfaction with the later Hasmonaeans caused a return to the hope of a Davidic Messiah.

is, however, doubtful if there is anywhere the *substitution* of a Levitical for a Davidic Messiah. Where the Levitical anointed one appears, he is beside the Davidic,[1] and E. J. Bickerman describes the view that the author of the Testaments of the Twelve Patriarchs cherished the concept of a Messiah from the tribe of Levi to be "a figment, created by modern readers of the work".[2] That a Messiah ben Joseph, or ben Ephraim, is found in still later works is beyond dispute.[3]

In the Book of Daniel we do not find the figure of the Messiah at all, though we do find the term, just as we have noted that we find it elsewhere in the Old Testament. In Daniel ix. 25 we read of an anointed leader, and in ix. 26 of the cutting off of the anointed one.[4] It is almost certain that the reference here is not to a future ideal person, but to a historical person. In any case, there is nothing whatever to connect him with the Davidic house, and there is no suggestion that he is the leader of the kingdom in the Golden Age. He is cut off before the consummation, and does not figure again in the vision.

That the figure of the Messiah does not appear in the Book of Daniel is not surprising, however.[5] For no member of the

---

[1] Cf. G. R. Beasley-Murray, in *Journal of Theological Studies*, xlviii, 1949, pp. 5 ff.

[2] Cf. *Journal of Biblical Literature*, lxiv, 1950, p. 252.

[3] Cf. J. Drummond, "The Jewish Messiah", 1877, pp. 356 ff.; M.-J. Lagrange, "Le Messianisme chez les juifs", 1909, pp. 251 ff.; G. H. Dix, "The Messiah ben Joseph", in *Journal of Theological Studies*, xxvii, 1926, pp. 130 ff.; C. C. Torrey, "The Messiah Son of Ephraim", in *Journal of Biblical Literature*, lxvi, 1947, pp. 253 ff.

[4] The A.V. renders by *Messiah* in these two verses, thus importing into the term its technical sense. This is rightly corrected by R.V. and R.S.V. Cf. Bousset-Gressmann, "Die Religion des Judentums im späthellenistischen Zeitalter", 1926, p. 222: "In a whole series of promises of late hellenistic Judaism—Joel, Sir. xxiii, Isa. xxiv–xxvii, Daniel, 1 Enoch i–xxxvi, the Apocalypse of Weeks and the Similitudes of the same book, Jubilees, the Assumption of Moses, 2 Enoch, besides books in which the mention of the Messiah might have been expected, Tobit, Judith, 1 and 2 Maccabees, Wisdom, 1 Baruch—the figure of the Messiah is not found at all."

[5] The Qumran texts show that the Messianic concept was very much alive at the time when they were composed. But the Davidic Messiah lay still in the future. In the Rule of the Congregation there is a vague reference, "If God should cause the Messiah to be born in their time." In the Zadokite Work,

Davidic house headed the rising against Antiochus Epiphanes, and it would have been a sheer lack of realism to import a Davidic Messiah into the visions, and one entirely uncalled for, since the Davidic Messiah had fallen into the background in the Persian period. On the other hand, the alleged thought of a Levitical Messiah had certainly not yet arisen, and even if it had it would hardly have appeared relevant to the situation.[1] For while the Maccabaean rising was led by a priest and his sons, at the time of the outbreak Mattathias was an obscure priest, quite unlikely to have the Messianic concept transferred from the line of David to himself. Nor were the High Priests in that age such as to inspire the author of Daniel with any high hopes of their spiritual leadership. For the office was the reward of intrigue with the hated oppressor.

Hence, the Book of Daniel speaks only of divine rule exercised through the saints. Doubtless the author did not contemplate a kingdom without some human head, but to him the person of that head was a negligible detail, with which he did not concern himself. He did, however, use a figure for the kingdom which in course of time was influenced by the concept of the Messiah, and individualized to yield a

---

which almost certainly originated in the Qumran sect, it is indicated that the Messiah was expected to appear forty years after the death of the Teacher of Righteousness (see below, p. 84). A number of scholars now place the ministry of the Teacher of Righteousness in the middle of the second century B.C., while I place it somewhat earlier. But the author of the Book of Daniel expected the establishment of the enduring kingdom almost immediately when he wrote, when no Davidic leader was in view. It is understandable that when that expectation was not realized the Qumran sectaries should turn anew to the Scriptures and should cherish the hope that ere long a Davidic leader should arise to establish the kingdom.

[1] It is fast becoming normal to say that the Qumran sectaries expected a Levitical Messiah and a Davidic, but this is quite misleading. These sectaries certainly expected that in the Messianic age there would be an anointed priest beside the Davidic leader, but this does not justify the use of the term Messiah in the sense that it conveys to us. Cf. H. H. Rowley, in *Bulletin of the John Rylands Library*, xliv, 1961–2, pp. 122 ff., 144 ff. The use of the term Levitical Messiah arose among scholars who claimed to find the concept of a Levitical leader replacing that of a Davidic leader, and therefore Messianic in the same sense as the Davidic Messiah. It merely causes confusion to use the term for the priest who stands beside the Davidic leader as Joshua stood beside Zerubbabel in the immediately post-exilic period. Cf. A. J. B. Higgins, in *Vetus Testamentum*, iii, 1953, p. 330.

title for the leader of the kingdom. He used the figure of the Son of Man (Dan. vii. 13).

Endless discussion has gathered round this figure,[1] and opinions as to the reference have differed widely. To some it has seemed that the author of Daniel intended by it to portray a leader of the kingdom, comparable to the figure of the Messiah, and of this school Dr. W. O. E. Oesterley is representative.[2] Dr. W. F. Albright also thinks that the author of Daniel conceived of a pre-existent heavenly figure, destined to appear as Messiah, and that we have here a fusing of the Jewish figure of the Messiah with the Mesopotamian saviour Atrakhasis.[3] To Dr. T. W. Manson, on the other hand, the individualizing of the figure of the Son of Man is the outcome of the ministry of Jesus, and he believes that in Daniel, in the Similitudes of Enoch, and on the lips of our Lord, it is an ideal figure, standing for the manifestation of the kingdom of God on earth in a people wholly devoted to their heavenly King.[4] It is with diffidence that I

[1] Cf. my "Darius the Mede", pp. 62 ff. n., for some of the literature and views. A number of more recent references could now be added to the list.

[2] "The Jews and Judaism during the Greek Period", 1941, pp. 152 ff.

[3] "From the Stone Age to Christianity", 1940, pp. 290 ff. Cf. C. H. Kraeling, "Anthropos and Son of Man", 1927, and S. Mowinckel, "Ophaver til den senjødiske forestilling om Menneskesønnen", in *Norsk Teologisk Tidsskrift*, 1944, pp. 189–244. The latter is a richly documented study of the variety of views which have been propounded on the origin of the idea of the Son of Man. T. F. Glasson disposes of the whole question with great facility. He merely states that the comparison of Dan. vii with 1 En. xiv shows that the original Son of Man was Enoch, and the question is settled ("The Second Advent", 1945, pp. 15 ff.). Questions of literary dependence are never simple, and it is by no means self-evident that Dan. vii is dependent on 1 En. xiv. Indeed, Charles, on whom Glasson quite uncritically relies for his dating of the relevant section of 1 Enoch (see below, p. 96 n.), states that the dependence is the other way round ("The Book of Enoch", 2nd ed., 1912, p. 34; cf. below, pp. 97 f.). Similarly, Montgomery says that the passage in 1 Enoch is an expansion of the passage in Daniel ("A Critical and Exegetical Commentary on the Book of Daniel", 1927, p. 298). When, therefore, Glasson says that "the dependence of Daniel vii on 1 En. xiv is obvious" (*op. cit.*, p. 14), his confidence exceeds his cogency.

[4] "The Teaching of Jesus", 2nd ed., 1935, pp. 227 ff.; but cf. *Bulletin of the John Rylands Library*, xxxii, 1949–50, pp. 171 ff., esp. p. 191. Cf. H. Lietzmann, "Der Menschensohn", 1896; also N. Schmidt, in *Journal of Biblical Literature*, xlv, 1926, pp. 326 ff. S. J. Case (*ibid.*, xlvi, 1927, pp. 1 ff.) would reject the term altogether from the lips of Jesus, and suggests it was fathered on Him by His disciples because they were fond of it on their own account. He thinks it would be much easier to do this in the latter half of the first century than for Jesus so to

differ from any of these scholars, but I am compelled here to agree with the view of a great number of scholars, who stand midway between them. That the Son of Man in Daniel is not an individual figure seems to me certain. The first four kingdoms of the vision are symbolized by the four beasts rising from the sea, and it was therefore natural to symbolize the fifth kingdom by a single figure. To select a human figure instead of a beast was to differentiate its character from theirs at once, and to bring it from above[1] instead of from the sea was to emphasize its higher origin and nature. The interpretation of the vision clearly states that the fourth beast was a kingdom, and that the dominion was transferred from it to the saints of the Most High, thus equating the saints of the interpretation with the Son of Man of the vision. But, as I have said, I have little doubt that the author would have agreed that he did not contemplate a kingdom without a leader, and it is not surprising that later thought, under the influence of the comparable but different idea of the Messiah, should think of the leader, and should adopt the term "Son of Man" with an individual reference as his title.

But there is no evidence that the Son of Man was identified with the Messiah until the time of Jesus.[2] He does not seem

---

style Himself. W. G. Kümmel ("Die Eschatologie der Evangelien", 1936, p. 18) also observes that the primitive community used the term "Son of Man" commonly for Jesus. This leaves quite unexplained the strange fact that all our evidence outside the Gospels shows that this was not the title that first-century disciples delighted to use on their own account. Cf. C. H. Dodd, "The Parables of the Kingdom", 3rd ed., 1936, pp. 89 f., J. Héring, "Le royaume de Dieu et sa venue", 1937, pp. 88 f. Cf. also A. S. Peake ("The Servant of Yahweh", 1931, p. 227): "It is difficult to conceive a case much stronger on its positive side than that for the application of the title (*i.e.* Son of Man) to Himself by Jesus. The evidence that he used it is drawn from every one of our documentary sources."

[1] T. F. Glasson ("The Second Advent", 1945, p. 14) states that the meaning is that the Son of Man was borne on the clouds to heaven, and not that He came down from above. Cf. T. W. Manson, in *Bulletin of the John Rylands Library*, xxxii, 1949–50, p. 174. This view is rejected by J. Muilenburg in *Journal of Biblical Literature*, lxxix, 1960, p. 200.

[2] Albright (*op. cit.*, p. 292) thinks the term "Son of Man" was already Messianic, in the sense that it had been fused with the figure of the Messiah, before the time of Christ. Cf. W. Manson, "Jesus the Messiah", 1943, pp. 98 ff., 113 ff., 171 f. P. Parker (*Journal of Biblical Literature*, lx, 1941, pp. 151–7) goes to the extreme in the opposite view, and argues that in the Gospels the

to have applied the term "Messiah" or "Christ" to Himself during His ministry, but to have used the term "Son of Man" freely.[1] At His trial He was asked, "Art thou the Christ?" and replied, "I am: and ye shall see the Son of Man sitting on the right hand of power, and coming with the clouds of heaven" (Mark xiv. 61 f.). Here the term "Christ", or "Messiah", is brought into intimate connexion with a clear reference to the passage in Daniel, but it is significant that the question was couched in the terms, "Art thou the Christ?" It was not sufficient to use the term which had ever been on His lips, Son of Man, as it would have been if the two terms were already accepted as identical in their significance. An unequivocal answer was required to the question whether He accepted the title which He had never assumed for Himself, but which others had applied to Him. Moreover, if the two terms were already associated together there would have been no point in One who applied the one term to Himself charging His disciples, when Peter acknowledged Him as the Christ, to tell this to no man (Mark viii. 29 f.).[2]

While the earliest great apocalyptic work, the Book of Daniel, does not depict an individual leader of the enduring kingdom, it does depict in vivid terms the great human adversary of that kingdom, the leader of the last of the bestial empires, whose overthrow should inaugurate the new age. The term "Antichrist" is not employed, of course, and could

---

term is only Messianic in three unauthentic passages, and that on the lips of Jesus it was never related to an apocalyptic or Messianic context. Against this cf. G. Kittel, in *Deutsche Theologie*, 1936, p. 173.

[1] J. Héring (*op. cit.*, pp. 88 ff., 111 ff.) holds that Jesus believed in His future identity with the Son of Man of Daniel and Enoch, destined to appear in the clouds of heaven, but that He expressly repudiated the title of Messiah. This, I am persuaded, goes too far and rests on too radical a treatment of the Gospel texts. Cf. A. E. Garvie (*Expository Times*, xlix, 1937–8, p. 426, in a review of Héring): "My own impression is that the data in the Gospels are often treated very arbitrarily; and that this critic, as so many others, is only too ready to dismiss as unauthentic what does not fit into his scheme." Cf. also M. Goguel (*Revue d'Histoire et de Philosophie Religieuses*, vii, 1927, p. 56, in a review of R. Bultmann's "Jesus"): "Without the messianic consciousness the thought and work of Jesus remain incomprehensible."

[2] Cf. H. H. Rowley, "The Servant of the Lord", 1952, pp. 80 ff.

not be in a work which has no Messiah or Christ. Nor was the term coined until much later. But we have here the manifest prototype of Antichrist. Yet here again, the conception is not without preparation in the older literature.

In Ps. ii the peoples and their rulers are represented as conspiring against God and His anointed in a vain effort to overthrow the divinely established kingdom of the anointed. The word here rendered "anointed" is the word which, transliterated, gives "Messiah", and it is disputed whether it here has its eschatological meaning of future ideal ruler, or whether it is used in its ordinary sense of an anointed king.[1] The promise of a world-wide dominion would seem to favour the eschatological view, and in any case the psalm could readily be attached to that view, whatever its primary reference may have been. The opposition here is neither personified in an individual figure nor is there any hint of a single leader of its massed forces.

It was characteristic of Israelite thought to pass from the collective to the individual, however, and to represent the group by the single figure and then go on to treat this as a real individual. The concept of the Messiah began in the promise of the lasting glory of the Davidic house (2 Sam. vii. 16), and in the expectation that after the northern exile the restoration of the Davidic line would bring about the restoration of the national fortunes (Hos. iii. 5). The concept of the Son of Man began as a personifying of the saints, as we have seen, and later the personification became a person. The same thing probably happened with the concept of the Suffering Servant. What was at first a collective figure, representing the community, became the figure of an indi-

[1] Cf. A. R. Johnson, "Sacral Kingship in Ancient Israel", 1955, pp. 118 ff., where it is held that this psalm was used in the dramatic ritual to express the thought of the eventual fulfilment of the promise given to David in the supremacy over the Kings of the earth which his descendant and ideal successor should exercise. Dr. Julian Morgenstern, in a paper read before the American Oriental Society in 1942, has sought to establish that Psalm ii is an important historical document, bearing upon the overrunning of Judah in 485 B.C. by a coalition of nations, by whom Jerusalem was destroyed and the Temple burned, and a newly appointed Davidic king taken prisoner. Cf. *Hebrew Union College Annual*, xxvii, 1956, pp. 138 ff.

vidual who in himself embodied its mission.[1] In the same way it is not surprising that the hostility to the divine will and the divine kingdom should be concentrated in a single figure.

In Ezek. xxxviii and xxxix we find the figure of Gog, of the land of Magog, as the leader of the opposing forces. All the discussion that has centred round this figure has failed to yield any assured identification.[2] The name has been linked with that of Gyges of Lydia,[3] with the city of Carchemish, through the Amarna Gaga,[4] or with some lost myth.[5] A

[1] Cf. my "Israel's Mission to the World", 1939, p. 13: "In general I believe the author was personifying Israel, but in the fourth poem that personification is carried to a point where it is hard to escape the feeling that he really thought of an individual, so supremely the Servant of Yahweh that within the Servant community He stood out as its representative and leader, carrying its mission of service to a point no other could reach." Cf. also "The Servant of the Lord", 1952, pp. 49 ff.

[2] P. Auvray ("Ézéchiel" [Bible de Jérusalem], 2nd ed., 1957, p. 143) thinks it is vain to try to identify Gog. R. Augé ("Ezequiel" [Montserrat Bible], 1955, p. 341) thinks he is a fictitious character and that the author has here brought together traits of various historical personages. M. Schumpp (Das Buch Ezechiel [Herders Bibelkommentar], 1942, p. 197) contents himself with saying Gog is a historical, and not a mythical, figure. For surveys of the diverse views that have been advanced cf. W. Gronkowski, "La Messianisme d'Ézéchiel", 1930, pp. 162 ff.; G. Fohrer, "Die Hauptprobleme des Buches Ezechiel", 1952, pp. 195 f.; C. Kuhl, in Theologische Rundschau, N.F. xxiv, 1956–7, pp. 28 ff.

[3] So Fr. Delitzsch, "Wo lag das Paradies?", 1881, pp. 246 f.; Schrader, "Cuneiform Inscriptions and the Old Testament", Eng. trans., ii, 1888, p. 123; C. Steuernagel, "Lehrbuch der Einleitung in das Alte Testament", 1912, p. 592; J. L. Myres, in Palestine Exploration Fund Quarterly Statement, 1932, pp. 213 ff.; H. L. Ellison, in "The New Bible Dictionary", 1962, p. 480b; and many others. J. Herrmann ("Ezechiel" [Sellin's Kommentar], 1924, p. 245) erroneously says that Lagarde ("Gesammelte Abhandlungen", 1896, p. 158) already mentions the possibility of the identification of Gog with Gyges. This erroneous statement is repeated in W. Gronkowski, "Le Messianisme d'Ézéchiel", 1930, p. 163, and G. Fohrer, "Hauptprobleme des Buches Ezechiel", p. 196. C. H. Toy ("The Book of the Prophet Ezekiel" [Sacred Books of the Old Testament], 1899, p. 99) rejects the identification with Gyges.

[4] So O. Weber, in J. A. Knudtzon, "Die El-Amarna-Tafeln", ii, 1915, p. 1015. W. F. Albright (Journal of Biblical Literature, xliii, 1924, pp. 381 f.) objects to the connexion of Gaga with Carchemish, and thinks rather of Gašga, which is found in Hittite texts for a wild district on the confines of Armenia and Cappadocia.

[5] So Winckler, "Altorientalische Forschungen", 2 Reihe, 1898, pp. 160 ff., and in Schrader's "Die Keilinschriften und das Alte Testament", 3rd ed., 1903, p. 513. The whole figure of Antichrist is held by some writers to rest on the old Creation myth. So H. Gunkel, "Schöpfung und Chaos in Urzeit und Endzeit",

further suggestion is that the chapters were inspired by the
Scythian invasion in the seventh century.[1] Gog has been
identified with the younger Cyrus,[2] Alexander the Great,[3] or
with Antiochus Epiphanes,[4] or Antiochus Eupator,[5] or with
Mithridates VI.[6] Or again, it has been suggested that Gog
is a misleading secondary form of Magog, and that by
reversing the letters of Magog and reading it as a cipher, of
the type that uses the following letter of the alphabet for the
letter intended, we have Babylon.[7] It has also been suggested that Gog is the name of the god Ga-ga, which was
applied to the prince of *mât Ga-ga*, i.e. Magog.[8] Yet another

1895, pp. 323 ff., W. Bousset, "The Antichrist Legend", Eng. trans., 1896, pp.
144 ff. Cf. Bousset-Gressmann, "Die Religion des Judentums", pp. 254 ff. Cf.
also A. S. Kapelrud, "Joel Studies", 1948, pp. 104 ff. I. G. Matthews ("Ezekiel" [American Commentary on the Old Testament], 1939, pp. 142 f.) objects
that this would require that the name Gog be preserved in popular thought, and
for this we have no evidence beyond this passage.

[1] So C. von Orelli, "Das Buch Ezechiel", 1888, p. 148, 2nd ed., 1896, p. 150;
C. H. Toy, in "Encyclopaedia Biblica", ii, 1901, col. 1466; W. F. Lofthouse,
"Ezekiel" (Century Bible), p. 276; J. E. McFadyen, in Peake's "Commentary
on the Bible", 1920, p. 517; E. Bruston, in "La Bible du Centenaire", ii, 1947,
p. 679. A. Merx ("Die Prophetie des Joel", 1879, pp. 65 ff.) identified Gog with
"the northerner" of Joel ii. 20. Cf. also H. Gressmann, "Ursprung der
israelitisch-jüdischen Eschatologie", 1905, pp. 180 ff., and "Der Messias",
1929, p. 125.

[2] So N. Messel, "Ezechielfragen", 1945, pp. 125 f.

[3] So Winckler, "Altorientalische Forschungen", 2 Reihe, 1898, pp. 160 ff.,
where a lost Alexander myth is postulated. C. C. Torrey ("Pseudo-Ezekiel and
the Original Prophecy", 1931, pp. 95 f.) describes Winckler's theory as
"fantastic", but himself argues that Gog is a reflection of Alexander. So also
G. Dahl, in "Quantulacumque" (Kirsopp Lake Festschrift), 1937, pp. 281 ff.

[4] So L. Seinecke, "Geschichte des Volkes Israel", ii, 1884, pp. 13 f. J. G.
Aalders ("Gog en Magog in Ezechiël", 1951, pp. 148 ff., 170 f.) holds that the
chapters are a prediction of the defeat of the forces of Antiochus by the Maccabees.

[5] So G. R. Berry, in *Journal of Biblical Literature*, xli, 1922, pp. 224 f.

[6] So N. Schmidt, in "Encyclopaedia Biblica", iv, 1907, cols. 4332 f.

[7] So J. Böhmer, in *Zeitschrift für wissenschaftliche Theologie*, xl, 1897, pp. 347 f.;
L. Finkelstein, "The Pharisees", i, 1938, pp. 338 ff. Cf. also J. Meinhold,
"Einführung in das Alte Testament", 3rd ed., 1932, p. 268. E. König ("Die
messianischen Weissagungen des Alten Testaments", 1923, p. 250) rejects this
view. So also A. van den Born, in *Oudtestamentische Studiën*, x, 1954, pp. 197 f.
Cf. also R. H. Pfeiffer, "Introduction to the Old Testament", 1941, p. 534 n.,
and G. Fohrer, "Hauptprobleme des Buches Ezechiel", 1952, p. 94 n.

[8] So P. Dhorme, in *Revue Biblique*, N.S. xvi, 1919, p. 364. Cf. "Recueil
Édouard Dhorme", 1951, pp. 170 f. Cf. also J. Herrmann, "Ezechiel" [Kom-
mentar zum Alten Testament], 1924, p. 244 n.

view is that Gog is the Sumerian word *gug*, meaning *darkness*, and that Gog is therefore the personification of all that is dark and evil.[1] In any case, we have here the individualizing of the opposition in the figure of a monster of iniquity, who will treacherously attack his weak and unsuspecting neighbours, but who will be smitten and destroyed by the power of God in a resounding disaster.[2]

In the days when Israel's oppressors were ruled by a strong king, of outstanding personality and will, it was natural for him to focus in himself all the bitter hostility of the oppressed peoples, and to be regarded as the personification of all iniquity. Thus we find in the great taunt song of Isa. xiv the King of Babylon depicted as one who thought to ascend into heaven, and to exalt his throne above the stars of God, who aspired to be like God, but who was brought down to Sheol like any common individual, to the taunts of those he joined.

In the same way, in the Maccabaean age, it was natural that Antiochus Epiphanes should focus in himself all the hatred of the people he proscribed, and be thought of as the embodiment of the spirit of opposition to the divine will.[3]

---

[1] So Van Hoonacker, in *Zeitschrift für Assyriologie*, xxviii, 1914, p. 336. Cf. Albright's criticism in *Journal of Biblical Literature*, xliii, 1924, p. 381.

[2] The later references to the names Gog and Magog do not help us very much. The names are found in a topographical sense in Jub. viii. 25, ix. 8, and again in Sib. Or. iii. 319, where they are set in the midst of the rivers of Ethiopia. In the LXX version of Num. xxiv. 7 it is said that the kingdom of the one who shall arise from the seed of Jacob and rule many nations shall surpass that of Gog, but this adds no more to our knowledge of the figure of Gog than does Rev. xx. 8, where Gog and Magog seem both to be regarded as persons. Gog appears as the great adversary of the Messiah, whose armies will do battle against Israel and be destroyed by the Messiah, in the Targum of pseudo-Jonathan on Num. xxiv. 17, and again in the Fragment Targum on Num. xi. 26. For the references to Gog in the Talmud and other rabbinical literature see Volz, "Jüdische Eschatologie von Daniel bis Akiba", 1903, p. 176, or "Die Eschatologie der jüdischen Gemeinde", 1934, p. 150.

[3] A modern Jew protests against the injustice done to the name of Antiochus. He observes: "Posterity loves to pillory an individual for an evil of gradual growth; and the individual upon whom the odium of this attempt is regularly cast is Antiochus Epiphanes, the Seleucid emperor who reigned from 175–166 [*sic*] B.C.E. Yet he was less the promoter than the instrument of the policy which had its roots in the corruption of a part of the Jewish people" (N. Bentwich, "Hellenism", 1919, p. 93). It will be seen below that there is a measure of justification for this, though Antiochus cannot be cleared of a real measure of responsibility for the policy.

He is therefore depicted as the Little Horn, with a mouth speaking great things, thinking to change times and seasons, wearing out the saints and measuring himself even against the Most High (Dan. vii. 8, 25), or magnifying himself above every god, and speaking marvellous things against the God of gods (xi. 36).

We must now return to the predictive element in prophecy and apocalyptic. That the prophets were not merely preachers of righteousness, but foretellers of the future, is plain to every reader.[1] Their prophecies were not always fulfilled, indeed, and we know that Jeremiah found the non-fulfilment of his prophecies a serious problem, and roundly accused God of letting him down (Jer. xx. 7 ff.). But they none the less regarded the foretelling of the future as of the essence of their function. Similarly, the apocalyptists sought to sketch the future, and were confident of their power to do so. The pattern of the prophecies of the prophets and of the apocalyptists differed, however. Speaking generally, the prophets foretold the future that should arise out of the present, while the apocalyptists foretold the future that should break into the present. The prophets saw the events and policies of their day with penetrating eye, and perceived their inevitable outcome. When they saw wickedness and sin they saw the harvest it would bring, and so they were largely prophets of doom. Yet they did not prophesy unrelieved disaster. They looked, as we have seen, through the darkness to a brighter dawn in the more distant future, and had glimpses of the glory the righteous Remnant should inherit, when evil had run its course and consumed itself.

The apocalyptists had little faith in the present to beget the

[1] Charles ("Critical Commentary on the Book of Daniel", 1929, p. xxvi) makes the surprising statement: "Prophecy is a declaration, a forthtelling, of the will of God—not a foretelling. Prediction is not in any sense an essential of prophecy, though it may intervene as an accident—whether it be a justifiable accident is another question." The sufficient comment on this is found in Deut. xviii. 22. Cf. A. S. Peake ("The Servant of Yahweh", 1931, p. 83): "It is rather unfortunate that the reaction from the old-fashioned view that prophecy was in the main prediction has led to the prevalent belief that the prophets were scarcely concerned with the future at all. . . . For really the predictive element in prophecy was very prominent."

future. That is why they are so often, and so unfairly, called pessimists. They saw not wicked men heading for disaster so much as innocent men suffering direst agonies for their faith, the righteous Remnant in the crucible of affliction, and they looked for a great divine intervention in history in the immediate future. To the prophets the great world empires were the instrument in God's hand to execute His will on His faithless people, controlled by the God whose will all history unfolded. To the apocalyptists the great world empires were the adversaries of God, proudly resisting His will, which could not triumph through them, but only in their annihilation. Nevertheless, we must beware of making the contrast too sharp or too absolute, or of forgetting that in the prophets there are passages with a definitely apocalyptic flavour in this respect.

On the other hand, we must not ignore the curious difference in the form of prophecy in the prophets and in the apocalyptists. The prophets spoke from the standpoint of the present, while from the time of the issue of the Book of Daniel it became a characteristic of the apocalyptists that they threw themselves back into the past, under an assumed name, and put in the guise of prophecy things that were past in their own day as the prelude to their unfolding of the grand dénouement of history which they believed to be imminent.

It is commonly suggested that, owing to the prevailing belief that inspiration was dead, these writers were forced to assume a pseudonym to gain a hearing.[1] It is hard to believe that their first readers were under any illusions as to the antiquity of the books, or that pseudonymity was a mere trick to delude the reader.[2] For the ancient Hebrews were not

---

[1] So Charles, "A Critical History of the Doctrine of a Future Life", 2nd ed., 1913, pp. 196 ff.; J. B. Frey in Pirot's "Supplément au Dictionnaire de la Bible", i, 1928, col. 334.

[2] It is interesting to note that Charles believes that 1 En. vi–xxxvi dates from before 170 B.C. (on this, however, see below), and that it was written in Aramaic. It is hard to suppose that anyone in that age would have seriously expected to delude his contemporaries that a work in Aramaic was so ancient as the time of Enoch, and it is highly improbable that he would have ascribed to Enoch a work in that language. If he had resorted to pseudonymity in order

greatly interested in authorship, and we do not know the
name of the author of a single book of the Old Testament.
For even the prophetic books, though they undoubtedly contain genuine oracles of the prophets whose names they bear,
could not have been compiled by these prophets. Nor does
it seem to be observed that the Book of Ecclesiasticus is a
singular commentary on this theory. For the grandson of
Ben Sira claims this work for his grandfather in the second
century B.C., and there is no reason to doubt the claim or to
suppose that the intention of this claim was to ensure that
the work would not gain a hearing.

Some years ago I proposed the view that the pseudonymity
of the Book of Daniel grew out of its genesis,[1] and that it was
not consciously intended from the start, but that succeeding
writers slavishly copied this feature, as though it were part of
the technique of apocalyptic. I still think this is the most
probable explanation. For there is much to suggest that the
stories of the first part of the Book of Daniel were created one
by one, and circulated separately as stories with a message.
No author's name was attached to them, any more than to
all the other writings that have been gathered into the Old
Testament. But most of these stories were about Daniel.
They were timely and were superbly told. Hence, they
secured an immediate popularity in the circles for which they
were written. When the author came to write his visions,
therefore, also carrying a message of hope for the same circles,
he wrote them under the guise of Daniel, not in order to
deceive his readers, but in order to reveal his identity with
the author of the Daniel stories.[2] Pseudonymity was thus

---

to secure a hearing for himself from people who believed that inspiration was
dead, he might have been expected to complete the process by writing in the
language of inspiration.

[1] *Zeitschrift für die alttestamentliche Wissenschaft*, N.F. ix, 1932, pp. 266 ff.

[2] L. H. Brockington (*Journal of Theological Studies*, xlvi, 1945, p. 76) does me
less than justice here, and fails to realize the nature of the problem. He observes
that "to say that the author of Daniel wrote under the guise of Daniel 'to reveal
his identity with the author of the Daniel stories' sounds unconvincing".
Indeed, it sounds nonsense. But to say that the author wrote the pseudonymous
visions under the name of the hero of the anonymous stories in order to attach
visions and stories together, and to indicate their common authorship, is not

born of a living process, whose purpose was the precise opposite of deceit. It became artificial only when it was woodenly copied by imitators.[1]

It will be seen that this view not alone gives an explanation of the pseudonymity,[2] but explains why the apocalyptists wrote history under the guise of prophecy as the prelude to their prophecies. Among the stories of Daniel we find that

---

nonsense. It is safe to say that if a crime story appeared, written in the first person and bearing only the name of Lord Peter Wimsey on the title page, readers would not be long in associating the work with the authoress of "The Nine Tailors". To say that pseudonymity is integral to apocalyptic is to ignore the fact that the first half of the Book of Daniel is not pseudonymous, but anonymous. That is a vital element of the problem, which is ignored by all other views of the genesis of pseudonymity. Cf. J. Bloch, "On the Apocalyptic in Judaism", 1952, p. 51. S. B. Frost ("Old Testament Apocalyptic", 1952, p. 146) thinks my view is sufficiently overthrown by the observation that Glasson says the dependence of Daniel vii on 1 Enoch xiv is "obvious". As Charles, upon whom Glasson so often uncritically rests, held that the dependence was the other way round ("The Book of Enoch", 2nd ed., 1912, p. 34, and "Apocrypha and Pseudepigrapha", ii, 1913, p. 197), the choice of the word "obvious" is not convincing enough to settle that issue, let alone to dispose of my view.

[1] D. S. Russell ("Between the Testaments", 1960, pp. 114 ff.) suggests that the apocalyptists wrote pseudonymously because they regarded themselves as "extensions of the personality" of those whose names they used. It is very probable that the names under which they wrote were not chosen haphazard, and Principal Russell is probably right in suggesting that the name selected was related to the content of their writings. It is not probable, however, that this throws light on the origin of pseudonymity among the apocalyptists. For no possible reason could be suggested for the author of Daniel's selection of Daniel as the name under which to write, since a Daniel of the sixth century B.C. at the court of Nebuchadnezzar is otherwise quite unknown, and he had no known personality to "extend" until this book was written.

[2] H. Wheeler Robinson (*Congregational Quarterly*, xxii, 1944, p. 369) asks why the writer should need to explain pseudonymity away. The last word in this question is superfluous, for I have nowhere sought to explain it *away*. Wheeler Robinson further asks why we should not believe that some of the apocalyptists felt that they were actually expressing what the seer in whose name they spoke would have said if living in their age. But why should anyone feel it important to express what Daniel would have said, when Daniel is a figure only known to us from this book? In the case of the other apocalyptic writers the name of some well-known ancient was employed. But in this case this book created the reputation of Daniel, and did not come in under the wing of an already established reputation—save such as the author had established by the first part. That is why I have sought a view that fits the facts, and not an *a priori* view. There is, of course, a Dan'el well known to us to-day from the Ras Shamra texts of the fourteenth century B.C., whose name is spelt as in Ezek. xiv. 14, 20, xxviii. 3, and who fits the references there. But the Daniel of the Book of Daniel is a different person, represented as living in Babylon in the sixth century B.C., and known to us from no other literature independently of this book.

of Dan. ii, in which Daniel interprets the king's vision. There is no suggestion of pseudonymity here. It is merely a story of an ancient worthy who cleverly and supernaturally interpreted the king's dream, much as Joseph had interpreted Pharaoh's. If the dream was to carry a message of hope to the writer's contemporaries, as the other Daniel stories did, the intervening years had to be spanned in some way in the dream, and the author used for this purpose the idea of the four world empires, which he did not create, but took over. This feature of the form of the prophecy was but the corollary of his choice of Daniel as the hero of his stories. And when he wrote his visions under the guise of Daniel as his confession of a common authorship, he was bound to continue the same feature and bridge the gap between Daniel's ostensible age and his own. For the same reason the fiction of the sealing of the book had to be inserted, when it had become a book apparently by Daniel, instead of merely one about him, in order to convey the book, so to speak, from Daniel's day to his own. And all of this the imitators, always unable to distinguish between the accidents and the elements of what they copied, took over, and apocalyptic became esoteric. A further reason for the esoteric character was doubtless the danger of broadcasting its contents in some ages, and the necessity for limiting to the initiated the understanding of the meaning.

In treating thus of the preparation for apocalyptic in the earlier thought of the prophets I do not wish to ignore the influence of foreign thought on this literature. Many of its ideas are found outside Israel altogether, and doubtless have their roots far back in the past. The idea of four world empires, for instance, which was used with such effect by the author of the Book of Daniel in chapters ii and vii, is certainly much older than this work, and is found beyond the borders of Israel. Even where there is a manifest root in Israel, it may ultimately go back to a root without, or the idea may have been influenced by foreign thought. Thus, there may well have been widespread expectations that history was tending to a great cataclysm, when a monster of iniquity would head the forces of evil, and this idea may have been utilized by Ezekiel and by the author of Daniel in the depicting of Gog and the Little Horn.[1] Nor need we doubt that ancient mythological material was used by the apocalyptic writers. In treating of great cosmic events they would find the figures of cosmic myths appropriate to their purpose.

In particular, the influence of Persian thought must be recognized.[2] For alongside the eschatological passages in the prophets we must set the ideas of Zoroastrian eschatology, which were doubtless widely known in the Persian Empire.[3] Similarly, Persian angelology contributed to Jewish thought, to develop their ideas in this field. In the older literature of the Old Testament Yahweh has His messengers, and in His court He is surrounded by spirits (Job i. 6), including even the lying spirit who went forth to mislead the prophets in the days of Ahab (1 Kings xxii. 19 ff.). For the development of the doctrine, however, and for the ascription of names to the angels and the definition of their functions, we should look to Persian influence. The seven archangels, who are named in 1 En. xx, and some of whom figure in the Book of Daniel, are doubtless to be identified with the Amesha Spentas of Zoroastrian thought. Similarly, the sharp opposition in Persian thought between Ahura Mazda and Angra Mainyu may have contributed to the creation of the figure of Antichrist.

But whatever apocalyptic owes to prophecy, or to the apocalyptic element in the older prophecy, and whatever it owes to foreign ideas and influence, it owes more to the circumstances that gave it birth in the Maccabaean age. For the Book of Daniel is the first great apocalyptic work.[4] It was

[1] Cf. Bousset-Gressmann, "Die Religion des Judentums", p. 254. Cf., too, C. C. McCown, in *Harvard Theological Review*, xviii, 1925, pp. 257 ff., esp. p. 391.

[2] Cf. E. Meyer, "Ursprung und Anfänge des Christentums", ii, 4th ed., 1925, pp. 189 ff.; Oesterley, "The Jews and Judaism during the Greek Period", 1941, pp. 85 ff.; Albright, "From the Stone Age to Christianity", 1940, pp. 275 ff.

[3] Cf. E. Stave, "Über den Einfluss des Parsismus auf das Judentum", 1898; E. Böklen, "Die Verwandtschaft der jüdisch-christlichen mit der parsischen Eschatologie", 1902; L. H. Mills, "Avesta Eschatology compared with the Books of Daniel and Revelation", 1908; J. Scheftelowitz, "Die altpersischen Religion und das Judentum", 1920.

[4] Cf. Bousset-Gressmann, *op. cit.*, p. 12: "With Daniel begins the apocalyptic literature of Judaism."

born in some measure out of the past; but it was yet more certainly born out of the present. That this book was created in the Maccabaean age has been so far taken for granted, and will continue to be taken for granted here. There are still some writers who defend the sixth-century date, but the evidence against them seems to me to be overwhelming.[1] There are also not a few scholars who dissect the book, and assign parts of it to a date earlier than the Maccabaean age, and among these are some of the most distinguished of modern scholars.[2] But again I am not persuaded.[3] I find it easier to give an intelligible meaning to everything in the book in that age, and I find nothing which requires an earlier age. This does not mean, of course, that the author made up all the stories out of his own head. It means that he used older stories and traditions, and adapted them to his own purpose.

The situation in that age is too familiar to need more than a brief summary. Palestine had been for a hundred years under the rule of the Ptolemies of Egypt, until it was transferred to the rule of the Seleucids of Syria after the Battle of Paneion in 198 B.C. To many of the Jews the change was a welcome one, and they fondly imagined they would find the rule of the Seleucids to be less burdensome than the rule of the Ptolemies had proved. In fact, it was soon discovered to be far more burdensome. For Antiochus III, under whose rule they now passed, engaged in costly wars, and none more costly than his war with Rome, which both reduced the extent of his kingdom and involved him in the payment of a

[1] For my justification for this statement I must refer to what I have published elsewhere, in "The Aramaic of the Old Testament", 1929; "Darius the Mede", 1935; "The Belshazzar of Daniel and of History", in *The Expositor*, 9th series, ii, 1924, pp. 182 ff., 255 ff.; "The Historicity of the Fifth Chapter of Daniel", in *Journal of Theological Studies*, xxxii, 1931, pp. 12 ff.; "The Chaldaeans in the Book of Daniel", in *Expository Times*, xxxviii, 1926–7, pp. 423 ff.; "Early Aramaic Dialects and the Book of Daniel", in *Journal of the Royal Asiatic Society*, 1933, pp. 77 ff.

[2] Such as Hölscher, Welch, Baumgartner, Montgomery, Gressmann, and Eissfeldt.

[3] With this question I have dealt briefly in "Some Problems in the Book of Daniel", in *Expository Times*, xlvii, 1935–6, pp. 216 ff. See also "The Unity of the Book of Daniel", in "The Servant of the Lord", 1952, pp. 237 ff.

large indemnity to Rome, spread over a number of years. He was therefore compelled to impose heavier taxation on his subjects than the Ptolemies had imposed. His successor, Seleucus IV, at one time proposed to improve his finances by robbing the Jerusalem Temple of its treasures. Although this sacrilege was averted, it must have offended Jewish sentiment deeply that it was even contemplated. Then, in 175 B.C., Seleucus was murdered by his chief minister, Heliodorus, the man who had attempted to seize the Temple treasures. Heliodorus seems to have elevated to the throne the young son of Seleucus,[1] passing over his elder brother, Demetrius, who was a hostage in Rome. His idea was clearly to use the child as a cloak for his own ambitions, and to establish himself in effective control of the kingdom. But the brother of the murdered king appeared in Syria to dispute the upstart's control. Proclaiming himself king jointly with his nephew,[2] he soon rallied the country to himself, eliminated Heliodorus, and ere long his nephew also, leaving himself in sole possession of the kingdom. The elements among the Jews who were already disaffected towards the Seleucids would find new grounds for their disaffection in the fact that Antiochus was not the true heir to the throne, and that he had passed over Demetrius and put his young nephew out of the way. To this it should be added that Ptolemy Philometor, the reigning king of Egypt, had also some title to the throne, as a nephew of the murdered king, and there were not wanting those who held his claims to be greater than those of his uncle, Antiochus,[3] who had successfully intervened and seized the throne.

Moreover, the policy of hellenization, which Alexander the Great had begun, had been steadily carried on throughout the period of Ptolemaic rule in Palestine, and was now intensified under the Seleucids. In Alexandria there was a

[1] Cf. E. R. Bevan, "The House of Seleucus", ii, 1902, p. 126, and "Cambridge Ancient History", viii, 1930, pp. 498, 713 f.

[2] For evidence of this, cf. Bevan, "Cambridge Ancient History", *loc. cit.*

[3] Cf. Jerome on Dan. xi. 21 (Migne, "Patrologia Latina", xxv, 1845, col. 566), where it is said that there were some in Syria who favoured Ptolemy. It is probable that Syria here means Coele-Syria, or Palestine, as elsewhere in Jerome.

large Jewish colony, Greek in speech and thought, for whose use the Greek version of the Old Testament had already begun to be made, and the intercourse with this colony, as well as the administration of the Ptolemies, advanced Greek influence in Palestine throughout the period of their control. Many influential Jews welcomed this influence. Many others, however, resisted it as a menace to their faith and institutions. There was thus an inner division among the Jews, and it is vital to remember this as one of the most important factors that led to the crisis of the Maccabaean days.

There was another more sordid division in the rivalry of the house of Tobias and the High Priestly house of Onias. For while Palestine still belonged to the Ptolemies, Joseph, of the Tobiad house, secured the tax-farming rights for Palestine. Onias was the High Priest, and hence the one party had considerable influence in the religious life of the nation, while the other had great economic power. When Palestine came under the rule of the Seleucids Onias III was the High Priest, and the rivalry between the two parties was intense.

All these various factors soon began to react on one another. Onias welcomed the change to Seleucid rule, hoping to improve his position, and at the same time to check the hellenizing influence, which the Tobiads welcomed, and to maintain the strict observance of the practices of Judaism. He was soon outbidden by his rivals, however, who were not attached to the Ptolemies in any way, and whose hellenizing sympathies could soon be used to commend them to their new masters. For the Seleucids were as Greek as the Ptolemies, and as interested in the spread of Greek culture.

The situation was complicated by intermarriage between the rival houses, so that at this time we find bitter divisions within a single family, and when Onias went to the court of Seleucus IV to implore his aid, his own brother Jason headed the rival party. The murder of Seleucus at this time gave Jason an opportunity, which he immediately seized, to install himself as High Priest in his brother's room. Exploiting at once his own position and the royal bankruptcy, he got him-

46

self confirmed in the position by the offer of an increased contribution to the royal exchequer.

And now the work of hellenization was redoubled. For the hellenizing party was in full control of the administration of Jerusalem, and the new king, Antiochus IV, was particularly interested in this phase of the traditional policy of both the Ptolemaic and the Seleucid houses. Because of some supposed similarity between his own features and the traditional representations of Zeus, he posed as Zeus incarnate. Hence, he welcomed the hellenizing activities of the Jerusalem authorities, though it should not be forgotten that they were their activities, and not his.

The inner cleavage among the Jews was now very deep. Hostility to the ambition and power of Jason, resentment at the increased burden of taxation, the questioning of the title of Antiochus to the throne, and religious distrust of the policy of hellenization, all reinforced one another. The deposition of Onias and the conversion of the High Priesthood into the prize of the highest bidder shocked and scandalized the pious. This was intensified when Menelaus[1] outbade Jason and secured the office, and then had Onias murdered when he rebuked him.

Add to all this the king's ambition to add Egypt to his dominions. For Ptolemy Philometor and his brother Ptolemy Euergetes were contending for the kingdom, and Antiochus undertook the cause of Philometor, in order to secure the control of Egypt for himself, as he had secured that of Syria. But when the two brothers were reconciled he threw off the mask, and marched against them both. The brothers had made a timely appeal to Rome for protection, however, and when Antiochus arrived in Egypt he was confronted by the envoy of Rome, who demanded his immediate withdrawal. Antiochus knew that he was no match for the Roman legions,

[1] According to 2 Macc. iv. 23 ff., Menelaus was the brother of Simon, who is said in 2 Macc. iii. 4 to have been a Benjamite. But according to Josephus ("Antiquities", xii, 238 [XII, v, 1]) Menelaus was the brother of Onias, and therefore of the line of Aaron. In "Studia Orientalia Ioanni Pedersen dicata", 1953, pp. 303 ff., this question is discussed and reasons for preferring the evidence of 2 Maccabees are offered.

and so was compelled to withdraw his forces. His chagrin at this humiliation spurred him to vent his anger on the Jews, of whose disaffection he was well aware. He knew that the real strength of the opposition lay in the religious dislike of the policy of hellenization, yet it was quite impossible to conciliate that opposition, save by throwing over the only friends upon whom he could depend. Hence, he determined to destroy Judaism root and branch, in order to destroy the political disaffection with which it was allied. For the titular leaders of Judaism had no real interest in its faith, now that the High Priesthood had been so turned over to the hellenizing party.

Antiochus therefore forbade all the special practices of Judaism, including the observance of the Sabbath and the rite of circumcision, and turned the Temple into a temple of Zeus. An idol of Zeus, doubtless in the form of an image of the king himself, was set up in the Temple, and swine's flesh was offered there.[1] The Jews were bidden to sacrifice to idols and to eat unclean foods, and all copies of the Scriptures were ordered to be destroyed. Death was laid down as the penalty for resistance to the king's commands. Many paid that penalty, until Mattathias, a priest of Modein, slew an apostate Jew who was about to comply with the demand to offer heathen sacrifice, and then slew one of the royal officers. Thereupon the standard of revolt was raised, and a bitter struggle began.

---

[1] Jerome says that both an idol of Zeus and images of the king were set up (Commentary on Dan. xi. 31, in Migne, "Patrologia Latina", xxv, col. 569). Cf. Vulgate rendering in 1 Macc. i. 57, *abominandum idolum desolationis*. It is frequently said that Antiochus erected an altar but not an image. So C. F. Keil, "Commentar über die Bücher der Makkabäer", 1875, p. 53; E. Kautzsch, "Die Apokryphen und Pseudepigraphen des Alten Testaments", 1900, p. 36 n.; W. Fairweather and J. S. Black, "The First Book of Maccabees" (Cambridge Bible), 1908 ed., p. 70; W. O. E. Oesterley, in R. H. Charles, "Apocrypha and Pseudepigrapha", i, 1913, p. 70; H. Bévenot, "Die beiden Makkabäerbücher" (Bonner Bibel), 1931, p. 56; D. Schotz, "Erstes und zweites Buch der Makkabäer" (Echter Bibel), 1948, p. 8; F.-M. Abel, "Les livres des Maccabées" (Études Bibliques), 1949, p. 27. In "Studia Orientalia I. Pedersen dicata", pp. 309 ff., reasons are offered for preferring the view of Jerome. Cf. also H. Graetz, "Geschichte der Israeliten", ii. 2, 2nd ed., 1878, p. 315; C. Gutberlet, "Das erste Buch der Machabäer", 1920, p. 27.

48

In a most valuable study of this struggle, Bickermann[1] has argued that it was fundamentally a civil war between two Jewish parties, of which one was supported by the Government. Yet the Government was not a disinterested spectator, merely supporting this policy because its friends wanted it. Its friends were interested in the policy in part because they knew this would commend them to the Government, and into the complex causes that produced the rising there went external as well as internal factors. It is true that there is no evidence that Antiochus undertook any persecution elsewhere in order to enforce religious obedience, but it is unlikely that anywhere else in his dominions he would find such fierce opposition to the policy of hellenization as he found among the Jews. And the persecution was as much born of the opposition as the opposition was of the hellenization. There was action and reaction in the development of the situation, and religious and political elements were fused together in it. To regard Antiochus as the sole cause is, of course, wholly wrong. But to minimize his part in it would be equally wrong. Bickermann has shown that the religion Antiochus attempted to enforce in Palestine was a hellenized oriental cult, rather than a Greek cult, in which Baal-shamin was equated with Zeus, Allat was equated with Athena, and Dusara was equated with Dionysos. This marriage of hellenism with orientalism was characteristic of the Macedonian policy throughout, but the oriental element here was of the type which the prophets had always condemned rather than that which was embodied in Judaism, and any Jewish party which favoured it was guilty of as grave an offence against the spirit of Judaism as if it had been a purely Greek cult that was introduced.[2] The proscription of the Scriptures of Judaism is sufficient evidence that it was incompatible with Judaism.

In the light of this situation, the Book of Daniel can be readily understood. For if the author wished to hearten the faithful in the time of affliction and persecution, what better

---

[1] "Der Gott der Makkabäer", 1938.

[2] Cf. O. Eissfeldt, "Ba'alšamēm und Jahwe", in *Zeitschrift für die alttestamentliche Wissenschaft*, lvii (N.F. xvi), 1939, pp. 1–31.

medium could he have chosen than that of the stories of the first part of the book? They were entertaining, as well as charged with a message, and so they could easily be remembered and passed from mouth to mouth. That they were stories about Nebuchadnezzar and Belshazzar and Darius would make them innocuous superficially, but those for whom they were written would easily be given the clue to their understanding.[1] We have but to remember that a newspaper in German-occupied Paris during the war published a poem which read superficially as an attack on Britain and praise of Germany. But divided vertically and read as two stanzas, the meaning was precisely reversed.[2] It would be no harder to whisper the clue in Palestine than in Paris, and probably no harder to get past the friends of Antiochus than to get past the Paris censorship. The situation prevailing at the time offers sufficient reason to account for the taking of these ancient names, and the weaving of the things the author wanted to say into a framework of such knowledge about their owners as he had. He told of a king who carried off the sacred vessels of the house of God and brought them to the treasure house of his god (Dan. i. 2), and his readers might be reminded of Antiochus, who entered the sanctuary and took the golden altar and all the precious vessels, and carried them off to his own land (1 Macc. i. 21 ff.). He told of a king who set up a colossal image and commanded all men to worship it on pain of death (Dan. iii), and his readers might be reminded of the image set up in the Temple, colossal in its significance rather than its size, and of the dire penalties incurred by those who refused to worship it (1 Macc. i. 41 ff.). He told of a king who was plunged from the heights of his own vaunting pride into madness and contempt (Dan. iv), and his readers might be reminded of the king who called himself Epiphanes, God manifest in the flesh, but who was

[1] We may note in passing that the suggestion has been made that the figure of Gog was a similar substitute for Nebuchadnezzar in Ezek. xxxviii f. Cf. I. G. Matthews, "Ezekiel", 1935, p. 143. In that case, it would be a fitting irony of circumstance that turned Nebuchadnezzar into the lay figure of a later age.

[2] See *The Times*, April 25, 1941, p. 3.

called by others Epimanes, the madman.[1] He told of a king who committed sacrilege with the sacred vessels of the Temple, and of the swift doom he brought on himself, and his readers might be again reminded of the desecration of the Temple by Antiochus, and the prostitution of the sacred vessels to the service of the king, and they would take heart at the implied promise of a swift end for him.

Moreover, the stories were not merely about Nebuchadnezzar, and Belshazzar, and Darius, pillorying Antiochus under these names. They were stories first and foremost about loyal men who refused to compromise their faith, and who were delivered by God. They told of three who refused to worship the king's image, who showed superb courage and confidence in God, and who came unscathed through the flames (Dan. iii). But chiefly they were stories about Daniel, around whose name they therefore gathered as a whole. They told how he refused to eat unclean foods, how he fearlessly rebuked kings, how he refused to abandon his own religious practices, despite the threats of a monarch. All of this had meaning to men in the days of crisis in which the author lived.

And beyond this, the author wished to tell the faithful that the supreme moment of history was at hand, and that the latter end of the days had come. Yet a little while and their faithfulness would be rewarded, not alone by their individual deliverance, but by the breaking of the Golden Age, when evil should be finally destroyed and the enduring kingdom of God be established. To present this message in the form of a story about Nebuchadnezzar, he adopted the simple device of presenting it as the king's dream, in which the borrowed idea of four world empires was used to bridge the intervening period and bring him to the present, where the climax of the dream had to be located. Here the interpreter of the dream was the same Daniel. Subsequent messages, emphasizing the promise of the swift approach of the climax

[1] Cf. Polybius xxvi. 10 (Loeb ed., edited by W. R. Paton, v, 1927, pp. 480 f.); Athenaeus ii. 45 c, v. 193 d, x. 493 a (Loeb ed., edited by C. B. Gulick, i, 1927, pp. 196 f., ii, 1928, pp. 376 f., iv, 1930, pp. 488 f.).

of the age, and the great world judgement, to be followed by the glorious and everlasting kingdom of God, administered by the saints, were thrown into the form of visions seen by Daniel and interpreted to him by angels. Repeatedly is it indicated that this climax is to follow hard on the setting up of the appalling abomination, by which the readers would understand the altar and image erected in the Temple. For the name by which Zeus was worshipped would be Lord of Heaven, but for the first word *abomination* was substituted, rather than call this idol *Lord*, while a slight twist was given to the second word, to reflect the horror caused to the pious by this desecration. In its altered form the second word has associations also with the idea of madness, and it may be that there is a further punning reference to Antiochus in the thought of the "abomination of the Madman".[1]

This first great apocalypse, therefore, was born partly out of the past, and partly out of the situation of the hour. It was not written to be a puzzle for the curious, but to be a living source of strength to men in a situation on which we can look back with calm complacency, but which to them was the supreme moment of destiny. The author was not concerned with the historical exactness of the traditions with which he worked, for he was not a historian producing a work of scientific research. He had scant opportunity, and probably scant resources, available for that. He was concerned to play a part in the great events through which he was living, and to mediate a divine message to the tortured men around him. He took what traditions serviceable to his purpose he could, and he worked with such ideas as were current, so long as they fitted his main aim. And of these he fashioned a great work, which can be rightly understood only in the light of its genesis. Its success made it the model which others copied. Moreover, the non-fulfilment of its hopes led others to re-adapt them to the circumstances of their own time. The Ezra Apocalypse, for instance, re-interprets Dan. vii. There we read: "This is the interpretation of the vision which thou hast seen. The eagle which thou sawest come up from the sea

[1] Cf. *Zeitschrift für die alttest. Wissenschaft*, N.F. ix, 1932, pp. 264 f.

is the fourth kingdom which appeared in vision to thy brother Daniel; but it was not interpreted unto him as I now interpret it unto thee" (2 Esdr. xii. 10–12) Others without specific reference to the Book of Daniel sought to dress its hope of the approaching judgement in garments woven out of the situation of their own day. In one sense they completely misunderstood the book they copied. For they read it primarily as a prediction of the end, whereas it was primarily a word of power for men in dire need. As a prediction of the end it was a failure, but as a powerful spiritual force it was a great success, as the popularity that secured for it a place in the Canon testifies. In another sense, however, the imitators of the book did not misunderstand it. For, as we shall see, they were repeating for their generation the same essential service, and keeping alive the flame of hope in dark and difficult days.

CHAPTER TWO

The Apocalyptic Literature:
i. During the Last Two Centuries B.C.

THE PAST century has brought to light an unsuspected array of apocalyptic writings that followed the Book of Daniel. Only the swiftest and most cursory of glances can be taken at these, to see something of their individuality and of their contribution to the development of ideas. For while it was not without reason, as will appear, that only two great apocalypses were received into the Canon, the one in the Old Testament and the other in the New, all the works of this character that lay between them had their part tó play in the development. Our survey will therefore be limited to the period starting with the Book of Daniel and ending with the Book of Revelation. It will also be limited to apocalyptic works or passages, and will not take account of all the eschatological ideas found in non-apocalyptic works, though these ideas are often closely related to those found in the apocalypses. For we must distinguish between apocalyptic and eschatology. Just because so much eschatology enters into all apocalyptic, the two terms are commonly confused; but the ideas of apocalyptic eschatology may be found in works that could not be described as apocalypses. For instance, in the Pauline writings of the New Testament there are not a few of the ideas and expectations that we shall find in apocalyptic. For the Church took over and re-adapted these expectations. This, however, does not convert the Epistles of Paul into apocalyptic works, and they will therefore be left without reference. They have no place in a study of apocalyptic literature, though they have a place in the study of the influence of apocalyptic literature on the current of the Church's thought.

The Book of Daniel

Little need here be added to what has been already said about the Book of Daniel. That it dates from the Maccabaean period has been taken for granted, and reference has been made to its use of the idea of four world ages, culminating in the author's day, and to its use of the term "Son of Man" as a symbol for the expected enduring kingdom to be administered by the saints. Familiar is its use of symbolism, in the form of animals and horns for kingdoms and kings, and its use of numbers. For not alone do the four world empires figure in it, but also the seventy weeks. And always the climax is indicated as falling in the time of Antiochus Epiphanes, with the mysterious time, times and half a time, or specified number of days, or of evenings and mornings, pointing to the time when the Temple sacrifices were interrupted and the Temple desolate.

Of greater importance was the author's doctrine of the Kingdom of God. He conceived of it as a political kingdom, exercised in an earthly state, and administered by Jewish saints. But more significant than this, he conceived of it as a kingdom in which the will of God should be supreme and unchallenged. Every evil force should be overthrown, and all that exalted itself against God should be cast out. The kingdom should therefore endure for ever, just because it should contain within itself no seed of disintegration.

Nor can we ignore the contribution of this book to the development of thought on the future life. For here the resurrection of some of them that sleep in the earth, both good and bad, is distinctly taught (Dan. xii. 2). For this there were preparations in earlier Old Testament thought,[1] and the idea of resurrection can be found in foreign thought. But I believe that fundamentally the author's teaching did not arise from either, but from the inner dynamic of his own earlier stories. He had proclaimed that God was able to

---

[1] On the Old Testament preparation for the thought cf. my "Faith of Israel", 1956, pp. 150 ff.; E. F. Sutcliffe, "The Old Testament and the Future Life", 1946. For a valuable study of the subject in the post-exilic and intertestamental literature see K. Schubert, in *Biblische Zeitschrift*, N.F. vi, 1962, pp. 177 ff.

deliver men who trusted in Him and obeyed His will, and in his stories such men were always delivered. And he profoundly believed that God could so deliver. But the plain fact was that God did not deliver the men who suffered in Maccabaean days. Many were martyred ere the triumph of their cause came. Could it be that they whose loyalty and sacrifice had been in the service of the kingdom would be denied a share in it? That were an offence against justice, and the God of all the earth must do right. If He had not delivered them in the hour of their suffering it was because He purposed a more glorious vindication. For if they were to share in the joy of the kingdom, then they must be raised from the dead, since the kingdom was to be an earthly kingdom.[1] In the same way it had to be recognized that some of the enemies of the saints had died, while swift destruction seemed too slight a penalty for men who were guilty of such heinous sins. Hence, our author looked for their resurrection to an unceasing torment and dishonour. His ideas are therefore very different from those that became current in the Christian Church. He thinks of no general resurrection, but only the resurrection of some of the dead, and he thinks of that resurrection as imminent in his day, and as a resurrection to life on earth.

The angelology of this book is also interesting. In the older literature of the Old Testament angels figure as the messengers of God, but here we find the differentiation of their functions, and the attribution of names to them. Elsewhere in the Old Testament we find the Satan, with a defined function, but it must be remembered that at first this was not a proper name, but merely a title defining the function of a member of God's heavenly court. He was the Adversary, a sort of Public Prosecutor at the bar of divine justice, until he became thought of as the embodiment of the evil he had to expose, and his office of adversary became his name, Satan. Here, however, in the Book of Daniel, we find angels named in quite a different fashion. We find Gabriel and Michael,

[1] Cf. A. Causse, "Der Ursprung der jüdischen Lehre von der Auferstehung", 1908, pp. 39 ff.

and since the latter is called one of the chief princes (Dan. x. 13), it would seem that a hierarchy of angels was thought of. It is almost certain that here the author is reflecting the influence of Persian ideas, though it must be remembered that these ideas were working on a basis of Hebrew ideas that goes back to the very beginnings of Israelite literature.

The Ethiopic Book of Enoch (1 Enoch)

Three apocalyptic works connected with the name of Enoch[1] have come down to us,[2] known as the Ethiopic Book of Enoch, the Slavonic Book of Enoch, and the Hebrew Book of Enoch, according to the language in which they have reached us. Of these the third lies outside our period and will not call for consideration.[3] The Ethiopic is the oldest work, and it is generally recognized to be of composite authorship. Its earliest sections are sometimes dated earlier than the Book of Daniel, but on inadequate grounds.[4] They belong rather to the Maccabaean than to the pre-Maccabaean age, and probably come from a time very soon after the appearance of the Book of Daniel. Of these sections the ones that concern us are: (a) chapters vi–xxxvi; (b) chapters xciii. 1–10, xci. 12–17, known as the Apocalypse of Weeks; (c) chapters xci–civ, excluding the Apocalypse of Weeks; (d) chapters xxxvii–lxxi, known as the Similitudes of Enoch; (e) chapters lxxxiii–xc.[5]

In the first of these sections, containing chapters vi–xxxvi, we find that evil is traced to the fallen angels and their lust for the daughters of men (1 En. vi f.). This myth is an

---

[1] For a study of the origin and signification of the Enoch legend cf. P. Grelot, in *Recherches de Science Religieuse*, xlvi, 1958, pp. 5 ff., 181 ff.

[2] Cf. S. Mowinckel, "Henokskikkelsen i senjødisk apokalyptikk", in *Norsk Teologisk Tidsskrift*, 1940, pp. 206–36.

[3] See H. Odeberg, "3 Enoch", 1928. G. S. Scholem ("Major Trends in Jewish Mysticism", 1941, p. 44) brings this work down some centuries later than Odeberg places it.

[4] See Note A at the end of this chapter.

[5] C. P. van Andel ("De Struktuur van de Henoch-Traditie en het Nieuwe Testament", 1955) essays a study of the growth of 1 Enoch as a reflection of the history of the community within which the book came into being.

ancient one,[1] appearing first in Gen. vi. 1 ff., but here it is developed in the thought that though the Deluge had destroyed the children of these unions, their spirits still infest the earth as demons, and prove themselves to be the source of every kind of corruption (1 En. xv. 8 ff.). A great world judgement is awaited, where the fallen angels, demons, and men should receive the recompense of their deeds (1 En. x. 6, xvi. 1, xix. 1). It is probable that the author believed that before that judgement there would be a resurrection from Sheol of those now gathered there,[2] comparable with the expectation we have found in the Book of Daniel. In the conception of Sheol, however, there is an advance on the views found in the Old Testament. For here the souls in Sheol are not thought of as herded together, in a uniform condition of misery, but tentatively divided into groups according to their condition and experience in life (1 En. xxii). After the judgement the establishment of the Golden Age was looked for, with Jerusalem and the Temple as its centre (1 En. xxv. 5), and thither the tree of life should be brought, so that the righteous might feed thereon (1 En. xxv. 4 f.). There is no Messiah in the picture, and the bliss of the righteous is conceived in sensuous terms. They shall each beget a thousand children, and their material blessings will be unlimited (1 En. x. 17). Not wholly devoid of spiritual content, however, is the author's conception of the Golden Age, for truth and peace shall mark it for ever (1 En. xi. 1 f.).

The second of these sections, known as the Apocalypse of Weeks, consists of but a few verses, in which the history of the world is divided into ten periods, of which seven are past, and three are to come.[3] The seventh week is marked by apostasy, while the eighth week is the week of righteousness. The ninth should see the destruction of all the works of the godless, and

---

[1] For a study of this myth, cf. J. Morgenstern, "The Mythological Background of Psalm 82", in *Hebrew Union College Annual*, xiv, 1939, pp. 29–126. Cf. also A. Lods, "La chute des anges", in *Revue d'Histoire et de Philosophie Religieuses*, vii, 1927, pp. 295 ff.

[2] This is not explicitly stated, but is deduced by Charles from xxii. 13.

[3] J. P. Thorndike (*Revue de Qumran*, iii, 1961, pp. 163 ff.) finds in this Apocalypse of Weeks a secret history of the Qumran sect.

the tenth should witness the final judgement on the angels, the creation of a new heaven, and the inauguration of an eternity of sinless joy. The section is too brief for any of its ideas to be developed, but we observe the division of history into periods, comparable with the world empires of the Book of Daniel, culminating in a great and final judgement and in eternal bliss for the righteous.

The third of the sections, containing the rest of chapters xci–civ, depicts the persecuted righteous and their wicked oppressors. It is common to locate this section in the time of Alexander Jannaeus, in the first century B.C., and to interpret it of the conflict between the Pharisees and the Sadducees,[1] but Frey[2] finds the time of Antiochus Epiphanes to yield a more fitting background. The wicked are accused of apostasy and blasphemy and idolatry, of following foreign customs and renouncing their own, and Frey finds a reference to alliance with foreign foes which would point rather to the Maccabaean age than to the time of Alexander Jannaeus. The wicked are promised eternal torment in Sheol (1 En. xcix. 11, ciii. 7 f.), while the spirits of the righteous shall enter heaven's portals with joy (1 En. ciii. 3 f., civ. 2 ff.). It is to be observed that there is here nothing apocalyptic in the strict sense of the term. There is no coming kingdom on earth, but only in the Hereafter will the balance of desert and recompense be redressed. No deliverance is promised to the sufferers on this side of the grave, comparable with that held out in the stories of the Book of Daniel, and no return to earth to blissful experience, such as the Book of Daniel promised. It is, however, to be noted that the differentiation within Sheol, which we have above found in the first section of 1 Enoch, is here developed into the separation of the wicked and the righteous in Sheol and Heaven.

[1] So Charles, "The Book of Enoch", 2nd ed., 1912, pp. liii f., and "Apocrypha and Pseudepigrapha", ii, p. 171. Eissfeldt, however, thinks this is doubtful. Cf. "Einleitung in das Alte Testament", 2nd ed., pp. 765 f.

[2] In Pirot's "Supplément au Dictionnaire de la Bible", i, col. 367. J. Bonsirven ("La Bible Apocryphe", 1953, p. 71) dates these chapters "au commencement du second siècle avant J.-C.", where "second" is probably a slip for "premier".

In the section known as the Similitudes of Enoch[1] we find no reference to the fallen angels, but the wicked are said to be the subjects of the Satans (1 En. liv. 6), who, unlike the fallen angels, have access to heaven (1 En. xl. 7 f.). This was doubtless due to the account of the Satan's activity in the Prologue to the Book of Job, where also he was found in the court of God. The coming kingdom figures in the Similitudes, but its establishment is placed not in Jerusalem, but in a new heaven and a new earth (1 En. xlv. 4 f.). For this again there is Old Testament foundation in Isa. lxv. 17, lxvi. 22. We repeatedly find in the Similitudes the expression "Son of Man", alongside other designations of the leader of the coming kingdom. Many scholars have held that the work has been interpolated by a Christian editor, and in particular they have found the references to the Son of Man to

[1] Charles ("The Book of Enoch", 2nd ed., p. liv, and "Apocrypha and Pseudepigrapha", ii, p. 171) would date the Similitudes in the first century B.C., either between 94 and 79 B.C. or between 70 and 64 B.C. (cf. F. Martin, "Le Livre d'Hénoch", 1906, p. xcvii, and J. Bonsirven, "La Bible Apocryphe", 1953, p. 46), but again Eissfeldt would go back to a date in the second century B.C. ("Einleitung", 2nd ed., pp. 765 f.), while Frey argues cogently for the second century B.C. and maintains that a Maccabaean background is reflected (loc. cit., cols. 361 f.). He would assign the composition of this section to a date soon after the death of Antiochus Epiphanes (col. 364). It is to be noted that while fragments of the other sections of 1 Enoch have been found among the Dead Sea Scrolls, no fragments of the Similitudes have appeared. J. T. Milik ("Ten Years of Discovery in the Wilderness of Judaea", Eng. trans., 1959, p. 33) thinks this can scarcely be due to chance, and would date the Similitudes in the first or second century A.D. Cf. F. M. Cross, "The Ancient Library of Qumran", 1958, p. 150 n. This is a large conclusion to draw from silence, when all that we have from Qumran is a mass of fragments. The Habakkuk Commentary does not contain Hab. iii, and since the last page is incomplete, it is certain that it never contained it. Yet few would conclude that the Bible of Qumran did not contain this chapter. Similarly, no fragment of the Book of Esther has turned up at Qumran. Yet most scholars hesitate to draw bold conclusions from this. It may indeed be that these parts of the Bible and the Similitudes of Enoch did not exist in the Qumran Library, but the argument from the absence of fragments is most precarious. M. Delcor ("Essai sur le Midrash d'Habacuc", 1951, pp. 55 f., and Revue Biblique, lviii, 1951, pp. 535 ff.) finds some links between the Scrolls and the Similitudes. Older scholars who held the Similitudes to have been composed during the Christian era include A. Hilgenfeld, "Die jüdische Apokalyptik", 1857, pp. 148 ff.; and A. Kuenen, "The Religion of Israel", Eng. trans. by A. H. May, iii, 1883, p. 265. E. de Faye ("Les Apocalypses juives", 1892, pp. 212 ff.) and J. Drummond ("The Jewish Messiah", 1877, pp. 23 ff.) held the Similitudes to be of pre-Christian origin, but with Christian interpolations.

be accretions, and have accordingly removed them. It is sometimes noted that the oldest manuscript of the Similitudes does not go farther back than the fifteenth century, and that although the work was known to the early Fathers, none of them mention any of a whole series of striking parallels to the Gospels found in our present text. Messel[1] argues that the expression "Son of Man" is original in only two passages, where it designates not an individual, but the elect people, as in Dan. vii, and Manson[2] independently believes the term is a collective one in this work. He similarly holds that the other terms employed, "the Righteous One", "the Elect One", and "the Anointed One (Messiah)", are collective in their reference, while Messel[3] eliminates the term Messiah as unoriginal, and where he does not eliminate "the Elect One" treats it as collective.

It seems precarious to treat as interpolations all, or nearly all, of the Son of Man passages,[4] though scarcely less so to pronounce with any confidence against the interpolation hypothesis. It seems best, therefore, to concede them the benefit of the doubt, and to treat them as genuine until more conclusive reasons against them can be found.[5] It should be remembered, however, that even though we accept all of these passages, and even though we equate all of these terms, and treat them all as individual in their reference, that does not involve the equating of the Son of Man with the Messiah, in the technical sense of that term. For in the Similitudes there is no Messiah in the sense of a human deliverer, whether of Davidic or of any other descent, and there is nothing

[1] "Der Menschensohn in den Bilderreden des Henoch", 1922, pp. 3 ff.

[2] "The Teaching of Jesus", pp. 228 f. On the Son of Man in 1 Enoch, cf. Volz, "Eschatologie der jüdischen Gemeinde im neutest. Zeitalter", 1934, pp. 186 f. More recently Manson has modified his view to the extent of recognizing that the concept of the Son of Man is both individual and collective, with something of the fluidity of the concept of "corporate personality". Cf. *Bulletin of the John Rylands Library*, xxxii, 1949–50, pp. 188 ff.

[3] *Op. cit.*, p. 31.

[4] Cf. M. Goguel, in *Revue d'Histoire et de Philosophie Religieuses*, v, 1925, p. 526; also E. Sjöberg, "Der Menschensohn im äthiopischen Henochbuch", 1946, pp. 14 ff.

[5] Cf. S. Mowinckel, "He that Cometh", Eng. trans., 1956, p. 355, where it is held that these passages are integral to the text.

whatever here to associate that Old Testament hope, which
the New Testament expresses by the word Messiah, or Christ,
with the Son of Man. For here the Anointed One is a purely
transcendental figure. So, too, is the Son of Man, and while
the Book of Enoch may have exercised an influence on New
Testament thought and expression, if all of these passages are
genuine it could hardly have prepared men for our Lord's
appropriation of the title.[1] In Dan. vii the Son of Man is a
figure for the community of saints invested with power from
on high to rule in the eternal kingdom. In Enoch, if we
equate the terms mentioned above, we have a pre-existent

[1] R. Otto ("The Kingdom of God and the Son of Man", Eng. trans., 1938,
pp. 219 ff.) believes the Book of Enoch did very definitely prepare for our
Lord's use of the title, but that He did not appropriate the title, or teach that
He was the Son of Man. He finds 1 Enoch to express the idea that "a powerful
preacher alike of righteousness, the coming judgment and the blessed new age, a
prophet of the eschatological Son of Man, would be transported at the end of
his earthly career to God; that he would be exalted to become the one whom he
had proclaimed" (*ibid.*, p. 213). In the Book of Enoch he finds Enoch himself
exalted to be the Son of Man, on the basis of 1 En. lxxi. 14, where the text reads:
"Thou art the Son of Man". In the same way he thinks Jesus worked pro-
leptically with the powers of the Son of Man, but that it was not His calling to
teach the secret of His person. It should, however, be noted that in 1 En.
lxxi. 14 Charles believes something has fallen out of the text, and he reads:
"This is the Son of Man" ("The Book of Enoch", 1912, pp. 144 f.; cf. L. Gry,
in *Le Muséon*, ix, 1908, pp. 324 f.); so also P. Riessler, "Altjüdischen Schrifttum
ausserhalb der Bibel", 1928, p. 403. Martin ("Le Livre d'Hénoch", 1906, p.
161) retains the text and renders "Thou art the son of man", indicating by the
small *s* that he differentiates from the Son of Man of xlvi. 3, where, however,
analogous things are said of the Son of Man, as Martin himself agrees. S.
Mowinckel ("He that Cometh", pp. 442 f.; cf. *Norsk Teologisk Tidsskrift*, xlv,
1944, pp. 59 ff.) similarly retains the rendering "Thou art the Son of Man" in
lxxi. 14, but maintains that "Son of Man" is here not a technical term, but is
used in the ordinary sense, as a common noun, "that man who". Cf. H.
Lietzmann, "Der Menschensohn", 1896, p. 46, where both passages are
similarly rendered, xlvi. 3 being translated "this is a man", and lxxi. 14 "you
are a man". For others who retain the text in lxxi. 14, cf. H. H. Rowley, "The
Servant of the Lord", p. 77, n. 3. My difficulty with Otto's view is that if 1
Enoch identifies Enoch with the Son of Man, and if 1 Enoch influenced our
Lord's assumption of the title Son of Man, the implied identification of Himself
with Enoch might have been expected to leave some trace in the Gospels. Cf.
Glasson, "The Second Advent", 1945, pp. 48 ff. On 1 En. lxxi. 14 and the
whole problem, cf. S. Mowinckel, "Henok og 'Menneskesønnen'", in *Norsk
Teologisk Tidsskrift*, 1944, pp. 57–69. R. Laurence ("The Book of Enoch the
Prophet", 3rd ed., 1838, p. 46) rendered xlvi. 3 "This is the Son of man", and
(p. 84) lxxi. 14 (here numbered lxx. 17) "Thou art the offspring of man". J.
Bonsirven ("La Bible Apocryphe", 1953, p. 51) renders xlvi. 3 "It is the Son of
man", but lxxi. 14 is not included among the passages selected for translation.

Being,[1] seated on the throne of glory, possessing all dominion and pronouncing all judgement. This is no human figure, but rather the personifying of the Danielic concept of the Son of Man in a supramundane person who should be the representative and head of the kingdom that concept symbolized, and who should come down to dwell with men.[2] For Christians to read back their thought of the Person of Christ into this is one thing, but to equate it with any pre-Christian expectation of a deliverer that can properly be called the Messiah is quite another.

In the section of the book contained in chapters lxxxiii–xc we have recorded two visions, of which the first deals with the Deluge, and the second with the history of the world up to the final judgement. Once more we find reference to the myth of the fallen angels, to whom sin is traced. In the second vision we have a general sketch of the history of Israel, under the figure of sheep, down to the last attack of the Gentiles on the Jews, when a powerful horn sprouted on one of the sheep, against which the enemy had no power (1 En. xc. 9 ff.). This probably refers to the Maccabees.[3] The final assault of the

---

[1] T. W. Manson (*Bulletin of the John Rylands Library*, xxxii, 1949–50, pp. 178 ff.) maintains that the Son of Man is pre-existent only in the sense of having existed in the purpose of God from the beginning of time, and that he was now about to be given reality in the community of the saints, so that he could more fittingly be described as unborn than as pre-existing. Cf. M. Black, in *Expository Times*, lx, 1948–9, p. 14. For the view that he is a pre-existent, transcendental being, cf. W. Staerk, "Soter", 1933, pp. 72 ff., and "Die Erlösererwartung in den östlichen Religionen", 1938, pp. 438 ff.; A. H. Edelkoort, "De Christusverwachting in het Oude Testament", 1941, p. 500; E. Sjöberg, "Der Menschensohn im äthiopischen Henochbuch", pp. 83 ff.; S. Mowinckel, "He that Cometh", Eng. trans., pp. 370 ff.

[2] T. F. Glasson ("The Second Advent", 1945, pp. 14 ff., 25 ff.) agrees that the Similitudes of Enoch depend on Dan. vii, but assumes that the Son of Man began as an individual figure in 1 En. xiv, where it stands for Enoch himself, was then taken over by the author of Dan. vii and turned into a symbol of the collective body of the saints, and then taken over by the author of the Similitudes, but once again individualized. The statement of this improbable sequence can hardly be said to establish it.

[3] Schürer ("History of the Jewish People", II, iii, p. 66) observes: "Nothing but stubborn prejudice can prevent anyone from seeing that, by the symbolism of the lambs (xc. 6), the Maccabees are to be understood. . . . The fourth period extends from the commencement of the Maccabaean age on to the author's own day." Schürer identifies the great horn with John Hyrcanus. This would bring the composition of this section towards the end of the second

enemy should usher in the last judgement, when the wicked should be destroyed (1 En. xc. 20 ff.), and the surviving Gentiles should be converted and serve Israel (1 En. xc. 30). The righteous dead should arise (1 En. xc. 33), and the Messiah should arise to lead them (1 En. xc. 37). Here the actual term "Messiah" is not used, nor is there any thought of a scion of the house of David. But a human figure is clearly in mind, since he is described as a white bull that was born, to whom all creatures made petition, and into whose likeness they were transformed. In all this the influence of the Book of Daniel is clearly manifest. The use of the figures of sheep and bulls, and of horns, to symbolize men, bears the clearest marks of that influence, and the thought of the final great assault on the Jews, followed by the destruction of their foes and the resurrection of the righteous, closely resembles what we find in Daniel. At the same time the author holds himself free to bring in ideas from other sources, and to rework the whole into a new picture.

The Book of Jubilees

The Book of Jubilees derives its name from the fact that it divides history into jubilee periods of forty-nine years.[1] In

century B.C. Here Charles argues for an earlier date, not later than 161 B.C. ("The Book of Enoch", 2nd ed., p. liii, and "Apocrypha and Pseudepigrapha", ii, p. 171), and with this date Frey agrees (*loc. cit.*, col. 365). Cf. F. Martin, "Le Livre d'Hénoch", p. 96, and J. Bonsirven, "La Bible Apocryphe", p. 68.

[1] Much attention has been directed to the calendar of Jubilees in recent years, since the finding of the Dead Sea Scrolls. The Zadokite Work (see below pp. 80 ff.) favoured the same calendar, and there can be little doubt that the Zadokite Work came from the Qumran sect (see below, p. 86). This calendar of Jubilees was a fifty-two week calendar, in which all festivals fell on the same day each year. Cf. D. Barthélemy, in *Revue Biblique*, lix, 1952, pp. 199 ff.; A. Jaubert, in *Revue de l'Histoire des Religions*, cxlvi, 1954, pp. 140 ff., and *Vetus Testamentum*, iii, 1953, pp. 250 ff., vii, 1957, pp. 35 ff.; J. Morgenstern, in *Vetus Testamentum*, v, 1955, pp. 34 ff.; J. Obermann, in *Journal of Biblical Literature*, lxxv, 1956, pp. 285 ff.; S. Talmon, in "Aspects of the Dead Sea Scrolls" (Scripta Hierosolymitana IV), 1958, pp. 162 ff.; E. E. Ettisch, *Revue de Qumran*, iii, 1961, pp. 125 ff.; A. Strobel, *ibid.*, pp. 395 ff. Mlle Jaubert has argued that Jesus and His disciples kept the Passover according to this calendar, and has explained by this means the disagreement between the Synoptic Gospels and the Fourth Gospel as to whether the Last Supper was a Passover meal (cf. especially "La Date de la Cène", 1957, and in *New Testament Studies*, vii, 1960–1, pp. 1 ff.). For references to some of the scholars who have supported or opposed this view cf. *Bulletin of the John Rylands Library*, xliv, 1961–2, pp. 148 f.

the Pentateuch the jubilee year is the year that follows the seven sevens, i.e. the fiftieth year, but here there is no provision for this fiftieth year in the scheme, but only the reckoning by jubilee periods of forty-nine years. The book is also called the Little Genesis, where "little" does not refer to the size of the book, but to the detail into which it enters. Yet again it is called the Apocalypse of Moses, because in form it is a revelation made to Moses at Sinai. God is said to have there unfolded to Moses all history past and future (Jub. i. 4, 26), and to have commanded an angel of the presence to share in its literary preservation.

That the work really belongs to the second century B.C. has been generally agreed, though complete agreement as to the closer definition of the date has been wanting. Recently, however, earlier dates have been proposed, carrying the work back to the fourth or fifth century B.C., but on grounds which do not appear to be adequate.[1] All probability, indeed, points to a Maccabaean date.

When we turn to examine the eschatological teaching of the book, we find that the author appears to have thought that the Messianic age had already set in. But his conception of that age was quite other than the author of Daniel's. He looked for no catastrophic event, but for a gradual coming of the kingdom. Men's days would gradually grow longer, until they attained a thousand years (Jub. xxiii. 27). For this there was some preparation, indeed, in Isa. lxv. 20, where it is promised that death at a hundred years old shall be regarded as the death of an infant, or the premature cutting off of the sinner. According to Jub. xxiii. 11, it would appear that the great Judgement would precede this gradual establishment of the kingdom, as in Daniel and 1 En. lxxxiii–xc it preceded the dramatic establishment of that kingdom, but Charles finds this hard to reconcile with other ideas in the book, and concludes that to this author the kingdom was not eternal, and that it would end in the general judgement.[2]

[1] See Note B at the end of this chapter. A. Büchler (*Revue des Études juives*, lxxxii, 1926, pp. 253 ff.) argued that Jubilees was written in Greek. As fragments of the work in Hebrew have been found in the Qumran caves, this is most unlikely. [2] "The Book of Jubilees", 1902, p. 150.

No hint of the resurrection is found in the book, and nothing whatever is said about the dead, except in one passage, where we read: "And the righteous will see and be thankful, and rejoice with joy for ever and ever, and will see all their judgements and all their curses on their enemies. And their bones will rest in the earth, and their spirits will have much joy" (Jub. xxiii. 30 f.). An immortality of bliss is therefore the portion of the righteous in some undefined state, but there is no expectation of a resurrection to share in the Messianic kingdom on earth.

The author greatly exalts the house of Levi. In the Book of Genesis Levi's treachery against the Shechemites, in company with Simeon, is condemned (Gen. xxxiv. 30), and in the Blessing of Jacob a curse is pronounced on these two brothers for that act (Gen. xlix. 7). But in the Book of Jubilees this act is transformed into the execution of the judgement of Heaven against the Shechemites (Jub. xxx. 5). The descendants of Levi are promised both civil and ecclesiastical authority (Jub. xxxi. 14 f.). Here is a further argument against the pre-Maccabaean dating of the work, for civil and ecclesiastical authority was not concentrated in Levite hands until the Maccabaean family exercised both functions.[1] Yet it is to be noted that no Messianic role is ascribed to Levi, as in the Testaments of the Twelve Patriarchs. The only reference to the Messiah in the book intimates that he is to arise from the tribe of Judah (Jub. xxxi. 18), though the term

[1] S. Zeitlin (*Jewish Quarterly Review*, xxxv, 1944–5, pp. 458 f.) disputes the accuracy of this statement, and claims that up to the Maccabaean period civil and ecclesiastical authority was vested in the hands of the priests. It is indisputable that prior to the achievement of independence under Simon the final authority was successively exercised by the Achaemenids, the Ptolemies, and the Seleucids, under whom civil governors were appointed. Of these governors I have cited Zerubbabel and Bagoas, together with Nehemiah and Ezra, both of whom came to Jerusalem armed with powers by the Persian king. None of these were High Priests, nor is there the slightest evidence that they were subject to the authority of the High Priest (*ibid.*, xxvi, 1945–6, pp. 183 f.). Zeitlin prudently ignores this evidence, and claims that the transaction of business and the management of the city market, together with the collection of taxes, was in the hands of the High Priests (*ibid.*, p. 187). This is both disputable and irrelevant. For a text that promises that the descendants of Levi shall be judges and princes has far more extensive civil powers than these in mind, and scarcely conceives of them as collectors of taxes for an alien power!

"Messiah" is still not applied to him. As Charles observes, no role of any importance is assigned to him, and it would appear that he was regarded as subordinate to the priest. It would seem that at this time the hope of a Davidic leader who would one day arise was kept alive by the older prophecies, but the tribe of Levi occupied a more prominent position.[1]

Of the angelology of this book, Charles observes that it is in an advanced stage,[2] while Albright regards it as comparable with that of the Book of Job, and definitely more primitive than that of the Book of Daniel.[3] It is true we do not find the names of angels here, as we do in both Daniel and 1 Enoch, but there is a considerable development from the Book of Job. The angels are divided into various classes and ranks, and have each their various functions. On the other hand, we do not find here Satan in the court of God. Instead, we find the demons organized into a kingdom, ruled by Mastema,[4] who is to be equated with Satan. There is there-

---

[1] This is what we find also in the Dead Sea Scrolls, where in the Rule of the Congregation it is laid down that "if God should cause the Messiah to be born in their time" he should occupy a position subordinate to that of the priest. Fragments of the Book of Jubilees have been found among the Dead Sea Scrolls (cf. J. T. Milik, "Ten Years of Discovery in the Wilderness of Judaea", 1959, p. 32), and the sect of the Scrolls favoured the calendar of Jubilees. It is not therefore surprising to find a common attitude to the Messiah and the priest here and in the Scrolls.

[2] "The Book of Jubilees", p. lvi.

[3] Op. cit., pp. 266 f.

[4] Mastema does not occur as a proper name in the Dead Sea Scrolls, but in the War Scroll (col. xiii, line 11) Belial is described as "the angel of enmity (mśṭmh)", and in this Scroll and elsewhere the word "enmity" stands in other descriptions of his characteristics (cf. M. Burrows, "More Light on the Dead Sea Scrolls", 1958, p. 288; Y. Yadin, "The Scroll of the War of the Sons of Light against the Sons of Darkness", Eng. trans., 1962, pp. 233 f.). The same title "angel of enmity" is found in the Zadokite Work (xx. 2), where Charles ("Apocrypha and Pseudepigrapha", ii, p. 834) renders "the angel of Mastema", C. Rabin ("The Zadokite Documents", 2nd ed., 1958, p. 74) "the angel Mastema", but A. Dupont-Sommer ("The Essene Writings from Qumran", Eng. trans., 1961, p. 162) "the Angel of Hostility" (cf. T. H. Gaster, "The Scriptures of the Dead Sea Sect", 1957, p. 93 "the Angel of Obstruction"; G. Vermes, "The Dead Sea Scrolls in English", 1962, p. 109 "the Angel of Persecution"). It is easy to see how the word Mastema came to stand for the angel. On his character and activities cf. Yadin, loc. cit., p. 234. On Mastema in Jubilees, cf. M. Testuz, "Les Idées religieuses du livre des Jubilés", 1960, pp. 82 ff.

fore an advance in the direction of dualism beyond the Book of Job, and beyond the Book of Daniel.

The Testaments of the Twelve Patriarchs

The Testaments of the Twelve Patriarchs[1] purport to be the last words of the twelve sons of Jacob addressed to their children. In each Testament we find history, exhortation, and prophecy combined. It is generally agreed that in its present form the work is interpolated by Christian hands,[2]

---

[1] The Testaments were translated into Latin by Robert Grosseteste, Bishop of Lincoln, and an English version of this by A. Gilby was several times reprinted. In the edition of 1716, to which I have had access, there is no indication of the translator's name, but the Preface is signed by Richard Day.

[2] The older view was that it was a Christian work. See J. M. Vorstman, "Disquisitio de Testamentorum XII Patriarcharum origine et pretio", 1857. This view was revived by N. Messel in "Abhandlungen zur semitischen Religionskunde und Sprachwissenschaft" [Baudissin Festschrift], 1918, pp. 355 ff. E. J. Bickerman (*Journal of Biblical Literature*, lxix, 1950, p. 247 n.) surmised that this would be the last advocate of this view. This surmise was mistaken. M. de Jonge ("The Testaments of the Twelve Patriarchs", 1953) argues for a date around A.D. 200 for the composition of the work, but holds that the author used older Jewish materials, including a Testament of Levi and a Testament of Naphtali. (It is curious to note that Aramaic fragments of a Testament of Levi have been found at Qumran [see T. J. Milik, *Revue Biblique*, lxii, 1955, 398 ff.] and also Hebrew fragments of a Testament of Naphtali [cf. Milik, "Ten Years of Discovery in the Wilderness of Judaea", Eng. trans., p. 34], though neither of these facts was known when de Jonge wrote his dissertation. Fragments of an Aramaic Testament of Levi from the Cairo Genizah were published by R. H. Charles and A. Cowley in *Jewish Quarterly Review*, xix, 1906–7, pp. 566 ff.; and reprinted in R. H. Charles, "The Greek Versions of the Testaments of the Twelve Patriarchs", 1908, pp. 245 ff.; cf. P. Grelot, in *Revue Biblique*, lxiii, 1956, pp. 391 ff.) In *Revue Biblique*, lxii, 1955, pp. 297 f., Milik expresses disagreement with de Jonge's date, although he agrees that the work was composed in a Christian milieu. H. F. D. Sparks (*Journal of Theological Studies*, N.S. viii, 1955, pp. 287 ff.) hesitates to commit himself to de Jonge's view, while M. Philonenko ("Les Interpolations chrétiennes des Testaments des Douze Patriarches et les manuscrits de Qumran", 1960) rejects it. So also F.-M. Braun, in *Revue Biblique*, lxvii, 1960, pp. 516 ff., especially p. 543; and A. Dupont-Sommer, "The Essene Writings from Qumran", Eng. trans., 1961, pp. 301 ff. Cf. O. Eissfeldt, "Einleitung in das Alte Testament", 2nd ed., 1956, pp. 784 f. Cf. also the criticisms of de Jonge's thesis by A. S. van der Woude, "Die messianischen Vorstellungen der Gemeinde von Qumrân", 1957, pp. 191 ff. De Jonge has replied to van der Woude and Philonenko (*Novum Testamentum*, iv, 1960–1, pp. 182 ff.; cf. v, 1961–2, pp. 311 ff.), and now retracts the view that the Testaments are a Christian book using Jewish materials, but maintains that they underwent a thoroughgoing Christian redaction, and not merely received interpolations. The work was dated around the end of the third century B.C. by E. Meyer ("Ursprung und Anfänge des Christentums", ii, 1925, p. 44; cf. R. Eppel, "Le Piétisme juif dans les Testaments des douze Patriarches", 1930,

though there is less agreement as to the extent of the inter-polations.[1]

Charles finds a whole series of passages which look for the Messiah from the tribe of Levi,[2] but Lagrange disputes this interpretation.[3] He finds scant trace of any personal Messiah in the Testaments, but thinks that we have rather the appro-priation of the Messianic idea to the Hasmonaean house, which collectively fulfils the function of the Messiah. It is never easy to be certain whether we are dealing with a personification or with a person in Hebrew thought, but in any case the association with the Hasmonaean house seems more than doubtful. Already, before the discovery of the Dead Sea Scrolls, T. W. Manson had argued against such a view, and had suggested the probability that in Test. Levi

---

p. 32); in the second half of the 2nd century B.C. by Frey ("Supplément", i, cols. 383 ff.); at the end of the 2nd century B.C. by Charles ("The Testaments of the Twelve Patriarchs", 1908, p. lii; cf. R. H. Pfeiffer, "History of New Testa-ment Times", 1949, p. 64; J. Bonsirven, "La Bible Apocryphe", p. 116); in the 1st century B.C. by E. Schürer ("History of the Jewish People", Eng. trans., II, iii, 1890, p. 122) and C. C. Torrey ("The Apocryphal Literature", 1945, p. 131). O. Eissfeldt ("Einleitung in das Alte Testament", 2nd ed., 1956, pp. 785 f.) places it in the second century B.C. E. J. Bickerman (*Journal of Biblical Litera-ture*, lxix, 1950, pp. 245 ff.) argues for a date in the first quarter of the second century B.C., and A. Lods ("Histoire de la littérature hébraïque et juive", 1950, p. 822) assigns it to the period 128–63 B.C. It seems to me difficult to date the work so early as Bickerman does. The fact that what appear to be sources of the Testaments are found among the Qumran texts would put the composition of the Testaments later than their sources, yet those sources would scarcely have been composed earlier than Bickerman's date for the Testaments, and almost all scholars would put them later—and some much later.

[1] Charles finds a minimum of Christian interpolation, and therefore finds much influence of the Testaments upon the language of our Lord and of the New Testament. Others feel that once Christian interpolation is admitted, it is more likely that the similarities are to be explained by the dependence of the Testaments through interpolation than the other way round, especially as the Testaments left no trace in the literature of the early Fathers. Cf. A. Plummer, in *The Expositor*, 7th series, vi, 1908, pp. 490 f.; F. C. Burkitt, in *Journal of Theological Studies*, x, 1909, pp. 135 ff.; Lagrange, in *Revue Biblique*, xvii (N.S. v), 1908, p. 445 (in a review of Charles' edition of the Testaments). On this question see the admirable summary by Frey, in Pirot's "Supplément", i, cols. 381 ff.

[2] See "Testaments of the Twelve Patriarchs", 1908, p. xcviii. M. Philonenko (*op. cit.*) reduces the Christian interpolations to a minimum, and following Dupont-Sommer ("The Jewish Sect of Qumran and the Essenes", Eng. trans., 1954, pp. 38 ff., and "The Essene Writings", *loc. cit.*) holds that the Testaments were of Essene origin. Against this cf. Braun, *Revue Biblique*, lxvii, 1960, pp. 544 ff.

[3] "Le Judaïsme avant J.-C.", pp. 127 ff.

viii. 14 there was a reference to the "sons of Zadok" as the new name for the priesthood.[1] The priestly members of the Qumran sect were called "the sons of Zadok", and if, as now seems almost certain, the Testament of Levi is based on one of the texts treasured by the Qumran sect,[2] this suggestion finds new support.[3] It is certain that the Qumran sectaries did not regard the Hasmonaeans as fulfilling Messianic expectations, and it is more likely that, as in the Dead Sea Scrolls, the thought is of the true line of Zadok exercising the priesthood in the Messianic age. But the question is complicated by the disagreement as to how much of the text is original, and how much Christian interpolation.

Charles accepts as genuine a series of passages which describe the person and work of the Messiah ben Levi in the following terms: He shall walk with the sons of men in meekness and righteousness, and no sin shall be found in Him (T. Judah xxiv. 1);[4] He shall establish a new priesthood, and be a mediator for the Gentiles (T. Levi viii. 14);[5] He shall open the gates of Paradise to the righteous (T. Levi xviii. 10;

---

[1] *Journal of Theological Studies*, xlviii, 1947, pp. 59 ff. Charles ("The Testaments of the Twelve Patriarchs", 1908, p. 45) had argued that the new name was the revival of the name Melchizedek, but Manson shows the untenability of this view. [2] See p. 68, n. 2.

[3] T. J. Milik (*Revue Biblique*, lxii, 1955, p. 298) observes that "the 'Essene' character of the Testaments is incontestable". Already M.-J. Lagrange ("Le Judaïsme avant J.-C.", 1931, p. 130) had regarded the Testaments as of Essene origin. C. Rabin ("The Zadokite Documents", 2nd ed., 1958, p. 86) notes a number of parallels between the Zadokite Work and the Testaments. A. Dupont-Sommer (*Semitica*, iv, 1951–2, p. 49) claimed to find a reference to the Teacher of Righteousness of the Scrolls in the Testaments, but B. Otzen (*Studia Theologica*, vii, 1953 [1954], pp. 145 ff.) contests this claim. C. Rabin (*Journal of Theological Studies*, iii, 1952, pp. 127 f.) does not find the Teacher of the Scrolls mentioned, though he thinks Dupont-Sommer's claim to find the same title is worthy of consideration. On the links between the Testaments and the Scrolls, cf. also A. Michel, "Le Maître de Justice", 1954, pp. 44 ff.

[4] As the text stands, it refers to a Messiah ben Judah. But Charles presents reasons for thinking the words *from my seed* are secondary and therefore for associating the verse with the Messiah ben Levi, as elsewhere in the Testaments ("Testaments of the Twelve Patriarchs", p. 95).

[5] The rendering *be a mediator for the Gentiles* rests on a conjectural emendation of the reconstructed Hebrew original, which Charles makes. Moreover, the Greek MSS. again make the Messiah arise here *out of* Judah. But Charles holds that we should either follow certain Armenian MSS., which read *in* Judah, or eliminate the whole clause as an interpolation (*ibid.*, p. 45).

T. Dan v. 12), and give the saints to eat of the tree of life
(T. Levi xviii. 11). He shall make war against Beliar (T. Levi
xviii. 12; T. Dan v. 10),[1] who shall be cast into the fire for
ever (T. Judah xxv. 3), and sin shall come to an end (T. Levi
xviii. 9).[2] A Messiah ben Judah is found in T. Judah xxiv.
5 f., but here Charles finds a first-century addition to the text,[3]
and Lagrange agrees that it may not be original.[4]

G. R. Beasley-Murray, however, maintains that only two
passages refer to a Messiah ben Levi, while he finds stronger
evidence of a Messiah ben Judah than Charles would allow.[5]
After a careful study of the relevant passages of the Testaments he recognizes two Messiahs in the Testaments, of whom
the Messiah ben Judah is subordinate to the Messiah ben
Levi.[6] This is precisely what we find in the Dead Sea
Scrolls,[7] though here, as in dealing with the Scrolls, we should
be cautious in the use of the term Messiah. This term is not
used in the Testaments, though the thought is certainly
Messianic. The warlike character of the leader in the
Messianic age is clearly transferred to the Levitical leader,
and this, as Beasley-Murray observes,[8] doubtless reflects the
leadership of the priestly Maccabees.[9]

[1] As the text stands the Messiah here arises *from the tribe of Judah and of Levi*.
Charles eliminates the words *of Judah and*, on the grounds that the text is
grammatically irregular, and the order elsewhere in the Testaments is invariably *Levi and Judah* ("Testaments of the Twelve Patriarchs", p. 130).

[2] M. Black (*Expository Times*, lx, 1948–9, pp. 321 f.) thinks the whole of Test.
Levi xviii is a Christian interpolation (cf. J. R. Porter's criticism of Black's argument, *ibid.*, lxi, 1949–50, pp. 90 f., and Black's rejoinder, *ibid.*, pp. 157 f.).

[3] *Op. cit.*, p. 95.

[4] "Le Judaïsme avant J.-C.", p. 129.

[5] *Journal of Theological Studies*, xlviii, 1947, pp. 1 ff.

[6] C. C. Torrey (*Journal of the American Oriental Society*, lxii, 1942, p. 57, and
"The Apocryphal Literature", 1945, pp. 111 f.) thinks the Messiah ben
Ephraim and the Messiah ben Judah figured in 1 En. xc. 37 f. This is, of course,
a very different conception, and one that no other scholar has found in the
passage.

[7] Cf. *Bulletin of the John Rylands Library*, xliv, 1961–2, pp. 122 ff., 144 ff.

[8] *Loc. cit.*, p. 9.

[9] R. Eppel (*op. cit.*, p. 32) finds allusions in the Testaments to Jason and
Menelaus (174–170 B.C.), but none to the persecution of Antiochus or the
Maccabaean uprising. The references to the warlike Levitical leaders, however, almost certainly carry us down later than this. It seems to me possible, or
even probable, that the author idealized a conception which was based on the
achievements of the Maccabees, and thought of a coming priest who would

The figure of Beliar assumes great importance in the Testaments, and will come before us in later works. His name is a mutation of the word "Belial", which is found in the Old Testament. But in the Old Testament there is nothing to suggest that it is a proper name, borne by an evil spirit. Instead it is an abstract noun, whose meaning is probably "worthlessness". In the Book of Jubilees we read of "the spirit of Beliar" (Jub. i. 20) and "sons of Beliar" (Jub. xv. 33), where we might still read no more than an Old Testament significance into the term, were it not for the position Beliar has in the Testaments. For here he is the personification of iniquity, and the supreme adversary of God. It is to be observed that just as Satan is the personification of a function, so Beliar is the personification of an idea. And when Satan became identified with the evil which it was his function to expose he became the precise counterpart of Beliar. It is important to realize the genesis of these figures, and to remember that neither began as the person he became in the thought of men.

Here in the Testaments Beliar has become a person, who stands over against God, the embodiment of evil as God is of goodness. God is the Lord of light, and Beliar the lord of darkness (T. Joseph xx. 2), and the two are frequently set over against one another (e.g. in T. Sim. v. 3; T. Naph. ii. 6). Moreover, Beliar has under him spirits who obey his will (T. Iss. vii. 7), and apparently the seven arch-spirits of evil, corresponding to the seven archangels (T. Reub. ii. 1 f.), belong to his court. In the last days men will abandon God and serve Beliar (T. Iss. vi. 1), but the Messiah ben Levi will make war on him and release the captive souls he holds (T. Dan v. 10), will bind Beliar (T. Levi xviii. 12), and will cast him into everlasting fire (T. Judah xxv. 3). In the Testaments, therefore, Beliar corresponds to Antichrist, though he is in no sense a human figure. He is the personification of opposition to the will of God and the rule of the Messiah, however, and in that sense he fills the role which Antichrist

---

overthrow all the forces of evil (cf. my "Jewish Apocalyptic and the Dead Sea Scrolls", 1951, pp. 12 f.).

fills. The influence of Persian dualism, which has been admitted above as a possible factor in the depicting of the figure of Antiochus Epiphanes in the Book of Daniel, is more clearly and more directly seen here. For Beliar is a closer parallel to Angra Mainyu than any human figure could be. Nevertheless, we must beware of overstressing Persian influence, or of ignoring those elements of Hebrew thinking which were also real factors in the development, and which laid themselves so easily open to influence in this direction.

It may be noted that in a passage which Charles regards as coming from the hand of an interpolator in the first century B.C. it is said that the prince of the tribe of Dan is Satan (T. Dan v. 6), and Charles attaches great importance to this as being the earliest distinct expression known to us of the idea that Antichrist shall arise from the tribe of Dan, an idea which is well attested later, and which may explain the omission of Dan from the list of the twelve tribes in the New Testament Apocalypse.[1] While the verse shows the association of the tribe of Dan with evil, and hence may account for the rise of the expectation that Antichrist should arise from it, I can find no distinct expression of this expectation in the text, and no reference to Antichrist whatever. Nor can I agree that the New Testament Apocalypse associated Antichrist in any way with the tribe of Dan. Its Antichrist is quite clearly indicated, and is quite other.

In the realm of angelology, we may note some development in the Testaments, and in particular the conception of Michael as mediator between God and man (T. Dan vi. 2; T. Levi v. 6).

The doctrine of the resurrection is also developed here, and we read how Enoch, Noah, Shem, Abraham, Isaac, and Jacob shall arise in gladness, followed by the twelve sons of Jacob, followed in turn by all men, some of whom will rise unto glory and some unto shame. Then will take place the Last Judgement, when the Lord will first judge Israel and then all Gentiles (T. Benj. x. 6–8). After the destruction of Beliar, already referred to above, the saints will rest in Eden,

[1] *Op. cit.*, pp. 128 f.

and the righteous will rejoice in the New Jerusalem, and it shall be unto the glory of God for ever (T. Dan v. 12). Here the everlasting character of the Messianic kingdom is taught, but it is not certain whether it is conceived of as a kingdom on earth, or whether the New Jerusalem is to be equated with Paradise. Charles decides for the former,[1] in view of the fact that the following verse says that Jerusalem shall no longer endure desolation, nor Israel be led captive, for the Lord shall be in the midst of it. It may be added that Bousset explains the parallel passage in T. Levi xviii. 10 f., which states that Messiah will open the gates of Paradise and remove the threatening sword against Adam, and give the saints to eat of the tree of life, in connexion with the myth of the restoration of Paradise and the renewal of the whole earth.[2] In that case the alternatives which Charles considers in dealing with T. Dan v. 12 are not alternatives, and there is nothing to suggest that the New Jerusalem should be anywhere but on earth.[3] In that case the whole conception bears a close resemblance to that of the Book of Daniel, save that there the author's thought was probably limited to the resurrection of the persecuted and their persecutors in the struggle of which he was a partaker, whereas here it has become universalized in the resurrection of all men to receive the just recompense of their deeds on earth.

The Sibylline Oracles

From an early time the name and authority of the Sibyls were used by Jewish propagandists, and later by Christian propagandists, to spread their faith. The Sibylline Oracles are essentially cast in the form of prophecy, and prophecy of a cryptic type, but they are not fundamentally apocalyptic,

---

[1] *Op. cit.*, p. 131.

[2] Bousset-Gressmann, "Die Religion des Judentums", p. 261.

[3] The thought of the New Jerusalem may go back to Isa. liv. 11 f., with which should be compared Tobit xiii. 16 f.: "For Jerusalem shall be builded with sapphires and emeralds and precious stones, thy walls and towers and battlements with pure gold. And the streets of Jerusalem shall be paved with beryl and carbuncle and stones of Ophir." Cf. Rev. xxi. 10 ff. Cf. A. Causse, "Le mythe de la nouvelle Jérusalem du Deutéro Esaïe à la IIIe Sibylle", in *Revue d'Histoire et de Philosophie Religieuses*, xviii, 1938, pp. 377 ff.

and so do not as a whole come within our purview. In the Jewish Sibyllines, however, there are some apocalyptic passages which are akin to the works we are considering, and particularly in the third of the twelve books that still survive under the name of the Sibylline Oracles.[1] These are not all of a common date, and while iii. 97–819 is generally held to belong to the second century B.C.,[2] iii. 46–62 probably belongs to the first century B.C., and iii. 63–92 to the first century A.D.[3] Passages in the fifth book, belonging probably to the second century A.D., lie beyond our purview.

In the earliest of the three sections above referred to there is a description of the coming of the Messiah. There is no clear indication as to when this will take place, since transitions are abrupt, and no simple chronological sequence is observed. In this passage it is said that God shall send a king from the east, who will be the instrument of the divine will in establishing universal peace (Sib. Or. iii. 652 ff.). At his coming the Jews will prosper, and the earth will teem with production (Sib. Or. iii. 657 ff.), thus exciting the envy of the Gentiles, who will muster for vain attacks on Palestine (Sib. Or. iii. 660 ff.). Particularly will they seek to desecrate the Temple (Sib. Or. iii. 665 ff.), but God will destroy them with great portents in the heavens above and on earth beneath (Sib. Or. iii. 669 ff.). The judgement of war will be

[1] Some passages in the Sibylline Oracles have been held to refer to the Essenes. On this question cf. B. Noack, in *Dansk Teologisk Tidsskrift*, xxv, 1962, pp. 176 ff.

[2] Cf. *Zeitschrift für die alttestamentliche Wissenschaft*, N.F. iii, 1926, pp. 324 ff., and "Darius the Mede", 2nd ed., 1959, pp. 115 ff., where I present reasons for dating part of this section between 129 and 122 B.C.

[3] There are divergences of view as to whether Sib. Or. iii. 97–819 is a unity, and there is also some variation of view as to the date of this section and of iii. 46–62 within the centuries indicated. For Sib. Or. iii. 63–92 there is less agreement, some holding the passage to belong with the preceding passage, and so to date from the first century B.C. (so Schürer, "History of the Jewish People", II, iii, pp. 283 f., and Eissfeldt, "Einleitung in das Alte Testament", 2nd ed., 1956, p. 762), and some dating it in the Christian era. Bousset (Bousset-Gressmann, "Religion des Judentums", p. 242) places it as late as the third century A.D. Cf. Ewald ("Abhandlung über Entstehung, Inhalt und Werth der Sibyllischen Bücher", 1858, pp. 82 ff.), who dates iii. 1–96 *circa* A.D. 300. On the whole question, cf. Geffcken, "Komposition und Entstehungszeit der Oracula Sibyllina", 1902, pp. 1 ff., and Bousset in Herzog-Hauck, "Realencyklopädie für prot. Theologie und Kirche", xviii, 1906, pp. 265 ff.

poured out on earth, and men and beasts alike will be consumed (Sib. Or. iii. 690 ff.). The Jews will dwell in safety round the Temple, however, rejoicing in the gifts God will send, and in the peace which He shall maintain for them (Sib. Or. iii. 702 ff.). Aliens will be astonished at this proof of the divine favour, and will flock to the Temple to be converted and to ponder the law of God (Sib. Or. iii. 710 ff.). The blessings of the Messianic age are then described in terms of material prosperity and of peace (Sib. Or. iii. 741 ff.). Jerusalem will be the centre of the kingdom that is for all ages (Sib. Or. iii. 767 ff.), and to its Temple gifts will be brought from all lands (Sib. Or. iii. 772 ff.), while the prophets will be made judges and kings (Sib. Or. iii. 781 ff.).

Much of this is based on familiar Old Testament passages, and in particular the submission of the Gentiles to the Jews and to the Jewish faith, and the enduring peace and prosperity of the Messianic kingdom. The mustering of the Gentiles for a great attack on Palestine may owe something to Ps. ii. We may especially note the idea that a great and desolating war will herald the coming of the kingdom, and that it will be directed against Jerusalem and its Temple. This idea, which became part of the stock-in-trade of the apocalyptists, was doubtless derived from the Gog passages of the Book of Ezekiel and from the Book of Daniel, while the thought of the Jews dwelling in safety round the Temple may again rest on Ezek. xxxviii. 14, in the Gog section. Of more immediate interest to us is it to observe that while the Messiah figures in the establishment of the kingdom, he is a purely human figure, and he falls out of the picture thereafter. The kingdom is an earthly kingdom, and it is conceived in Jewish national terms. There is no thought of the resurrection, or of anything supramundane, save the power of the God Whose will shall be manifest in this great consummation of history.

The little section found in iii. 46–62 predicts that when Rome rules over Egypt "a holy prince shall come to wield the sceptre over all the world unto all ages of hurrying time".[1] Here it would seem that the Messiah is thought of as living for ever in the earthly kingdom over which he rules.

Again, in the section contained in iii. 63–92, it is predicted that Beliar will deceive many and lead them astray, including faithful Hebrews (Sib. Or. iii. 63 ff.), but he will be burned up by fiery energy, which the wrath of God will cause to break forth (Sib. Or. iii. 71 ff.). A woman will then reign over the whole world, until God shall bring all the universe into ruin, when heaven and earth will be alike consumed in a vast conflagration (Sib. Or. iii. 75 ff.).

Here there is no Messiah and no kingdom, but only complete destruction. The chief interest of the section is in the figures of Beliar and the woman, who seem successively to play the part of Antichrist. Bousset finds in the woman a reflection of the Dragon myth,[2] but Lanchester thinks Rome is intended.[3] We are reminded of the Great Harlot in the New Testament Apocalypse, whose origin may have something in common with this figure. Beliar, who appears to be destroyed before she arises, comes from Sebaste. He is therefore commonly identified with Simon Magus. In that case the passage is of particular interest, as presenting the idea of the incarnation of Beliar in a human form. This is an idea that we shall meet again. Brief though this passage is, it is therefore of some importance for the study of the growth and development of the ideas of the apocalyptists.

The Psalms of Solomon

The Psalms of Solomon as a whole clearly do not belong to apocalyptic literature, but it is usual to include them in any survey, because of the familiar Psalm xvii, which is so important to the student of the thought of the apocalyptists. Yet even this Psalm may more properly be called Messianic than apocalyptic. Nevertheless, it has something in common

---

[1] Translation of Lanchester, in Charles, "Apocrypha and Pseudepigrapha", ii, p. 379.

[2] "Antichrist", Eng. trans., pp. 90 f. Those who date this section in the first century B.C. identify with Cleopatra. So Schürer, "History of the Jewish People", II, iii, p. 284, and Eissfeldt, "Einleitung", 2nd ed., p. 762.

[3] *Loc. cit.*, ii, p. 371.

with apocalyptic, in that it prefaces its prediction with a historical survey.

It is generally agreed that the Psalms of Solomon belong to the middle of the first century B.C.[1] It is not surprising, therefore, that the Hasmonaean house, which many scholars have associated with the Messianism of some of the texts considered above, cannot be found here reflected in the Messianism of the Psalms. There is no reference to any Messiah ben Levi at all. Instead, hope has returned to the house of David, and the expected deliverer is from his seed.

The great Messianic Psalm xvii attaches its hopes unequivocally to the line of David. The following psalm carries the title, "Again of the Anointed of the Lord", where the word "Christ", or Messiah, is employed, though there is no specific mention of a Davidic Messiah in the psalm. It would seem, however, that the term "Messiah", in its technical use, was now attached to the Messianic concept of an ideal deliverer who should arise in the future.

After a historical review the Psalmist cries: "Behold, O Lord, and raise up unto them their king, the son of David" (Ps. Sol. xvii. 23 [21]),[2] and the rest of the psalm describes the glories of the Messianic age. The Messiah will be wise and righteous (25 [23]), and pure from sin (41 [36]), and God will make him strong through His holy spirit (42 [37]). He is therefore conceived of as a definitely human figure. He will shatter unrighteous rulers, and cleanse Jerusalem from Gentile oppressors (24 f. [22]), and will destroy with the word of his mouth all godless nations (27 [24]). He will reign

---

[1] The Psalms of Solomon are generally pronounced Pharisaic. J. O'Dell (*Revue de Qumran*, iii, 1961, pp. 241 ff.) contests this, and argues that the Psalms came from Hasidic circles. He says, "There were without a doubt a number of deeply spiritual and eschatologically orientated men who belonged neither to the Pharisees, Sadducees, nor to the priestly-minded Qumran Essenes, but were nonetheless religious Jews. Such a man, or group of men, was the author of the Psalms of Solomon" (p. 257). Cf. P. Grelot's criticism of this in "La Venue du Messie", 1962, p. 26.

[2] The figures in brackets represent the numbers of the verses in the text of O. Gebhardt ("Die Psalmen Salomo's", 1895), which is the best edition of the text. The other figures are those of Swete's edition in the Cambridge Septuagint, usually followed in English works. See also the edition of J. Viteau, "Les Psaumes de Salomon", 1911.

over Israel (23 [21]), and will gather together a holy people, whom he will judge, and among whom he will divide the land, to which no alien shall henceforth be admitted (28–31 [26–28]). He will judge the nations, and reduce them to subjection to his yoke (31 f. [29 f.]), and will strike fear into every heart (38 f. [34 f.]). His rule will be marked by perfect righteousness and holiness, so that nations shall come from the ends of the earth to see his glory, bringing exiled Jews as their gifts (34–36 [31 f.]).

The Messianic kingdom is here thought of once more in definitely Jewish national terms. It is an earthly kingdom, with its centre at Jerusalem, and the Gentiles will be reduced to servitude. That it will be an eternal kingdom is implied in the promise that never again shall alien dwell in Palestine (31 [28]), and that the Messiah will smite the earth with the word of his mouth for ever (39 [35]), though Charles believes that the Messiah is thought of as mortal, and his kingdom as a temporary one.[1]

In Psalm xviii, which, as has been said, uses the term "Christ", or Messiah, instead of the Son of David, we have a similar picture, though more slightly sketched, and it cannot be doubted that the same figure is in mind. Here the Messiah manifests the spirit of wisdom and righteousness and strength, and wields the rod of chastening (8 [7]). The cleansing of Israel is thought of as a preparation for his coming (6 [5]), and he will be the instrument of the goodness of God (7 [6]), and will direct every man in the works of righteousness (9 [8]).

In neither of these psalms is there any suggestion of the resurrection, and no thought save of those who will be alive at the time of the Messiah's rule. "Blessed be they that shall be in those days, in that they shall see the good fortune of Israel" (Ps. Sol. xvii. 50 [43]); "Blessed shall be they that shall be in those days, in that they shall see the goodness of the Lord" (Ps. Sol. xviii. 7 [6]).

Elsewhere in the Psalms of Solomon we do not find any reference to the Messiah, though in Ps. xi we have a descrip-

[1] "Critical History of the Doctrine of the Future Life", pp. 269 f.

tion of Jerusalem's coming good time, when her exiles shall be gathered together.[1] We do, however, find some references to the resurrection. It is a resurrection of the righteous only, and it is to eternal life (Ps. Sol. iii. 16 [12]), whereas sinners perish for ever (Ps. Sol. xv. 15 [13]). Thought on this theme was clearly active, and each writer was ready to remould what he took over and to bring in new elements to modify the whole picture. Here there was no background of crisis, as in the case of the Book of Daniel and some of the other works with which we are concerned, and so speculation on the destiny of the individual was not brought into association with a great cataclysm that should inaugurate the Messianic kingdom.[2]

The Zadokite Work

In 1910 two fragments of a work which issued from a Jewish sect of the New Covenant were recovered from the Cairo Genizah. It is usually referred to by English authors as the Zadokite Work,[3] though it is only an inference that it bore some such title as "The Book of Zadok".[4] By German authors

[1] Viteau (op. cit., p. 2) describes Psalm xi as a Messianic psalm. On the Messianic thought of the Psalms of Solomon, cf. ibid., pp. 63 ff.

[2] M. Delcor ("Essai sur le Midrash d'Habacuc", 1951, pp. 50 ff., and Revue Biblique, lviii, 1951, pp. 531 ff.) has argued for some links between the Psalms of Solomon and the Dead Sea Scrolls, and so H. J. Schoeps (Zeitschrift für Religions- und Geistesgeschichte, iii, 1951, pp. 327 ff., and Zeitschrift für die alttestamentliche Wissenschaft, lxiii, 1951, pp. 256 ff.). On the links between the Psalms of Solomon and the Scrolls, as well as the diversities between them, cf. A. Michel, "Le Maître de Justice", 1954, pp. 62 ff.

[3] It is called the Zadokite Work because of the interest it shows in the priestly family of Zadok. The priestly members of the sect from which it emanated are referred to as the "sons of Zadok", and in the Dead Sea Scrolls we find the same thing (cf. Bulletin of the John Rylands Library, xliv, 1961–2, p. 126 n.). On the association of the Zadokite Work with the Qumran sect, see below, p. 86. It has been argued that Ecclesiasticus shows many Qumran links (cf. M. R. Lehmann, in Revue de Qumran, iii, 1961, pp. 102 ff., and J. Carmignac, ibid., pp. 209 ff.). It may be added that in the Hebrew text there is a passage not found in the other texts, and that this extols the sons of Zadok. On this passage and the views which have been held on its original place in the text, cf. "The Zadokite Fragments and the Dead Sea Scrolls", 1952, p. 26 n., where I give some references to the literature on the question.

[4] For the considerable literature which has been written about this work, see Rost, "Die Damaskusschrift" (in Lietzmann's "Kleine Texte"), 1933, pp. 4 ff. An excellent edition of the text, with translation and notes, has been issued by C. Rabin, "The Zadokite Documents", 2nd ed., 1958.

it is more often referred to as the *Damaskusschrift*, because the sect had its headquarters at Damascus when it withdrew from Jerusalem. Its date cannot be determined with any security, and the widest differences are found between the dates to which various scholars assign it. Eduard Meyer[1] assigned it to the pre-Maccabaean era, Barnes[2] to the Maccabaean, Ward[3] to about 80 B.C., Bertholet[4] to *circa* 63 B.C., Charles[5] to the period between 18 B.C. and 8 B.C., Lagrange[6] to the end of the second century A.D., Büchler[7] to the seventh or eighth century A.D., and Marmorstein[8] to the eleventh century A.D. Few works can have occasioned wider diversity of view as to their age.[9] The possible range of dates has now been definitely limited by the finding of fragments of this work among the Qumran Scrolls,[10] which were almost certainly deposited in the caves around Qumran in A.D. 68.[11] In the first edition of the present book I said that I would prefer not to attempt a closer definition of its age than to say it fell somewhere in the last century and a half before the Christian era. Since the finding of the Qumran Scrolls I have argued that the composition of the Zadokite Work probably fell about the middle of the second century B.C.[12] While some scholars would put it later,[13] there can be

[1] "Ursprung und Anfänge des Christentums", ii, 4th ed., 1925, pp. 47 ff.

[2] *Journal of Theological Studies*, xii, 1911, pp. 301 ff. Barnes finds the verse "From the day on which the only Teacher was taken away until the time when all the men of war who went with the Man of Falsehood were consumed there is a period of about forty years" (Zad. Work ix. 39B) to refer to the period from the murder of Onias to the surrender of the heathen garrison in Jerusalem to Simon in 142 B.C. [3] *Bibliotheca Sacra*, lxxxi, 1911, pp. 429 ff.

[4] "Beiträge zur alttestmentlichen Wissenschaft" (Budde Festschrift), 1920, pp. 31 ff. [5] "Apocrypha and Pseudepigrapha", ii, pp. 793 f.

[6] *Revue Biblique*, xxi (N.S. ix), 1912, pp. 213 ff., and "Le Judaïsme avant J.-C.", pp. 331 ff.

[7] *Jewish Quarterly Review*, N.S. iii, 1912–13, pp. 429 ff.

[8] *Theologisch Tijdschrift*, lii, 1918, pp. 92 ff.

[9] For fuller references to the literature and the variety of dates proposed, cf. "The Zadokite Fragments and the Dead Sea Scrolls", 1952, pp. 1 f.

[10] See below, p. 86.

[11] See especially R. de Vaux, "L'Archéologie et les manuscrits de la Mer Morte", 1961.

[12] Cf. "The Zadokite Fragments and the Dead Sea Scrolls", p. 77 (not later than 131 B.C.). Cf. also *Ephemerides Theologicae Lovanienses*, xxviii, 1952, p. 274; *Bulletin of the John Rylands Library*, xxxv, 1952, p. 144; *Theologische Zeitschrift*, xiii, 1957, pp. 530 ff. [13] See below, p. 87.

little doubt that it fell somewhere in the pre-Christian period, and therefore belongs here. Once more, the work as a whole is hardly an apocalyptic work, and its title to a place in our study may be disputed. It is included here because by some writers it is so included,[1] and because of the interest of some of its eschatological ideas. Gressmann, indeed, holds that it is essentially an apocalyptic work.[2]

The grounds on which Charles bases his dating of the book are germane to our subject, since they rest on the Messianic expectations of the author. Here the Messiah is looked for "from Aaron and Israel" (Zad. Work ix. 10B, 29B, xv. 4).[3] Charles believes that this revived hope of a Messiah ben Levi arose during the reign of Herod the Great, when hope centred on the two sons of Mariamne, one of whom was expected to be the Messiah. He thinks the unusual phrase "from Aaron and Israel" differentiates it from the earlier hope of the Testaments of the Twelve Patriarchs, and that this strange expression was chosen to indicate the sons of Mariamne, because they were descended from Aaron on their mother's side, since she was of the Hasmonaean line, while on their father's side they were from Israel, *i.e.* from the non-Levitical tribes. The date of the work could not then be placed later than 8 B.C., because they were put to death in that year.

This is more ingenious than convincing. Charles agrees that their descent from Aaron was not above suspicion, since it was through their mother, and believes it was on that account that the word "and from Israel" had to be added to bring in their paternal certification. He does not, however, observe that the son of the Idumaean Antipater and the Nabataean Cypros could hardly provide an "Israelite" descent that was not above suspicion.[4] I am not, therefore,

---

[1] So Volz, "Die Eschatologie der jüdischen Gemeinde im neutest. Zeitalter", 1934, pp. 14 ff. Volz observes that its style frequently reminds us of the mysterious quality of the apocalyptic style.

[2] *Zeitschrift der deutschen morgenländischen Gesellschaft*, lxvi, 1912, pp. 491 ff.

[3] Some have proposed to read "The Messiahs of Aaron and Israel"; see below, p. 91.

[4] J. L. Teicher (*Journal of Jewish Studies*, ii, 1950–1, pp. 134 ff.) argued that the reference is to Jesus, who was of the line of David on his father's side and of the tribe of Levi on his mother's. But it is impossible that the Zadokite Work is

persuaded that Mariamne's sons were in question,[1] and as Charles dates the origin of the sect in the period 196–176 B.C., it could have been written much earlier than he dates it.[2] Since there is a reference to the Book of Jubilees in Zad. Work xx. 1, however, it must be dated later than that work.

M.-J. Lagrange[3] and F. F. Hvidberg[4] argued that the expression indicated the expectation that the Messiah would arise within the sect, and in the light of the Qumran Scrolls this has seemed to me most probable.[5]

Turning to the figure of the Messiah and the expected development of history, we find the belief that a period of great wickedness will continue until the Messiah arises (Zad. Work xv. 4). Prior to the Messiah himself, however, another

---

late enough for this, and Teicher's general view of the Scrolls as Christian documents from anti-Pauline Ebionite circles has found little favour.

[1] K. Kohler (*American Journal of Theology*, xv, 1911, pp. 404 ff.) argued that the expression "from Aaron and Israel" points to the Samaritan line of the priestly house of Zadok. Volz (*op. cit.*, pp. 192 f.) thinks a priestly Messiah, comparable to the Messiah ben Levi of the Testaments of the Twelve Patriarchs, is intended. On this, see below, pp. 90 ff.

[2] The Zadokite Work opens with a reference to the period of 390 years after the time of Nebuchadnezzar, and Charles ("Apocrypha and Pseudepigrapha", ii, pp. 792, 800) regarded this as approximately accurate as the date of the origin of the sect, while E. Meyer ("Die Gemeinde des Neuen Bundes im Lande Damaskus", 1919, pp. 13 f.) held it to be a precise figure. In "The Zadokite Fragments and the Dead Sea Scrolls", pp. 62, 64, I recognized that no exact chronology of the Persian period is reflected in ancient Jewish works, and that therefore this figure has no evidential value, but argued that it is nevertheless approximately correct, though this is quite accidental. F. F. Hvidberg (*Zeitschrift für die alttestamentliche Wissenschaft*, N.F. x, 1933, pp. 309 ff.) thought the figure 390 rested on a calculation of the period from the birth of Shem to the birth of Abraham, while I. Rabinowitz (*Journal of Biblical Literature*, lxxiii, 1954, pp. 11 ff.) thought the reference was to a period of 390 years *before* the destruction of Jerusalem by Nebuchadnezzar. E. Wiesenberg (*Vetus Testamentum*, v, 1955, p. 308) thinks the passage unhistorically located the beginnings of the sect in the time of Nebuchadnezzar, while J. L. Teicher (*Journal of Jewish Studies*, iv, 1953, p. 52) found the figure to be symbolical, and not historical. I examine this question in "Mélanges Bibliques" (Robert Festschrift), 1957, pp. 341 ff.

[3] Cf. *Rev. Biblique*, N.S. xi, 1914, p. 135.

[4] Cf. "Menigheden af den Nye Pagt i Damascus", 1928, p. 281.

[5] Cf. "The Zadokite Fragments and the Dead Sea Scrolls", 1952, p. 41. In the Manual of Discipline from Qumran the sect, which is almost certainly to be identified with that from which the Zadokite Work emanated (see below p. 86), describes itself as a "house of holiness for Israel . . . and a house of unity (or community) for Aaron". The sect conceived itself, therefore, to represent Israel and Aaron. Cf. also W. S. LaSor, *Vetus Testamentum*, vi, 1956, pp. 425 ff.

figure will arise, who is variously referred to as the Teacher of Righteousness[1] (Zad. Work i. 7, viii. 10, ix. 53), the Unique Teacher[2] (Zad. Work ix. 29B, 39B), or the Teacher (Zad. Work ix. 50). It is said that the Teacher of Righteousness will arise in the end of the days (Zad. Work viii. 10), and that from the Unique Teacher until all men of war are consumed, *i.e.* until the Messianic age, shall be forty years (Zad. Work ix. 39B). Through the period of evil a Remnant shall be found to maintain their faithfulness (Zad. Work ii. 9), and when the Messiah comes he shall make them know his holy spirit (Zad. Work ii. 10). There are several references to those who have proved faithless to the New Covenant (Zad. Work ix. 10 ff., 28 ff., 49B), and they are to be destroyed by the Messiah, together with those of Judah who do wickedly in the days of testing (Zad. Work ix. 49B), or they shall be visited for destruction through the hand of Belial (Zad. Work ix. 12). Summary judgement will be executed on the people (Zad. Work ix. 48B), while those who hold fast to God are for the life of eternity (Zad. Work v. 6).[3]

It is to be noted that Beliar figures again in this work, though his name is here given in the Old Testament form Belial. He is, however, quite definitely a personal character. He appears to be the prince of the evil spirits, since we find a reference to "any man ruled by the spirits of Belial" (Zad. Work xiv. 5), and he is said to be let loose against Israel (Zad. Work vi. 9), and to have three nets with which he catches

---

[1] It is probable that this title should be translated "the True Teacher", but "the Teacher of Righteousness" has become so established that it is here retained.

[2] This should perhaps be rendered "the Teacher of the Community".

[3] Cf. Schousboe, "La secte juive de l'Alliance Nouvelle au pays de Damas et le Christianisme naissant", 1942. In this the author advances the view that the Zadokite Work emanated from the followers of John the Baptist shortly after the Destruction of the Temple in A.D. 70, and that much of it was a polemic against the Christians. He identifies the Teacher of Righteousness and the Unique Teacher with John the Baptist, who is also the Messiah from Aaron and Israel; he also finds references to Jesus as the Man of Insolence, and to the persecution of the Johannine community by the Christians, marked by bloodshed. Until concrete evidence is offered that the early Christians were of this character, this must stand as a difficulty in the way of the acceptance of this theory.

Israel (Zad. Work vi. 10). He is also said to have raised against Moses Jochanneh and his brother (Zad. Work vii. 19), who are probably to be identified with Jannes and Jambres (2 Tim. iii. 8).

Only a fragment of this work has survived, and it may be on that account that we learn so little of the nature of the Messianic kingdom. Nor is there any judgement on Belial and his hosts. The most interesting of the ideas presented in the surviving fragments are the ideas of the Forerunner of the Messiah, who shall precede his advent by forty years, and the idea of the faithless members of the Messianic community that awaits the advent of the Messiah.

The Qumran Scrolls

The Dead Sea Scrolls which began to come to light in 1947[1] have brought new interest to the study of the inter-testamental literature, and their relevance for the study of the apocalyptic writings is beyond question.[2] Scrolls from more than one locality have come to the light, and not all have yet been published. Of those that have been made available, it is the Scrolls from the Qumran caves which are relevant to our study. It is impossible here to take account of

---

[1] Innumerable accounts of the discovery of the Scrolls and of the contents of the find have been published. J. M. Allegro's Pelican Book "The Dead Sea Scrolls", 1956, gives an excellent account of the discovery and texts found, marred only by highly tendentious interpretations of their significance resting on imaginative supplementation of the Scrolls. Other accounts may be found in M. Burrows, "The Dead Sea Scrolls", 1955, and "More Light on the Dead Sea Scrolls", 1958; Y. Yadin, "The Message of the Scrolls", 1957; J. T. Milik, "Ten Years of Discovery in the Wilderness of Judaea", Eng. trans., 1959; F. M. Cross, "The Ancient Library of Qumran and Modern Biblical Studies", 1958; F. F. Bruce, "Second Thoughts on the Dead Sea Scrolls", 2nd ed., 1961; E. F. Sutcliffe, "The Monks of Qumran", 1960. The major publications of the texts themselves are: M. Burrows, "The Dead Sea Scrolls of St. Mark's Monastery", i, 1950; ii. 2, 1951; E. L. Sukenik, "The Dead Sea Scrolls of the Hebrew University", 1955; D. Barthélemy and J. T. Milik, "Qumran Cave I" (Discoveries in the Judaean Desert, i), 1955; N. Avigad and Y. Yadin, "A Genesis Apocryphon", 1956. Translations of the texts are given in T. H. Gaster, "The Scriptures of the Dead Sea Sect", 1957; E. F. Sutcliffe, "The Scrolls of Qumran", 1960; J. Maier, "Die Texte vom Toten Meer", 1960; A. Dupont-Sommer, "The Essene Writings from Qumran", Eng. trans., 1961; G. Vermes, "The Dead Sea Scrolls in English", 1962.

[2] Cf. my "Jewish Apocalyptic and the Dead Sea Scrolls", 1957.

the vast literature which has already grown up around them,[1] or to examine all the eschatological ideas which they contain.[2] None of the texts can be described as an apocalyptic work of quite the character of most of the works we are examining, but it is impossible to leave them wholly out of account. Yet any elaborate study of them here would throw the present brief study of the apocalyptic writings of our period completely out of balance.

When the first Scrolls came to light it was quickly perceived that they must be studied in association with the Zadokite Work, and it was believed that that work must have emanated from the sect of the Scrolls.[3] The finding of fragments of the Zadokite Work among the Scrolls[4] has confirmed this, though differences between the practice reflected in the Scrolls and the Zadokite Work must be recognized, and they have been differently accounted for.[5] The Teacher of Righteousness, who figures in the Zadokite Work, figures also in the Habakkuk Commentary and in some others of the Scrolls, and while the references here, as in the Zadokite Work, are cryptic, all must be taken into account in trying to determine the period when he lived.[6]

It is generally accepted that the sect came into existence in

---

[1] For the Bibliography of the Scrolls cf. C. Burchard, "Bibliographie zu den Handschriften vom Toten Meer", 1957; W. S. LaSor, "Bibliography of the Dead Sea Scrolls, 1948–1957", 1958. The *Revue de Qumran* is devoted wholly to the Scrolls and contains supplementary bibliographies.

[2] Cf. especially A. S. van der Woude, "Die messianischen Vorstellungen der Gemeinde von Qumran", 1957. On the theological ideas of the Scrolls cf. F. Nötscher, "Zur theologischen Terminologie der Qumrantexte", 1956, and "Gotteswege und Menschenwege in der Bibel und in Qumran", 1958.

[3] Attention was drawn by O. Eissfeldt (*Theologische Literaturzeitung*, lxxiv, 1949, cols. 597 ff.) to a letter of the Nestorian Patriarch Timotheus I mentioning the discovery of MSS. in a cave near the Dead Sea about A.D. 800, and this was followed by attention to passages in the tenth-century Karaite Kirkisānī's writings mentioning the "Cave Sect" (cf. R. de Vaux, in *Revue Biblique*, lvii, 1950, pp. 421 ff.). From this it was concluded that the texts to which Timotheus refers came into Karaite hands and were later copied, and it was late copies of one of these which were found in the Cairo Genizah.

[4] Cf. M. Baillet, in *Revue Biblique*, lxiii, 1956, p. 55; J. T. Milik, *ibid.*, p. 61. See also "Les 'petites grottes' de Qumran", 1962, pp. 128 ff., 181.

[5] On this cf. what I have written in *Theologische Zeitschrift*, 1957, pp. 530 ff.

[6] Cf. "The Teacher of Righteousness and the Dead Sea Scrolls", in *Bulletin of the John Rylands Library*, xl, 1957–8, pp. 114 ff., where I discuss this question.

the second century B.C.,[1] though a few scholars are still un-persuaded of this.[2] The archaeological evidence points convincingly to the deposit of the Scrolls in the Qumran caves in the year A.D. 68,[3] and this sets the Qumran Scrolls firmly within our period. For our present purpose it is immaterial to define their age with precision. Leaving aside the few scholars who place the origin of the sect after the beginning of the Christian era, three main dates for the period of activity of the Teacher of Righteousness have been advanced.[4] The view for which Dupont-Sommer has been the chief protagonist[5] locates his ministry in the first century B.C., and puts his death in the middle of that century. Others have argued[6] that his ministry began towards the end of the second century B.C. and ended in the reign of Alexander Jannaeus. The third view places his ministry earlier in the second century B.C. Some think he belongs to the middle of that century, and identify his great opponent with Jonathan or Simon.[7] To

[1] The excavation of the Qumran centre shows that it was probably already occupied by the sect towards the close of the second century B.C. Cf. R. de Vaux, "L'Archéologie et les manuscrits de la Mer Morte", 1961.

[2] S. Zeitlin, in a long series of articles in the *Jewish Quarterly Review*, is the stoutest champion of the medieval origin of the Scrolls. Others who earlier approximated to this view have abandoned it. J. L. Teicher argued for the Ebionite origin of the Scrolls in a series of articles in the *Journal of Jewish Studies*. C. Roth ("The Historical Background of the Dead Sea Scrolls", 1958) maintains that the Scrolls emanated from the Zealots in the first century of our era. So also G. R. Driver; cf. *Ephemerides Theologicae Lovanienses*, xxxiii, 1957, pp. 798 f. H. E. del Medico ("The Riddle of the Scrolls", Eng. trans., 1958) proposed a succession of post-Christian dates for the Scrolls.

[3] Cf. R. de Vaux, "L'Archéologie et les manuscrits de la Mer Morte", 1961.

[4] I discuss these in *Bulletin of the John Rylands Library*, xxxv, 1952–3, pp. 111 ff., and xl, 1957–8, pp. 114 ff.; *Ephemerides Theologicae Lovanienses*, xxviii, 1952, pp. 257 ff.; *Palestine Exploration Quarterly*, lxxxviii, 1956, pp. 92–109; and in "The Zadokite Fragments and the Dead Sea Scrolls", 1952.

[5] Cf. "The Dead Sea Scrolls", Eng. trans., 1952; "The Jewish Sect of Qumran and the Essenes", Eng. trans., 1954; "The Essene Writings from Qumran", Eng. trans., 1961. Cf. also K. Elliger, "Studien zum Habakuk-Kommentar vom Toten Meer", 1953.

[6] Cf. M. H. Segal, in *Journal of Biblical Literature*, lxx, 1951, pp. 131 ff.; M. Delcor, "Essai sur le Midrash d'Habacuc", 1951; J. M. Allegro, "The Dead Sea Scrolls", 1956; F. F. Bruce, "Second Thoughts on the Dead Sea Scrolls", 1956, 2nd ed., 1961.

[7] Cf. F. M. Cross, "The Ancient History of Qumrân", 1958; J. T. Milik, "Ten Years of Discovery", Eng. trans., 1959; E. F. Sutcliffe, "The Monks of Qumran", 1960; R. de Vaux, "L'Archéologie et les manuscrits de la Mer Morte", 1961.

this date the trend seems to be turning at present. The view for which I have argued,[1] and which still seems to me the most probable, is that the Teacher is to be identified with Onias III, whose death in 171 B.C. is referred to in Dan. ix. 27.[2]

That the sect of the Scrolls is to be identified in some way with the Essenes is widely,[3] though not universally,[4] believed. The difference between the practices of the Essenes, as they are reflected in our previously known sources,[5] and the practices of the Qumran sect may be accounted for by the fact that in the Scrolls we see them from the inside and at an earlier point of their history.

The texts in which the Teacher of Righteousness is mentioned show that eschatological significance was given to his ministry. The Book of Habakkuk is declared to set forth what should happen in the last days (Hab. Comm. VII. 1), and the Teacher of Righteousness, to whom all the mysteries of the words of the prophets were revealed (Hab. Comm. VII. 4), interpreted them to the final generation at the end of the days (Hab. Comm. II. 6 f.). His opponents were the last priests of Jerusalem (Hab. Comm. IX. 4). The time of judge-

[1] In the works mentioned on p. 87, n. 4. Cf. also "The Dead Sea Scrolls from Qumran", 1958. This view is also advocated by A. Michel, "Le Maître de Justice", 1954; E. Stauffer, in *Theologische Literaturzeitung*, lxxvi, 1951, cols. 667 ff.; I. Rabinowitz, in *Journal of Biblical Literature*, lxxi, 1952, pp. 19 ff., and *Vetus Testamentum*, iii, 1953, pp. 175 ff.; H. Bardtke, "Die Handschriftenfunde am Toten Meer", 1952, pp. 143 ff. C. Roth ("The Historical Background of the Dead Sea Scrolls", 1958, p. 37) holds that the Habakkuk Commentary should be placed either in the time of Antiochus Epiphanes or in the Jewish War. But whereas he chooses the latter date, I choose the former.

[2] M. Black ("The Scrolls and Christian Origins", 1961, p. 20) says that "to all other theories it may be objected that the Founder of a movement so famous and influential as that of the Hasidim must have left some trace in our known historical records, and in no single case except that of Onias can this be reasonably claimed".

[3] This has been particularly presented by Dupont-Sommer, in the works mentioned on p. 87, n. 5. It is found in very many works by others, and is often presented as certain.

[4] For some writers who reject the Essene identification, cf. *Bulletin of the John Rylands Library*, xliv, 1961-2, p. 121 n.

[5] The relevant passages from the principal sources are cited in E. F. Sutcliffe, "The Monks of Qumran", pp. 224 ff.; A. Dupont-Sommer, "The Essene Writings from Qumran", pp. 20 ff.; M. Black, "The Scrolls and Christian Origins", pp. 173 ff.

ment was coming when those who had been faithful to the Teacher of Righteousness would be delivered (Hab. Comm. VIII. 1 ff.), while the wicked would be punished (VII. 15 ff.) by the hands of the elect (Hab. Comm. V. 4 f.), when God should destroy all the wicked who served idols (XIII. 2 ff.). Then the elect would be leaders and princes (Comm. on Ps. xxxvii, II. 5), and the penitents of the desert, by which the members of the Qumran sect would appear to be indicated, would live for a thousand generations (Comm. on Ps. xxxvii, II. 1).

In the Manual of Discipline there is a section on the two spirits in man and the two ways to which they lead.[1] Here it is said that those who follow the spirit of light will have everlasting bliss (Man. Disc. IV. 6 ff.), while those who follow the spirit of darkness will suffer everlasting torment and shame and destruction by fire in the regions of darkness (Man. Disc. IV. 11 ff.), and the time when God will bring falsehood to an end and destroy it and enthrone truth for ever is envisaged (Man. Disc. IV. 18 ff.).

Some fragments of a Book of Mysteries[2] have been found. Here the coming glories are described, and the broken words of the second column suggest that here were described the rewards and punishments that should hereafter rectify the inequalities of this life. Some further tiny fragments of what appears to be a description of the New Jerusalem have been published,[3] and further texts of this class may be expected.[4]

The Battle Scroll[5] tells of the war against the Kittim which should last seven years, and which should be followed by successive battles against other nations for a further thirty-three years and usher in the Kingdom of God. This links

[1] Much has been written on this passage. Cf. P. Wernberg-Møller, in *Revue de Qumran*, iii, 1961, pp. 413 ff., where references to the literature on the passage will be found.

[2] Cf. "Qumran Cave I", pp. 101 ff. and *Revue Biblique*, lxiii, 1956, p. 61.

[3] Cf. "Qumran Cave I", pp. 134 ff., and *Revue Biblique*, lxii, 1955, pp. 222 ff.

[4] While the present work has been in the press, some have been published in "Les 'petites grottes' de Qumran", pp. 84 ff., 184 ff.

[5] Y. Yadin has published an excellent edition of this Scroll, "The Scroll of the War of the Sons of Light against the Sons of Darkness", Eng. trans., 1962.

clearly with the expectation of the Book of Daniel, but re-interprets it. There it was believed that the death of Antio-chus would herald the establishment of the Kingdom; but here the perspective becomes longer, and the forty years of the war should probably be equated with the forty years of the expected period between the death of the Teacher of Righteousness and the coming of the Messiah referred to in the Zadokite Work.[1]

Some have thought the Teacher of Righteousness was expected to rise from the dead and to be the Messiah,[2] but there is no clear indication of this in any of the Scrolls,[3] and it seems to be definitely ruled out by the Rule of the Con-gregation.[4] There we are told that "if God should cause the Messiah to be born in their time" he should yield precedence to the priest at the meal which is described. It is clear that he is the civil Messiah and not the priestly leader of the sect. The priestly leader would be an anointed priest, and the word *māshiaḥ* means "anointed"; but the term is not applied to him in this text. There is therefore no reason to import into the text the overtones that the word Messiah carries for us. If he were thought of as the resurrected Teacher of Righteous-ness it would be quite incredible that there should be no hint of this in the text. He is simply referred to as "the priest", and it is clear that he is thought of as the priest who should be presiding over the meal of the sect in the time of the Messiah.

Of the Messianic hopes and interests of the Qumran sect there can be no doubt. The members believed that they were living in the time of the end, and by their purity of life

---

[1] Cf. also Comm. on Ps. xxxvii, I. 6 ff., where it is said that "at the end of the forty years they will be blotted out and not a [wicked] man will survive".

[2] So Dupont-Sommer, "The Dead Sea Scrolls", Eng. trans., pp. 34 f., 44, and "The Essene Writings from Qumran", Eng. trans., p. 108 n.; C. T. Fritsch, "The Qumrān Community", 1956, p. 82.

[3] Many writers have emphasized this. Some references may be found in *Bulletin of the John Rylands Library*, xliv, 1961–2, p. 125 n. G. F. Moore (*Harvard Theological Review*, iv, 1911, p. 342) rejected this view when it was advanced after the publication of the Zadokite Work, observing that if the author had intended to identify the Teacher of Righteousness with the coming Messiah he would have expressed so singular and significant a belief unmistakably.

[4] For the text of this Scroll see "Qumran Cave I", pp. 108 ff.

and study of the Bible they sought to prepare themselves for the life of the Kingdom. They appear to have been especially interested in the prophetic books of the Old Testament, and more than one of the texts recovered consisted of a catena of Scripture texts with comments. Here a special interest in the passages which have commonly been interpreted in the Church as Messianic is shown, and among the texts commented on or collected are Gen. xlix. 10,[1] Deut. xviii. 18 f.,[2] Num. xxiv. 15 ff.,[3] Deut. xxxiii. 8 ff.[4] There is also a comment on the promise to David in 2 Sam. vii,[5] which makes it quite clear that a scion of David was expected to rule in the Messianic age. Any idea that the Teacher of Righteousness was expected to combine in himself the offices of priest and Messiah, such as Charles put forward on the basis of the expression in the Zadokite Work, is therefore definitely excluded by both this text and the Rule of the Congregation.

In the Manual of Discipline there is a reference to "The Messiahs of Aaron and Israel",[6] and on the basis of this it has been proposed to emend the reading in the Zadokite Work,[7] and to read the plural in the places where the text has "the Messiah of Aaron and Israel".[8] This is a very doubtful procedure,[9] since the expression is found there three times, and M. Black has made the alternative proposal to render by the singular here, taking the final *yōdh* as the *yōdh compaginis* instead of the plural construct ending.[10] It is, however, again to be noted that the expression does not mean more than "the anointed ones of Aaron and Israel", and may simply indicate

[1] Cf. J. M. Allegro, in *Journal of Biblical Literature*, lxxv, 1956, pp. 174 ff.

[2] Cf. *ibid.*, p. 183.   [3] Cf. *ibid.*, pp. 183 f.

[4] Cf. *ibid.*, p. 184.   [5] Cf. *ibid.*, pp. 176 f.

[6] Man. Disc. IX. 11.

[7] Cf. J. T. Milik, in *Verbum Domini*, xxx, 1952, pp. 39 f.; also K. G. Kuhn, in "The Scrolls and the New Testament", ed. by K. Stendahl, 1958, p. 59. J. Liver (*Harvard Theological Review*, lii, 1959, p. 152) says it is now conclusively proved that the singular is a scribal error or an emendation.

[8] Zad. Work, ix. 10B, 29B, xv. 4.

[9] Cf. W. S. LaSor, in *Vetus Testamentum*, vi, 1956, pp. 425 ff.; A. S. van der Woude, "Die messianischen Vorstellungen der Gemeinde von Qumran", 1957, pp. 77 ff.; W. H. Brownlee, in "The Scrolls and the New Testament", p. 45; M. Delcor, in *Revue Thomiste*, lviii, 1958, pp. 762, 773.

[10] Cf. *Scottish Journal of Theology*, vi, 1953, p. 6 n., and *Svensk exegetisk Årsbok*, xviii–xix, 1955, pp. 87 ff.

that in the Messianic age it was expected that there would be a priestly leader and a civil leader,[1] just as in the time of Zerubbabel the priest stood beside the civil leader. That the priest would have precedence over the civil leader is made clear in the Scroll of Benedictions, and this is similar to what we have found in the Testaments of the Twelve Patriarchs.

The angelology of the Qumran sect is reflected in the text known as the Angelic Liturgy.[2] This makes it apparent that seven "chief princes",[3] or archangels, were believed in. Belial appears very frequently as the leader of the evil spirits, and the dualism of good and evil, light and darkness, is characteristic of the thought of the Qumran sect.[4]

In all these works at which we have looked, coming from the second and first centuries B.C., we see the emergence of ideas which are found in the New Testament. All are concerned with the end of the age and the dawn of a new age, and with the destiny of the righteous and the evil, but all manifest a certain fluidity in their thought. They build freely on the basis of ideas culled from the Old Testament or from one another, but the building each rears has a character of its own. And each contributes something to the stream of ideas that flowed into the New Testament.

[1] T. H. Gaster ("The Scriptures of the Dead Sea Sect", 1957, p. 29) maintains that there is nothing "Messianic" about this text at all, and that the civil leader is simply the duly anointed King of Israel at any future epoch. But this rests on an emendation of the text, Gaster changing it to yield "in the event that the awaited (King) should be present" (p. 287), whereas the manuscript clearly has "if God should cause the *māshiaḥ* to be born". For other emendations which have been proposed, see *Bulletin of the John Rylands Library*, xliv, 1960-1, p. 145 n.

[2] Cf. J. Strugnell, in "Congress Volume. Oxford, 1959" (Supplements to *Vetus Testamentum*, vii), 1960, pp. 318 ff.

[3] The word for "prince" is that used of Gog in Ezek. xxxviii. 2 f., xxxix. 1, and not that used in Dan. x. 13, 20 f.

[4] This dualism has been traced by some writers to Zoroastrian influence, but this is contested by Wernberg-Møller (*Revue de Qumran*, iii, 1961, pp. 412 ff.), who approves the view of K. Schubert (*Theologische Literaturzeitung*, lxxviii, 1953, col. 501) that in the Scrolls we do not find a cosmic dualism but a relative dualism. Similarly, M. Treves (*Revue de Qumran*, iii, 1961, pp. 449 ff.) maintains that the doctrine of the two spirits is quite unlike Zoroastrian dualism, and holds that the two spirits "are simply the tendencies or propensities which are implanted in every man's heart". Cf. also W. Grossouw, in *Studia Catholica*, xxvi, 1951, pp. 293 ff.; F. Nötscher, "Zur theologischen Terminologie der Qumrantexte", 1956, p. 84.

NOTE A. THE DATE OF THE EARLIEST SECTIONS OF THE ETHIOPIC BOOK OF ENOCH

Two sections of the Ethiopic Book of Enoch are commonly dated earlier than the Book of Daniel, and as this would mean that much of what has been said in Chapter I is without basis, some examination of the question is called for, and some justification for the dating I have followed.[1]

R. H. Charles, that indefatigable pioneer worker in the field of apocalyptic, to whom all students of the subject are profoundly indebted for a whole series of publications,[2] believed that 1 Enoch is a composite work, and that the section contained in chapters vi–xxxvi was definitely pre-Maccabaean,[3] and the short Apocalypse of Weeks, contained in xciii. 1–10, xci. 12–17, may also have been.[4] But 1 En. vi–xxxvi is a pseudonymous work, in that it was written as though from the hand of Enoch in ancient days. If this is older than the Book of Daniel, then the author of that book could have copied this feature from 1 Enoch, and the suggestion that Daniel set the fashion in this respect, but owed its own pseudonymity to the living development out of which it grew, is quite worthless. For the pseudonymity of 1 En. vi–xxxvi we should have no relevant precedent, and we should be left without any explanation, save the suggestion that in no other way could a hearing be obtained, since it was believed that inspiration was dead. In this suggestion it seems to be tacitly implied that the hearing desired was inclusion in the Canon, and recognition as inspired Scripture. That suggestion seems to me quite groundless, and the idea

---

[1] It is unnecessary to examine the view of J. C. K. Hofmann (*Zeitschrift der deutschen morgenländischen Gesellschaft*, vi, 1852, pp. 87 ff.) that the whole book of 1 Enoch was of Christian origin.

[2] G. Ricciotti calls him "il grande e benmerito editore di Apocrifi" (see *Proceedings of the British Academy*, xvii, 1931, p. 445), and Burkitt adds the observation that his works "have not only instructed his own countrymen, but have also lightened the labours of scholars all over the civilized world" (*ibid.*).

[3] "The Book of Enoch", 2nd ed., 1912, pp. lii f., 1 f.; "Apocrypha and Pseudepigrapha", ii, 1913, p. 170.

[4] "The Book of Enoch", p. liii; "Apocrypha and Pseudepigrapha", ii, p. 171. It should be noted, however, that Charles adds: "But the date is wholly doubtful."

that any book was written with the conscious purpose of securing a place in the sacred corpus rests on the most unreal conception of the process of canonization. Yet no process, comparable to that which has been suggested for the Book of Daniel, can be traced, whereby the author of this book might have been led to pseudonymity.

Moreover, the author of Daniel could have found many of his ideas here, and we need not have looked farther afield for their source. The seven archangels are here named, and their functions defined (1 En. xx); the term "Watcher", which is used for an angel in Dan. iv, is found frequently in this section of 1 Enoch; the idea of the resurrection is found in 1 En. xxii. 13; the thought of the throne of God being set up on earth at the time of the final judgement is found in 1 En. xxv. 3. All of these ideas are found in the Book of Daniel, and if this work is earlier than that it should be given a very important place in the account of the rise of apocalyptic, and it, and not Daniel, should be regarded as the first great apocalyptic work.

Not all scholars are agreed, indeed, that this section is so early as Charles places it. Eissfeldt assigns it to a date not later than about 150 B.C.,[1] while Schürer would place it towards the end of the second century B.C.[2] Bousset put it between 164 B.C. and 80 B.C.,[3] and Beer between 167 B.C. and 64 B.C.,[4] while Baldensperger,[5] Causse,[6] and Klausner[7] assigned it to the reign of John Hyrcanus, Torrey[8] to the

---

[1] "Einleitung in das Alte Testament", 2nd ed., 1956, p. 766.

[2] "History of the Jewish People", Eng. trans., II, iii, 1890, p. 66.

[3] Bousset-Gressmann, "Religion des Judentums", p. 12.

[4] In Kautzsch, "Apokrypha und Pseudepigrapha", ii, 1900, p. 232.

[5] "Das Selbstbewusstsein Jesu im Lichte der messianischen Hoffnungen seiner Zeit", 1892, pp. 8 ff. (3rd ed., 1903, pp. 10 ff.). Cf. E. Stave, who assigns the oldest parts of the book of Enoch to the later Maccabaean age ("Über den Einfluss des Parsismus auf das Judentum", 1898, p. 190).

[6] "Les 'pauvres' d'Israël", 1922, p. 143 n. So, too, König, "Die messianischen Weissagungen des Alten Testaments", 1923, pp. 325 f.

[7] "Ha-ra'yon ham-Meshiḥi be-Yiśrael", 1927, pp. 174 ff. Klausner dates the earlier part of 1 Enoch (which in his view consists of i–xxxvi and lxxii–cviii) circa 110 B.C.—either in the time of John Hyrcanus or in that of Alexander Jannaeus.

[8] "The Apocryphal Literature", 1945, pp. 110 ff. Torrey assigns the whole book to "the first decade of the last century B.C. probably in or soon after the year 95". He declares that "no part of the book appears to be earlier than this".

reign of Alexander Jannaeus, and Kaplan[1] to the reign of Herod the Great. On the other hand, the view of Charles is in close agreement with that of Martin,[2] and it was at first accepted by Lagrange,[3] who, however, later felt that while this date was probable, it was possible that the section came from the early days of the Maccabaean revolt.[4] Frey assigns it with similar vagueness to the reign of Antiochus Epiphanes.[5]

It is when we examine the reasons on which Charles bases his view that the weakness of the case for the pre-Maccabaean dating becomes apparent. He advances three reasons. These are: (a) that these chapters were known to the author of chapters lxxxiii–xc, who wrote before the death of Judas Maccabaeus in 161 B.C.; (b) that they make no reference to the persecution of Antiochus Epiphanes, and (c) that their original language was Aramaic.[6]

So far as the first of these reasons is concerned, it may be noted that the Book of Daniel was also known to the author of 1 En. lxxxiii–xc, since, as Charles himself notes, the conception of the seventy shepherds of 1 En. lxxxix. 59 is an extension of the conception of the seventy years of Jeremiah, and the seventy weeks of Daniel.[7] Since Charles dates the Book of Daniel in the period of the Maccabaean revolt, a date anterior to that age is not required to make it possible for the author of the later section of 1 Enoch to show a knowledge of chapters vi–xxxvi.

Similarly, the argument from the language is best

---

[1] *Anglican Theological Review*, xii, 1929–30, pp. 534 ff. Kaplan argues that the greater part of the Book of Enoch, including the section vi–xxxvi, is not earlier than the time of Herod.

[2] "Le Livre d'Hénoch", 1906, p. xcv. Martin dates it from the beginning of the persecution of Antiochus, and before the outbreak of the Maccabaean revolt. Cf. J. Bonsirven, "La Bible Apocryphe", 1953, p. 28.

[3] "Le messianisme chez les juifs", 1909, p. 62.

[4] "Le Judaïsme avant J.-C.", 2nd ed., 1931, p. 113.

[5] In Pirot's "Supplément au Dictionnaire de la Bible", i, 1928, col. 358.

[6] On the language or languages in which 1 Enoch was written, cf. F. Zimmerman (*Journal of Biblical Literature*, lx, 1941, pp. 159–72) and C. C. Torrey (*Journal of the American Oriental Society*, lxii, 1942, pp. 52–60). The former follows Charles in arguing for a bilingual origin, while the latter argues that Aramaic was the original language of the whole.

[7] "Apocrypha and Pseudepigrapha", ii, p. 255.

answered by Charles himself. For in writing of this section of 1 Enoch he argues that when a nation is trying to recover its independence it seeks to revive its national language, and hence Aramaic would not be used in a Maccabaean work. Yet when Charles writes of the Book of Daniel he adopts a similar *a priori* argument, but exactly reversed in content. For he holds that the whole of the Book of Daniel was issued in Aramaic in that very age, and that the parts now standing in Hebrew were an early translation from Aramaic. To support this doubtful proposition he argues that it must have been so, since "to get in touch with his countrymen and to bring home to them the ideals for which they stood, *the author of Daniel could not do otherwise than write in Aramaic.* Only through the medium of the vernacular was this possible, and the vernacular of his day was Aramaic." [1] So, then, 1 En. vi–xxxvi could not be Maccabaean because it was issued in Aramaic, and Daniel must be issued in Aramaic because it was Maccabaean! [2] Such an argument is manifestly worthless, and if the Book of Daniel, which on Charles's view and on mine was an important weapon in the campaign for independence, was written in part or in whole in Aramaic, it is impossible to maintain that another work could not have been written in Aramaic in that age.

We are left, then, with the purely negative argument that there is no reference to the persecution of Antiochus Epiphanes. This could not be materially relevant, unless it were shown that the work contains specific references to contemporary events up to a point prior to that persecution, and hence that there is good reason to suppose that the author would have referred to the persecution if he had known of it. But the author does not follow the course of history, and hence

---

[1] "Critical Commentary on the Book of Daniel", 1929, p. xlv. The italics are Charles's.

[2] T. F. Glasson ("The Second Advent", 1945, p. 14) quite uncritically pronounces Charles's reasons for dating this section of 1 Enoch good, and therefore shares the view that the fact that it was written in Aramaic is evidence that it could not have been Maccabaean. He also quite uncritically follows Charles in declaring that the Book of Daniel is Maccabaean, and that it was originally written in Aramaic (pp. 14, 16). But whereas Charles's inconsistency was distributed in different works, Glasson's is achieved within three pages.

specific references to events either prior to or during the persecution are outside his purpose.[1] It may be noted, however, that Frey[2] sees evidence of a period of persecution and martyrdom in 1 En. ix. 10: "And now, behold, the souls of those who have died are crying and making their suit to the gates of heaven, and their lamentations have ascended: and cannot cease because of the lawless deeds which are wrought on the earth." Similarly, Lagrange[3] thinks the reference to Abel in 1 En. xxii. 7 is equally to those who, like him, have suffered martyrdom at the hands of the wicked, and Charles also observes that Abel stands for a class.[4] It is possible, therefore, that here we have something which gains relevance in a background of persecution.

Moreover, it may be observed that while the myth of the fallen angels is an ancient one,[5] the author may have been induced to use it partly by its applicability to Antiochus Epiphanes, who claimed to be of divine origin. The fruits of the unions of the fallen angels with women were monsters, and the physical monsters of the myth could well point to the spiritual monster, Antiochus. Further, the reference in 1 En. xix. 1 to idolatry as due to these unions might well suggest the idolatry Antiochus was attempting to force on the nation.

Finally, it may be observed that Charles, with complete inconsistency, but with sound observation, states that the writer of 1 En. xiv. 18–22 drew on Dan. vii. 9 f.[6] Since, on

---

[1] It may be noted that Steuernagel observed that this section offers no handle for dating, and hence made no attempt to date it. Cf. "Lehrbuch der Einleitung in das Alte Testament", 1912, p. 816.

[2] In Pirot's "Supplément", i, col. 358.

[3] "Le Judaïsme avant J.-C.", p. 112.

[4] "The Book of Enoch", p. 47.

[5] Cf. Gen. vi. 1 ff.

[6] "The Book of Enoch", 2nd ed., 1912, p. 34, and "Apocrypha and Pseudepigrapha", ii, 1913, p. 197. In his Century Bible commentary, "The Book of Daniel", 1911, p. 76, he had merely observed on Dan. vii. 9 f.: "We might compare 1 En. xiv. 18–22." In his larger work, "A Critical and Exegetical Commentary on the Book of Daniel", 1929, p. 183, he added to this observation "(pre-Maccabean in date)", showing that he had by now realized his inconsistency, though without going to the length of reversing the dependence so inconsistently stated in his works on 1 Enoch.

Charles's hypothesis, 1 En. xiv was written before the Book of Daniel, the inconsistency is manifest.

There seems no reason, therefore, to place this section of the book before the date of Daniel, and I prefer to find rather an inferior imitator of Daniel at work here. He lacks the brilliance of the story-teller of the first half of Daniel, and equally the precision and force of the creator of the visions of the second half. The author of the Book of Daniel is also a far more effective moral and spiritual teacher. To him the evil kingdoms rise out of the sea, and he castigates the vices of pride, sacrilege, and overweening ambition, evils that spring out of the human heart and for which men stand rebuked; whereas to the author of this section of 1 Enoch all evil comes from the fallen angels. Its origin lies in heaven, and man has no more responsibility for it than he would have for a disease which attacked and destroyed him. It should be added that the passionate summons to utter loyalty to God that marks the Daniel stories is also lacking here. Altogether the work of this writer is completely outclassed in style, imagination, and brilliance by the Book of Daniel. He shows little originality or versatility, compared with the author of Daniel, and it is altogether more probable that the less original work is the dependent one.

The other section of 1 Enoch which has been referred to a date earlier than the Maccabaean rising is the Apocalypse of Weeks, contained in xciii. 1–10, xci. 12–17. Eissfeldt[1] here agrees with Charles and Martin[2] in placing it so early, and this view is based simply on the claim that there is no reference to the persecution of Antiochus. But again, this could not be conclusive in so brief a passage, cast throughout in such vague and general terms. Lagrange[3] and Frey[4] find reference to this persecution in xciii. 9 f., and xci. 12, and it must be agreed that such a background would fit the reference, though it could not be said to be demanded as the

[1] "Einleitung in das Alte Testament", 2nd ed., p. 765. So also Beer in Kautzsch, "Apokrypha und Pseudepigrapha", ii, p. 230.

[2] "Le Livre d'Hénoch", 1906, pp. xciv f.

[3] "Le messianisme chez les juifs", pp. 78 f.

[4] In Pirot's "Supplément", i, col. 365.

only possible background.[1] For these verses describe the seventh week as marked by apostasy, and tell how at its close the elect righteous will have a sword put into their hands to execute judgement on their oppressors. Lagrange believes the reference to be to the first victories of Jonathan, and he therefore dates this section *circa* 152 B.C. Without attempting such precision we may agree that no age better fits these conditions than the Maccabaean age.[2] We may also observe that it is unlikely that this fragment represents the original Enoch book, and that it is much more likely that it was attached to an already existing Enoch collection. In itself it offers no explanation of the choice of Enoch for its pseudonym, if this were the earliest of the pseudonymous, apocalyptic works, and in the absence of any compelling, or even moderately strong, reason for placing it before the Book of Daniel, I do not place it there.[3]

NOTE B. THE DATE OF THE BOOK OF JUBILEES

By most writers it has been agreed that the Book of Jubilees belongs to the second century B.C. The most usual date to which it is ascribed is at the end of the century, in the reign of John Hyrcanus,[4] but Frey[5] puts it somewhat earlier,

[1] A. C. Welch (*The Expositor*, 8th series, xxv, 1923, pp. 273 ff.) holds that this Apocalypse of Weeks dates from the Roman period.

[2] Cf. A. Causse ("Les 'pauvres' d'Israël", 1922, p. 143 n.), who says that the Apocalypse of Weeks is slightly later than Daniel.

[3] For the curious it may be recorded that R. Laurence ("The Book of Enoch the Prophet", 3rd ed., 1838, p. xxxvii), who regarded the work as a unity, assigned its composition to a date but a few years before the beginning of the Christian era.

[4] M. Testuz ("Les Idées religieuses du livre des Jubilés", 1960) accepts the usual date, and holds that the work was written by an early Essene, who regarded the reign of Hyrcanus I as the beginning of the Kingdom of God, around 110 B.C. (pp. 7, 32 ff.). For a criticism of this view, and especially of the idea that the Essenes supported the Hasmonaeans, see my review in *Theologische Literaturzeitung*, lxxxvi, 1961, cols. 423 ff. Since the finding of the fragments of Jubilees among the Dead Sea Scrolls, it has become common to assume that the work emanated from the Qumran sect. B. Noack (*Svensk exegetisk Årsbok*, xxii-xxiii, 1957–8, pp. 191 ff.) pleads for more caution in such an assignment.

[5] In Pirot's "Supplément", i, col. 375. Cf. G. F. Moore, "Judaism in the First Centuries of the Christian Era", i, 1927, p. 199: "in the latter half of the second century before the Christian Era".

at the beginning of the second half of the century, while
Klausner [1] puts it at the beginning of the first century B.C.,
and Torrey [2] in the latter half of the same century. Some
indeed have placed it much later, [3] and Headlam placed it as
late as A.D. 50 to 60. [4] The usual dating has been more
seriously challenged, however, from the other side. Albright [5]
assigns it to the end of the fourth or the beginning of the third
century B.C., while Zeitlin [6] assigns it to the early post-exilic
period. It is necessary to examine these views in some detail,
since their acceptance would have important consequences
for the understanding of the rise and development of apocalyptic, and would certainly invalidate at some points the
account which has been given in Chapter I. As the Book of
Jubilees is not pseudonymous, however, an earlier dating
would not invalidate the view of the origin of pseudonymity
which has been suggested.

Zeitlin bases much on the fact that the Book of Jubilees
does not hesitate to oppose many of the Pentateuchal laws
and traditions, and hence supposes that it must have been
written in the pre-hellenistic period, when it could be hoped
that opposition to the Pentateuch would not be wholly futile.
Albright agrees that it must date from before the final fixing
of the Pentateuchal laws, though he cannot assign it to the
pre-hellenistic period. He recognizes that its outlook is
essentially pre-hellenistic, but finds the numerous Greek
geographical names fatal to a date earlier than the end of the
fourth century B.C. He then concludes that the canonical
form of the Pentateuch cannot be older than about 300 B.C.
I do not think it can be tacitly assumed that no one would
venture to oppose any Pentateuchal law after the fixation of

---

[1] "Ha-ra'yon ham-Meshiḥi be-Yiśrael", 1927, pp. 189 ff.

[2] "The Apocryphal Literature", 1945, pp. 126 ff.

[3] N. Messel ("Die Einheitlichkeit der judischen Eschatologie", 1915, p. 14)
follows Baldensperger in assigning it to the middle of the first century B.C.,
circa 63 B.C. (cf. Baldensperger, op. cit., p. 24, 3rd ed., 1903, p. 32).

[4] In Hastings' "Dictionary of the Bible", ii, 1899, p. 791.

[5] "From the Stone Age to Christianity", 1940, pp. 266 f.

[6] Jewish Quarterly Review, xxx, 1939-40, pp. 1 ff. Cf. ibid., xxxvi, 1945-6, pp.
12 ff., and on the other side L. Finkelstein, Harvard Theological Review, xxxvi,
1943, pp. 19 ff.

the accepted form of the collection. In the Maccabaean age there was a serious effort, supported by the most influential circles, to abolish the Pentateuchal law altogether, and to substitute a hellenized cult. And even the Pharisees, as Zeitlin himself points out,[1] felt themselves at liberty to reject the *lex talionis*, and thus to oppose an important Pentateuchal law.

Much more weight is attached by Zeitlin to the question of the calendar. He observes that the author protests vigorously against the change from the solar to the solar–lunar calendar, and that the work clearly dates from a time when the change of calendar was recent, and was still an issue among the Jews. This could not have been in the Maccabaean period, he argues, for then the true duration of the solar year was universally known, and the calendar had been changed for centuries. Hence the issue must long ago have become a dead one. The very designation of the months by numerals rather than by names, he holds, shows that this book could not have been written in a later period.

All this is less convincing than may at first appear. For Morgenstern had already argued[2] that a gradual change in the calendar employed occupied a long period in the post-exilic age. He believes that the growing Hellenic influence in the Seleucid period helped to bring this about. He had also pointed out that "the system of indicating the months by number continued to be used throughout the entire post-exilic Biblical literature, and is even employed in the majority of the apocryphal and pseudepigraphical writings".[3] It can-

---

[1] *Jewish Quarterly Review*, xxx, p. 2.

[2] *Hebrew Union College Annual*, i, 1924, pp. 13 ff. See, especially, pp. 19 ff., 73 ff.

[3] *Ibid.*, p. 19. Cf. U. Cassuto, "Encyclopaedia Judaica", ix, 1932, p. 799. Zeitlin (*Jewish Quarterly Review*, xxxv, 1944–5, pp. 458 f.) has challenged me to adduce any proof of this statement of Morgenstern's, and I have supplied it in the same journal (xxxvi, 1945–6, pp. 184–7). It may be summarized here. In Zechariah the reference by number is found four times, twice with Babylonian name attached in what are usually held to be late glosses. In Haggai the reference by number is uniformly found (five times). In Ezra we find the Babylonian name once, in an Aramaic source, and in the Memoirs of Nehemiah the same usage is found three times. These offer no secure evidence of contemporary Palestinian usage, but may reflect the usage of the Persian Court. We know from the Elephantine papyri that in official Aramaic documents in

not therefore be tacitly assumed that the calendar issue was wholly dead in the Maccabaean age. Indeed, we read in Dan. vii. 25 that the Little Horn should "think to change times and the law". With great plausibility Morgenstern suggests that this may refer to a calendar revision which Antiochus sought to promote.[1] He also argues that the calendar of the Book of Jubilees is closely similar to the original solar calendar of the Hebrews.[2] In that case it may well have been that in a time of debate about the calendar, and pressure to effect changes, the author of the Book of Jubilees advocated a return to older ways. It may be added that Morgenstern brings forward some evidence to suggest that the calendar of the astronomical part of 1 Enoch (un-referred to above) agreed with that of the Book of Jubilees, and also that the author of 1 Maccabees seems to have dated

---

Egypt the Babylonian names were used (alongside the Egyptian names). Else-where in the Books of Ezra and Nehemiah we find the reference by number only (fourteen times). In the Book of Esther we find the Babylonian names eleven times, seven of them with the numbers attached, and once we find the number only. As the Book of Esther is commonly dated in the middle of the second century B.C., we have no certain pre-Maccabaean evidence for the use of the Babylonian names in Palestinian Hebrew usage. The Additions to the Book of Esther follow the usage of that book, giving four occurrences of the Babylonian names, of which two have the number added. In 1 Esdras, in a passage depending on the above-mentioned passage in Ezra, we find the reference by name only, and elsewhere we find the reference by name and number once, and by number only five times. In 1 Maccabees the name is found seven times, twice with the number added, and the number only four times. In 2 Maccabees the Babylonian names are found four times, with number added once, and Greek names stand twice. In 1 Enoch dates are given by number three times, and never by the Babylonian name. In the Testaments of the Twelve Pat-riarchs the reference by number is used in the only relevant passage. In 2 Enoch (on whose date see below) we find the reference by number once, and by name four times. 2 Baruch uses the dating by number in its only passage, and the Biblical Antiquities of pseudo-Philo has the same usage in its only two occur-rences. In view of this evidence it is idle to suppose that we have in the exclusive use of numbers in Jubilees—a usage which is shared with 1 Enoch, the Testa-ments of the Twelve Patriarchs, 2 Baruch and pseudo-Philo—a valid canon for the pre-Maccabaean dating of the book. Further, the Book of Judith has the same usage in its only passage. Zeitlin for some reason claims that the reference here is not to the month of the calendar year, but "to the chronology of the king, the twenty-second day of the first month of the eighteenth year of his kingdom" (*ibid.*, xxxvi, 1945–6, p. 189). For this astonishing statement no evidence and no parallels are adduced.

[1] *Hebrew Union College Annual*, i, p. 75 n.
[2] *Ibid.*, p. 67.

the beginning of the year in agreement with the author of Jubilees.[1]

Both Zeitlin and Albright reverse the usually accepted relationship between the Book of Jubilees and the Ethiopic Book of Enoch. In Jub. iv. 17 f. we read that Enoch "was the first among men born on the earth to learn writing and knowledge and wisdom, and to write down the signs of heaven. . . . And he was the first to write a testimony . . . and he recounted the weeks of the jubilees." Zeitlin thinks the author of 1 Enoch based his book on this verse,[2] while Albright thinks the reference is to an older, lost book of Enoch.[3] Zeitlin's suggestion is an admission that there are sections of the present Ethiopian Enoch which well correspond to the reference, and it would seem needless to posit an older similar work. In any case, no weight could rest on such an assumption.

But if no strong case can be made out for the pre-Maccabaean dating it remains to be asked what kind of case can be made out for a later date. For no great weight could be placed on the suggestion recorded above for the interpretation of Dan. vii. 25. Albright declares the arguments advanced in favour of a Maccabaean date feeble,[4] and they are certainly not so strong as could be desired. They do seem, however, to be more cogent than those on the other side.

The work comes from a time when men have forgotten "commandment, and covenant, and feasts, and months, and Sabbaths, and jubilees" (Jub. xxiii. 19), when they "forsake the covenant which the Lord made between them and him" (Jub. xxiii. 16). The author accordingly lays much emphasis on the Sabbath, and on the death penalty appropriate to those who do not observe it (Jub. ii. 17 ff., l. 6 ff.); on the

---

[1] *Ibid.*, pp. 65 ff., 56. Cf. Moore, "Judaism in the First Centuries of the Christian Era", i, 1927, p. 194. Moore adds: "Into this eccentric calendar system it is unnecessary to enter here. The motive for it was probably not the mere charm of symmetry, but the desire to create a distinctively Jewish division of time fundamentally unlike those of other peoples, and particularly that of the Greeks. In the reaction against Hellenism in the second century such a motive is intelligible enough."   [2] *Loc. cit.*, p. 12.

[3] *Op. cit.*, p. 266.

[4] *Ibid.*, p. 267.

feast of weeks (Jub. vi. 17 ff.); on the feast of tabernacles (Jub. xvi. 20 ff.); on the Day of Atonement (Jub. xxxiv. 18 ff.); on the Passover (Jub. xlix. 1 ff.); on new moons (Jub. vi. 23 ff.). He warns his readers to observe Jewish food laws (Jub. vi. 7, 10 ff., vii. 31 ff., xxi. 18), to avoid eating or associating with Gentiles (Jub. xxii. 16), and especially to avoid intermarriage with them (Jub. xxii. 20, xxx. 7 ff.). He complains of idolatry (Jub. xi. 4) and warns against its folly (Jub. xx. 7 ff., xxi. 3 ff.); and against Gentile customs of sacrificing to the dead, worshipping evil spirits, and eating over graves (Jub. xxii. 17). It is true that a loyal Jew in any age might adopt all these positions, but in no age could they find a more appropriate setting than in the Maccabaean. For then the keeping of the Sabbath had been prohibited (1 Macc. i. 45; 2 Macc. vi. 6), idolatry had been commanded (1 Macc. i. 47), and the eating of unclean foods enforced (2 Macc. vi. 7). Nor could the protest against association with Gentiles ever be more urgently justified than in the age which witnessed the promotion of Greek customs in Jerusalem.

Further, the author knows by experience an age when circumcision has become a vital issue. He knows of the days when Jews refrained from circumcising their children, and treated their members like Gentiles (Jub. xv. 33 f.), and he enjoins the observance of this rite under the severest penalties (Jub. xv. 11 ff., 26). In Maccabaean days we know this was a living issue. Antiochus forbade circumcision under penalty of death (1 Macc. i. 48, 60 f.), and many underwent a surgical operation to remove its traces (1 Macc. i. 15), while on the other hand, the Maccabaean patriots forcibly circumcised the uncircumcised children (1 Macc. ii. 46). Again, the author of Jubilees warns his readers against being seen naked, like the Gentiles (Jub. iii. 31). The reference is quite clearly to the Greek nudity in the athletic games, and this alone would make a pre-hellenistic date for the book impossible. But even within the hellenistic age, we have no knowledge of a time when this was a live issue, except in the Maccabaean age, when Jason established a Greek palaestra in Jerusalem, and even priests neglected their duties in order to join in the games (2 Macc. iv. 7 ff.).[1]

While, therefore, the case for a Maccabaean date is by no means irresistible, every probability points to it, and similarly every probability points against the earlier dates suggested. There is nothing in the indications of date contained in the book inconsistent with the Maccabaean date, whereas in some respects their consistency with an earlier date cannot be established by any known facts. Moreover, there are some features which are peculiarly consistent with the Maccabaean dating, and the case for this date is very much stronger than we are often able to make for the dating on internal evidence of works of this kind.

[1] L. Finkelstein (*Harvard Theological Review*, xxxvi, 1943, pp. 19 ff.) puts much emphasis on this last consideration, and maintains that the Book of Jubilees cannot be earlier than the high priesthood of Jason—175 B.C.—but maintains that it must date from before the profanation of the Temple by Antiochus, because there is no reference to the persecution. But there is a reference to the question of circumcision, which, according to 1 Maccabees, was forbidden at the same time as the forbidding of the sacrifices of the Temple. This would seem, therefore, to carry us to the period of the persecution, as would also some of the other points noted above.

CHAPTER THREE

The Apocalyptic Literature:
ii. During the First Century A.D.

D URING THE first century of the Christian era there
was much continued activity in the production of
apocalyptic literature. The widespread expectancy
of the approach of the Messianic kingdom forms the background of the preaching of John the Baptist and of Jesus, and
in the political sphere pseudo-Messiahs were not unknown.[1]
Moreover, the growing restlessness of the Jews and the bitter
hostility to Rome pointed to a violent outburst in the not
distant future, and that exaggerated perspective that gave a
cosmic significance to Jewish concerns revived the hopes that
had found expression in the Book of Daniel, and applied
them to the situation of the hour. In the Church the Neronic
persecution, and later the Domitianic, in a different way
revived the expectation of the Book of Daniel, and led men
to expect that the faithfulness which embraced a martyr's
death, and the refusal to acknowledge the divine pretensions
of a king, would speedily give place to the glorious vindication
of the divinely established kingdom. It is not, therefore,
surprising that both in Synagogue and in Church apocalyptic
works were written during this century. The writers worked
with a common stock of ideas, many of which we have
already found, and they differently combined them and
worked them up. Their originality is not fundamentally in
the ideas they express, but in the pattern they make of those
ideas.

The Assumption of Moses

In early lists of apocryphal books there is mention of a
Testament of Moses and an Assumption of Moses. We have

[1] Cf. Bultmann, "Jesus and the Word", Eng. trans., 1935, pp. 20 f.

preserved for us but one book, which bears the title of the Assumption of Moses, and which was cited under this title as early as the Nicene Council,[1] but which bears the character of a Testament of Moses. For it is cast in the form of Moses' final charge to Joshua, in which he unfolds to him the future course of history. Charles thinks the two works above referred to were early combined, but that the bulk of the second has not survived.[2]

There is a rapid survey of history down to the Seleucid era in the first four chapters. The fifth chapter describes the inner divisions of the Jews in that era, and the apostasy of many. It is probable that chapter viii has been displaced, and that it should immediately follow chapter v. In that case it contains an account of the persecution of Antiochus Epiphanes, which it excellently fits, and which is otherwise surprisingly passed over without mention. Charles transfers chapter ix along with chapter viii, and identifies the mysterious figure of the Levite Taxo, who should exhort his seven sons to faithfulness, with Eleazar, of 2 Macc. vi. 18 ff. I find difficulty in accepting this view,[3] and prefer to follow the view of C. Lattey,[4] that chapter viii only should be transferred to follow chapter v, and that chapter ix depicts under the cryptic name of Taxo a contemporary or an expected figure.

Reverting to chapter vi, the history continues with an account of the Hasmonaeans, compressed into a single critical verse, and of an insolent alien king, who is clearly Herod the Great. Since it is stated that his children shall succeed him, but shall reign for shorter periods than their father, the work must have been written before any of Herod's sons exceeded the length of his reign. The date of the work is thus narrowly limited to the first three decades of the Christian era. There

[1] Cf. Mansi, "Sacrorum Conciliorum nova et amplissima collectio", ii, 1759, col. 844, where Ass. Mos. i. 14 is quoted.

[2] "The Assumption of Moses", 1897, pp. xlv ff. On the original language of the work, which is of no moment for our present study, cf. D. H. Wallace, in *Theologische Zeitschrift*, xi, 1955, pp. 321 ff.

[3] Cf. Note C at the end of this chapter.

[4] *Catholic Biblical Quarterly*, January 1942, pp. 9 ff. I am indebted to Father Lattey for an offprint of this article, to which I should otherwise have had no access.

is a reference to the savage conduct of Varus, who suppressed a Jewish rebellion in 4 B.C., and the statement that he should crucify some makes it clear that we are now in the age of Roman rule. Burkitt[1] and Ferrar[2] would assign the work to a date soon after the removal of Archelaus in A.D. 6, but Lattey[3] offers good reason to suppose it was rather later than this, and probably not long before A.D. 30.

The author believed that now the time of the end had come, and so he here passes from his historical survey, with the sons of Herod, to his announcement of the *dénouement* of history. "When this is done the times shall be ended, in a moment the course shall be ended, the four hours shall come" (Ass. Mos. vii. 1). Chapter ix describes how Taxo should exhort his sons to join him in a fast, to be followed by withdrawal to a cave, where they would die rather than transgress the law of God. Their death would be avenged of God, and the kingdom of God, whose glories are described in chapter x, would then come.

It will be seen that the parallel in form to the visions of the Book of Daniel is here very close. The author runs over the course of history from the time of the putative author to his own day, which he indicates very clearly, and expects the Messianic age to be imminent when he writes. Like the author of the Book of Daniel, he does not expect that kingdom to be established by human valour, but by divine intervention. It has been observed above that while the author of the Book of Daniel clearly approved of the Maccabaean rising, he did not build his hopes upon it.[4] His stories inculcated a loyalty in suffering rather than heroism in battle, and it was by a sudden divine intervention that the kingdom was to come. The author of the Assumption of Moses makes no reference to the Maccabees, but he holds up to honour Taxo, whose purpose was to embrace death rather than be

---

[1] In Hastings' "Dictionary of the Bible", iii, p. 448.

[2] "The Assumption of Moses", 1918, p. 9.

[3] *Loc. cit.*, p. 13. The generally accepted date for this work is somewhere near the beginning of the Christian era. S. Zeitlin (*Jewish Quarterly Review*, xxxviii, 1947–8, p. 35) dates its composition A.D. 140.

[4] In Dan. xi. 34 the Maccabaean rising is referred to as "a little help".

disloyal, precisely like Daniel's purpose, and that of the three who were cast into the fire. In his account of the establishment of the kingdom, the author of the Assumption of Moses makes no reference whatever to any human instrumentality that will even help.

When we examine the description of the kingdom in chapter x we find that it will appear suddenly throughout creation (Ass. Mos. x. 1), when the heavenly One will arise from His royal throne and go forth from His habitation (Ass. Mos. x. 3), to the accompaniment of signs on earth and in the heavens (Ass. Mos. x. 4–6). The angel—Michael is apparently intended, though he is not named—will avenge Israel on her foes (Ass. Mos. x. 2), and the Eternal God will Himself punish the Gentiles and destroy their idols (Ass. Mos. x. 7), and Satan shall be no more (Ass. Mos. x. 1). Israel, on the contrary, shall be made happy (Ass. Mos. x. 8), and one element in her joy shall be to see her foes in Gehenna (Ass. Mos. x. 10), while she herself is exalted to heaven (Ass. Mos. x. 9). From this it is clear that no kingdom on earth is expected and no Messiah enters into the picture. The thought is therefore quite different from that of the Book of Daniel and of other works at which we have looked, where a millennium[1] on earth was dreamt of. Again, there is here no thought of a great assault of the wicked on the saints as the prelude to the end, such as we find in the Book of Daniel, or in 1 En. lxxxiii–xc and in the Sibylline Oracles. The scene is wholly supramundane, after the destruction of the material universe that will herald the foundation of the Kingdom of Heaven. There is therefore no resurrection, either of the righteous or of the wicked, but there is bliss in Heaven for the righteous, and torment in Gehenna for the Gentiles. The satisfaction with which the author contemplates that torment is one of the least pleasing features of his anticipations. The nearest approach to his view in the earlier works at which we have looked is in the section of 1 Enoch contained in chapters xci–

---

[1] The word *millennium* is here used with reference to the quality of the life of the kingdom, and not to its duration for a thousand years. The latter idea will first come before us later.

civ, where also eternal bliss for the righteous in heaven and eternal torment for the wicked is anticipated, in contrast to the view of the Psalms of Solomon, where the wicked perish for ever. Beliar does not figure in the Assumption of Moses, but the prince of evil is Satan. It might have been expected that he would be subjected to torment with his followers, as Beliar in the Testaments of the Twelve Patriarchs is subjected to everlasting torment, but here he is just annihilated.

The Slavonic Book of Enoch (2 Enoch)

It has already been said that three books of Enoch are now known. The second is variously referred to as the Book of the Secrets of Enoch, the Slavonic Enoch, or 2 Enoch. It is known only in a Slavonic version.[1] Charles dates it with certainty before the destruction of the Temple in A.D. 70, and with probability in the first half of the first century A.D.[2] Already, in 1914 Burkitt was doubtful of this date,[3] and later he was convinced by astronomical evidence adduced by Mrs. Maunder and J. K. Fotheringham[4] that it was wrong. This evidence points to a date not earlier than the seventh century A.D., and Kirsopp Lake pronounces it "as convincing evidence as has ever been produced for the dating of a document of uncertain origin".[5] In view of this evidence, and its acceptance by so wise a guide in the field of apocalyptic as Burkitt,[6] it is improbable that the first-century date will maintain itself. The work has come down to us in shorter and longer forms. N. Schmidt argued[7] that the shorter form was the original, and in this Vaillant agrees.[8] This form is found in manuscripts dating not earlier than the fourth century, and it was a Slavonic translation of a lost Greek work. Vaillant

---

[1] The most recent edition of the text, with French translation, is by A. Vaillant, "Le livre des Secrets d'Hénoch", 1952.

[2] Charles and Morfill, "The Book of the Secrets of Enoch", 1896, p. xxvi.

[3] "Jewish and Christian Apocalypses", 1914, pp. 75 f.

[4] See the debate between Fotheringham and Charles in *Journal of Theological Studies*, xx, 1919, p. 252; xxii, 1921, pp. 161 ff.; xxiii, 1922, pp. 49 ff.

[5] *Harvard Theological Review*, xvi, 1923, p. 398.

[6] *Proceedings of the British Academy*, xvii, 1931, pp. 442 f.

[7] *Journal of the American Oriental Society*, xli, 1921, pp. 307 ff.

[8] *Op. cit.*, pp. iii ff.

holds that this was a Christian work, which rested on a Jewish work, and that the longer form, which Charles wrongly regarded as the original, was the creation of Slavonic editors of the thirteenth century to the sixteenth.[1] Schmidt, on the other hand, says there are no signs of distinctively Christian influence in the shorter text, and holds that the Greek original came from the first century A.D.,[2] while the expanded edition also rests on a Greek original,[3] dating perhaps from before the fifth century.[4] Yet since the earlier date is followed by Charles, and also by Bonwetsch,[5] in the editions of the book most commonly used, and is given in various other handbooks,[6] it seems well to include 2 Enoch here, but with the recognition that it probably lies well beyond the limits of our period.[7]

The book is cast in the form of a vision of Enoch, in which he is conducted by two angels through the seven heavens[8]

[1] A. Weiser ("Introduction to the Old Testament", Eng. trans., 1961, p. 430) is doubtful whether this view is to be accepted.   [2] *Loc. cit.*, p. 312.
[3] *Loc. cit.*, p. 310.   [4] *Loc. cit.*, p. 312.
[5] "Die Bücher der Geheimnisse Henochs", 1922, p. xix.
[6] Cf. A. Harnack, "Geschichte der alttestamentlichen Litteratur bis Eusebius", II i, 1897, p. 564 (towards the beginning of our era); E. Littmann, "Jewish Encyclopedia", v, 1903, p. 182 (between 50 B.C. and A.D. 70); E. Schürer, "Geschichte des jüdischen Volkes", 4th ed., iii, 1909, pp. 290 ff. (not in the Eng. trans., which was made from the 2nd ed.; not later than the end of the first or the beginning of the second century A.D.); Charles, "Apocrypha and Pseudepigrapha", ii, 1913, p. 429 (between 30 B.C. and A.D. 70); J. Klausner, "Ha-ra'yon ham Meshiḥi be-Yiśrael", 1927, p. 241 (A.D. 30–40); Bousset-Gressmann, "Die Religion des Judentums", 1926, p. 22 (in the Herodian and post-Herodian period); P. Riessler "Altjüdisches Schrifttum ausserhalb der Bibel", 1927, p. 1297 (before A.D. 70); O. Eissfeldt, "Einleitung in das Alte Testament", 2nd ed., 1956, p. 769 (in its present form not earlier than seventh century, but resting on a Jewish work of not later than A.D. 70); P. Volz, "Die Eschatologie der jüdischen Gemeinde", 1934, p. 34 (first century A.D.); W. O. E. Oesterley in Manson's "Companion to the Bible", 1939, pp. 93 ff. (middle of first century A.D.); A. Tricot, "Initiation Biblique", 1939, p. 542 (before A.D. 70); A. Bentzen, "Indledning til det Gamle Testamente", 1941, I, i, p. 216 (before A.D. 70). Cf., too, A. Lods, "De quelques récits de voyage au pays de morts", 1940, p. 14 (between A.D. 63 and A.D. 70); also J. Bonsirven, "La Bible Apocryphe", 1953, p. 227 (early in the first century A.D.).
[7] Cf. C. C. Torrey ("The Apocryphal Literature", 1945, p. 110 n.), who observes that "it is not clear that it is of Jewish origin, nor that the claim of an early date is justified".
[8] For a description of the plurality of the heavens, cf. T. Levi ii. 7. Also 3 Bar. ii ff. As 3 Baruch is probably to be dated not earlier than the second century A.D., it will not figure in this study.

and shown all they contain. In the first heaven he sees the
angels who guard the snow and ice, and the dew.[1] In the
second are the fallen angels, suffering torment and awaiting
their final doom.[2] In the third heaven he sees the Paradise of
the righteous, and also the place of torment for the wicked.[3]
In the fourth heaven are the sun, moon, and stars, and the
angels who attend them. In the fifth heaven are the Watchers,
with their chief, Satan.[4] These Watchers are the angels
whose revolt against God preceded the sin of their followers
with mortal women, and so they are separated from their
followers, who figure in the second heaven. In the sixth
heaven are the angels who are charged with the regulation of
all the forces of Nature. In the seventh heaven is God Himself, with the archangels and all the celestial glory of His
court.

The second part of the book records the revelations now
made to Enoch at the command of God. For thirty days and
thirty nights the angel ceased not to talk, and Enoch wrote
down all he said, recording all that heaven contained and all
that pertained to man. He also wrote about the souls of the
unborn, for all souls are said to have been created from
eternity (2 En. xxiii. 5).[5] The seer is given an account of
creation, down to the sin of Adam, and is then told the duration of the world. This will follow the plan of Creation, but
with a thousand years for each day (2 En. xxxiii). At the
beginning of the eighth thousand years time shall come to an
end. There shall be no computation and no end; neither
years nor months, nor weeks, nor days, nor hours (2 En.
xxxiii. 2).[6] It is therefore implied that the seventh thousand
years shall be a period of rest, corresponding to the Sabbath

---

[1] Cf. T. Levi iii. 2, where it is said that fire, snow, and ice are here made
ready for the day of judgement.

[2] In T. Levi iii. 3 the second heaven contains the hosts of the armies destined
to work vengeance on the spirits of deceit and on Beliar.

[3] In 3 Bar. iv ff. the third heaven contains Hades, while the souls of the
righteous are in the fourth heaven (3 Bar. x. 5).

[4] Here called Satanael (2 En. xviii. 3). Vaillant (*op. cit.*, p. 93) assigns this
verse to the reviser.

[5] This passage is again attributed by Vaillant (*op. cit.*, p. 97) to the reviser.

[6] Again, Vaillant (*op. cit.*, pp. 103, 105) assigns this to the reviser.

of the Creation.[1] We have here, therefore, the idea of the millennium, in the strict sense of a thousand-year period, and if Charles's dating of the book could be relied on it would be the first expression of this idea known to us. There is, however, no reference to the Messiah, and no details of the Messianic period are given. The story is resumed and carried down to the Flood, and Enoch is then given thirty days to go and teach his sons, after which he is again carried to heaven. In the meantime he has given to his sons much detailed instruction for the regulating of their lives, and deposited with them the three hundred and sixty-six books which he has written.

Here we have an excellent example of the type of apocalyptic work that betrays no consciousness of crisis, but that is written in calm detachment. Its world is neat and schematic, and it is indifferent to the trivialities of human history, which are of no account to the purpose of God.

The Life of Adam and Eve

The Life of Adam and Eve is found in two forms, the one represented by the Latin manuscripts and the other by the Greek. The latter is alternatively and erroneously called the Apocalypse of Moses, but the retention of the title is useful to distinguish the Greek form from the Latin form in references. Charles holds the work to date from a time between A.D. 60 and A.D. 300,[2] but probably near the beginning of this period. He finds it to be a Jewish work with Christian interpolations. It is cast in the form of a story of the experiences of Adam and Eve, after their expulsion from Paradise. The apocalyptic material it contains is not considerable.

In one passage we have recorded the vision of Adam, in which he learned what God would do to man in the future (Vita xxv–xxix). Here there is foreshadowed the giving of

---

[1] In the Assumption of Moses, the establishment of the Golden Age is placed 4,250 years after the Creation. For the death of Moses is placed in the two thousand five hundredth year from the Creation (Ass. Mos. i. 2), and the Great Assize 1,750 years later (Ass. Mos. x. 11).

[2] In "Apocrypha and Pseudepigrapha", ii, pp. 126 f., 129.

the Law, the building of the Temple, the exile and the return, the creation of the second Temple, and the final wickedness until God Himself shall dwell with men on earth, and the wicked be punished and the righteous be saved for eternity (Vita xxix. 7).

Here there is nothing more specific than the vague hope of a Golden Age in the future, when the injustices of the present shall be rectified. There is no indication as to when that age will dawn, and no thought of any Messiah. There is, however, the belief that its coming will be preceded by an age of great wickedness, though again there is no suggestion of an Antichrist.

Elsewhere in the work, however, we find the statement that the Messiah, the Son of God, will come after five thousand five hundred years (Vita xlii. 2).[1] This passage is considered by Charles to be a Christian interpolation, in which case it is of no value for discovering the author's views. He makes a number of references, however, to the day of judgement and the resurrection. He believes that the final judgement will be a judgement of fire, in contrast to the judgement by water in the Flood (Vita xlix. 3), while alongside several references to the day of resurrection (Apoc. Mos. x. 2, xxviii. 4, xlii. 2), he has some which make it clear that the resurrection of all flesh is in mind (Apoc. Mos. xiii. 3, xli. 3). In the passage that tells of the burial of Adam in the paradise on earth (Apoc. Mos. xxxviii. 5), there is the strange statement: "God spake to the archangels: Go away to Paradise in the third heaven, and strew linen clothes and cover the body of Adam" (Apoc. Mos. xl. 1). This shows acquaintance with the idea of a heavenly Paradise in the third heaven, which we have found in 2 Enoch, and also seems to imply that the body which is buried in the earth has its counterpart in the heavenly Paradise, and that this is the body that awaits the resurrection. This is of interest as a preparation for the insistence on the importance of the resurrection of the body which we shall meet later.

[1] For other ideas as to the duration of the world, cf. Volz, "Eschatologie der jüdischen Gemeinde im neutest. Zeitalter", 1934, pp. 143 ff.

4 Ezra (2 Esdras)

The Apocalypse of Ezra consists of chapters iii–xiv of the book which stands in the Apocrypha as 2 Esdras. It is commonly referred to as 4 Ezra, according to the numeration it has in the Appendix to the Vulgate. It consists of seven visions which Ezra is said to have seen in Babylon, but by general agreement its date of composition belongs in the main to the first century A.D.

There is less agreement, however, as to the unity of the work.[1] For our purpose the conflict of opinion here is not vital, since it is admitted even by the defenders of the unity of the work that there is a medley of ideas in it. Thus Lagrange says: "The mosaic is in the ideas, not in the documents. The author had before him certain traditional elements; he could neither fuse them, nor eliminate those that were incompatible with his main theme."[2] We may therefore examine separately the principal passages which express the ideas of apocalyptic eschatology.

In the first vision the seer is informed that the end of the present age is not far off (2 Esdr. iv. 44 ff.), and is told that the signs of the end shall be widespread desolation, portents in the heavens and monstrous births, and universal wickedness (2 Esdr. v. 1 ff.). It is also said that he shall rule, whom the inhabitants of the world do not look for (2 Esdr. v. 6). This probably indicates Antichrist,[3] but provides no clues for any identification.

---

[1] See Note D at the end of this chapter.

[2] *Revue Biblique*, xiv (N.S. ii), 1905, p. 487. Cf. Vaganay, "Le problème eschatologique dans le iv⁰ livre d'Esdras", 1906, pp. 13, 15; Gry, "Les dires prophétiques d'Esdras", i, 1938, p. xcvi. Also F. C. Porter ("The Messages of the Apocalyptical Writers", 1905, p. 336): "Each of them (2 Baruch and 2 Esdras) contains a variety of eschatological material, derived certainly in large part from various traditional sources, and not worked together into a consistent or orderly whole. It is because of such diversities that some regard these books as composite, but it is probably better to say that they have each a proper author and a real unity, but that the authors, like others of their class, are very dependent on traditions, and are not anxious, perhaps are not able, to harmonize them."

[3] Cf. B. Rigaux, "L'Antéchrist", 1932, p. 487; Bousset-Gressmann, "Die Religion des Judentums", p. 255.

In the second vision little is added, save a reference to the sealing of the world that is to pass away, and the opening of the book of judgement (2 Esdr. vi. 20), and the blast of the trumpet that shall herald the end (2 Esdr. vi. 23). All of these are ideas that we meet again in the Book of Revelation.

In the third vision the seer is told how the New Jerusalem[1] will appear (2 Esdr. vii. 26) and the Messiah[2] will be revealed, together with those who had not tasted death[3] (2 Esdr. vii. 28). The Messiah will remain for four hundred years and then die, and all men will die with him, and for seven years there will be complete silence in the earth (2 Esdr. vii. 29 f.). Then will come the resurrection of all men for the great judgement (2 Esdr. vii. 31 ff.). Gehenna and Paradise will stand over against one another (2 Esdr. vii. 36), and the judgement period will continue for a week of years (2 Esdr. vii. 43).

Here, it will be noticed, the New Jerusalem appears at the beginning of the Messianic period, and its bliss is temporary. The Messiah is mortal, and he does not figure in the judgement scene. The explanation of the four hundred years of the Messianic period is given from a passage in the Talmud,[4] which cites Ps. xc. 15: "Make us glad according to the days wherein thou hast afflicted us," in association with Gen. xv. 13: "And they shall afflict them four hundred years." It will be observed, too, that the resurrection is here a universal one, and that it is a resurrection only for judgement. The execution of the judgement takes place in Gehenna and Paradise, and not on earth. There is, therefore, here no enduring earthly kingdom.

[1] For the correction of the text cf. Violet, "Die Apokalypsen des Ezra und des Baruch", 1924, p. 73; Oesterley, "II Esdras", p. 70. The Latin text, represented in R.V., is held to rest on a corruption of the Greek. Gry, however, prefers to explain the versions in terms of a corruption of an Aramaic form (*op. cit.*, i, p. 147).

[2] The R.V., following the Latin, reads "my son Jesus", but this is clearly a Christian alteration of the text to which the other versions witness. Cf. Volz, "Eschatologie der jüdischen Gemeinde", pp. 37 f.

[3] The text reads, "those that be with him". This is probably to be interpreted by 2 Esdr. vi. 26.

[4] Cf. Box, "The Ezra-Apocalypse", pp. 115 f. L. Vaganay (*op. cit.*, p. 99) doubts the originality of the figure 400 in the Ezra text.

In the fourth vision the seer beholds a sorrowful woman, who represents Jerusalem in all its misery and desolation (2 Esdr. ix. 38 ff.). The sanctuary is laid waste and the altar broken down (2 Esdr. x. 21); the cultus and sacred song are no more (2 Esdr. x. 22), and exile, bondage, and dishonour are the portion of all the people (2 Esdr. x. 22). This passage is of importance as a clue to the date of the work, and it plainly indicates a time after A.D. 70. Suddenly the woman is transfigured, and now she takes the form of that which in her transfigured state she represents. She is no longer a woman, but the New Jerusalem, surpassing in beauty (2 Esdr. x. 25 ff.).

The fifth vision is the Eagle vision, in which Daniel's vision is reinterpreted. This vision is similar in type to the vision of Dan. vii, and is quite different from the visions that have preceded it. For here for the first time we have a symbolic sketch of history as the prelude to the prediction. The vision is of a twelve-winged and three-headed eagle (2 Esdr. xi. 1 ff.), and the interpretation declares that the eagle represents the fourth kingdom of Daniel's vision, now expounded differently (2 Esdr. xii. 10). It is certain that here it stands for the Roman Empire, whose emperors are indicated under the figure of wings and heads. The three heads probably represent Vespasian, Titus, and Domitian. The author then looked for the Messianic kingdom in Domitian's days, for he represents a lion as appearing in the reign of the third of these heads, and as destroying the eagle, under whose rule men were groaning (2 Esdr. xi. 36 ff.). The lion is declared to be the Messiah, and the Syriac text adds that he is from the seed of David (2 Esdr. xii. 31 f.). He will execute judgement on the oppressors, but will deliver the righteous with mercy, and will make them joyful until the day of judgement (2 Esdr. xii. 34).

Little is said here of the reign of the Messiah, and he functions only in a role of deliverance. Clearly there is no thought of an everlasting reign for him. He merely brings joy that shall last until the unspecified time of the judgement.

The sixth vision is also associated with Dan. vii, and it attached itself to the figure of the Son of Man. The seer beheld a storm-tossed sea, and one in the likeness of a man rising from it and coming with the clouds of heaven (2 Esdr. xiii. 1 ff.). A multitude of men gathered to make war against him, and he made for himself a mountain, later explained as Mount Zion, and flew upon it (2 Esdr. xiii. 6). Then he faced his foes and consumed them with no weapon but the breath of his mouth (2 Esdr. xiii. 9 ff.), and thereafter called unto him another multitude, which was peaceable (2 Esdr. xiii. 12 f.). In the interpretation the deliverer is called "my Son" (2 Esdr. xiii. 32), making it clear that an individual deliverer is in mind. He is to be identified with the Messiah, though he can hardly be equated with the Messiah of the preceding vision. For here we have no human figure of the seed of David, but a transcendental figure. Again, he is merely a deliverer of the oppressed saints, and there is little indication of the joys to which he will save them.

The seventh vision brings to the seer the assurance that he will be taken out of the world to be with "my Son", together with others such as himself, until the time of the end (2 Esdr. xiv. 9), and it is indicated that the end is not far off (2 Esdr. xiv. 11 ff.). There is here little fresh contribution, but it is to be noted that again the deliverer is not a human figure, but a pre-existent transcendental figure, who will descend to fulfil his task.

It is unnecessary further to emphasize the variety of the ideas that are here gathered together. It is clear that we have no systematic presentation of a self-consistent whole, but a series of visions, each of which presents its own aspect of the expected consummation of the ages. Its links with the past apocalyptic writings are manifest, and equally its links with the works that succeeded it, and especially with the Book of Revelation. As a moment in the development of apocalyptic thought it is of the greatest importance.

The Apocalypse of Baruch

The Apocalypse of Baruch has been preserved in a single manuscript in a Syriac translation.[1] On the question of its unity, date, and relation to 4 Ezra there is no agreement, though most scholars believe that it is dependent on 4 Ezra. Lagrange says: "The Apocalypse of Baruch is cast in the same mould as that of Ezra, but the metal is less noble. One of the two authors has imitated, and the imitator must be Baruch, whose images are less natural, and whose theological reflection is more advanced."[2] On the other hand, Schürer is not persuaded that the dependence is not the other way round.[3]

The unity of the book is again disputed, and there is some disagreement as to whether it belongs to the first or second century A.D.[4] In view of its association with 4 Ezra we may bring it within our purview, and review its eschatological ideas.

The first relevant section is found in chapters xxvii ff. Here twelve varieties of disasters which will mark the twelve periods before the dawn of the Messianic age are described (2 Bar. xxvii. 1 ff.), and after the manner of the Book of Daniel the date of the end is cryptically indicated, so that the wise will understand (2 Bar. xxviii. 1). As rendered by Charles, the clue reads: "For the measure and reckoning of that time are two parts weeks of seven weeks" (2 Bar. xxviii. 2). This is not very lucid, but Violet thinks it means two weeks of years, each consisting of seven weeks, or forty-nine years.[5] As to the point from which this reckoning of ninety-eight years is to be made, however, nothing is said, though

---

[1] There is also a Greek Apocalypse of Baruch, often referred to as 3 Baruch. The text is printed in M. R. James, "Apocrypha Anecdota", Second Series, 1897, pp. 84 ff., and an English translation is included in Charles, "Apocrypha and Pseudepigrapha", vol. ii. This work is probably not to be dated earlier than the second century A.D., and it therefore lies outside our period.

[2] "Le messianisme chez les juifs", 1909, p. 109.

[3] "History of the Jewish People", II, iii, pp. 89 ff. So, too, Kabisch, *Jahrbücher für protestantische Theologie*, xviii, 1892, p. 103.

[4] See Note D at the end of this chapter.

[5] "Die Apokalypsen des Ezra und des Baruch", 1924, p. 243.

Violet suggests that it might have been from the Augustan era.[1] Then the Messiah will begin to be revealed (2 Bar. xxix. 3).

Of the person of the Messiah nothing is said, but the glories of the Messianic age are described in sensuous terms. Behemoth and Leviathan will be eaten for food, and the earth will yield the richest fruits (2 Bar. xxix. 4 f.). On one vine there will be a thousand branches, and each branch will bear a thousand bunches, and each bunch will contain a thousand grapes, and each grape will produce a *cor*, say a hundred and twenty gallons, of wine (2 Bar. xxix. 5)! Finally, when the advent of the Messiah is fulfilled he will return in glory, and all who have fallen asleep in hope of him will rise (2 Bar. xxx. 1). Charles interprets this to mean that at the end of Messiah's reign he will return to Heaven. In that case the resurrection is not to earthly bliss. It is equally possible, however, that what is meant is that the Messiah will come to earth, and that the resurrection is to share in the glory of his earthly reign. In this sense Violet understands it.[2] In support of this it may be noted that the phrase "when the time of the advent of the Messiah is *fulfilled*" can be understood in connexion with the earlier expression, "the Messiah will then *begin* to be revealed". What stands between describes the marks of his coming, not its consequences.

The second section is found in chapters xxxvi ff. It describes the seer's dream and its interpretation, and in the interpretation we find the familiar scheme of the four world empires (2 Bar. xxxix. 3 ff.). The fourth is harsh and cruel, and its dominions are widespread (2 Bar. xxxix. 5), but little is said to make specific its identification with Rome, which is doubtless intended. Then the principate of the Messiah will be revealed (2 Bar. xxxix. 7), and he will put to the sword the hosts of the last leader of that time, who will himself be taken to Zion to be judged (2 Bar. xl. 1). The principate of

[1] Cf. Gry, in *Revue Biblique*, xlviii, 1939, p. 351, where it is argued that the reckoning is from the Battle of Actium, 31 B.C.

[2] *Op. cit.*, p. 246.

the Messiah will then endure so long as the world itself shall endure (2 Bar. xl. 3).

Here it is quite clear that the Messianic kingdom is an earthly one. It is clear, too, that it will be brought about by a warlike Messiah, who will not destroy merely by the word of his mouth, but by the sword of his hand. Moreover, we find Antichrist here in the person of the last leader of the hosts of iniquity. He is apparently a human figure, and presumably the last king of the fourth kingdom, though this is not unequivocally stated. The Messiah's kingdom appears to last so long as time shall last, and beyond its horizons there is nothing to be seen.

The third relevant section is found in chapters liii ff. It contains a vision and its interpretation, unfolding the course of history under the figure of a cloud which poured waters on the earth. Of these some were black and some bright, but the black were more numerous. Finally, the last black waters represent the desperate state of the world on the eve of the Messianic age (2 Bar. lxx. 1 ff.). Then the Most High will come and make war with the leaders of this evil age, and they that survive the war will be swallowed up by an earthquake, and they that survive the earthquake will die by famine (2 Bar. lxx. 7 f.). Then the time of the Messiah will come, when he will execute judgement on all peoples, according to their treatment of Israel (2 Bar. lxxii. 1 ff.). The Golden Age of peace and prosperity, when pain and weariness will be abolished, will then dawn (2 Bar. lxxiii. 1 ff.).

The Messianic kingdom is here conceived of again in sensuous terms as an earthly kingdom, but the person of the Messiah is completely vague. The kingdom is thought of in nationalistic terms, because Israel is thought of as the people of God, so that men's attitude to God can be known by their attitude to His people.

One other passage claims our attention. This is the section contained in chapters xlix ff., in which the form of the resurrection body is discussed. Here it is declared that at the resurrection men will have restored to them the precise body they had in life, in order that identity may be established with certainty (2 Bar. l. 2 ff.).[1] Here we are reminded of that passage in the Life of Adam and Eve which suggested that the counterpart of the earthly body was buried in the heavenly Paradise, to await the resurrection. Here in the Apocalypse of Baruch, however, we find some development of the thought. For while it is insisted that the raised body must be identical with the body had in life, it is added that this body will be changed, so that the new body will reflect the curse of condemnation or the glory of justification (2 Bar. li. 1 ff.).[2] It is clear that a resurrection of both good and evil is in mind, and that it is a resurrection to earth.

It should perhaps be added that Dr. M. R. James[3] believes that the author of the Apocalypse of Baruch was acquainted with another work, which he dates about this time, but which is not an apocalyptic work, and which does not fall to be considered independently here. This is the Biblical Antiquities of pseudo-Philo. James believes this is a Jewish work of the first century A.D., written after the destruction of Jerusalem in A.D. 70, and a product of the same school as 4 Ezra and the Apocalypse of Baruch.[4] The grounds on which it is located in that age are interesting.[5] For in pseudo-Philo xix. 7 reference is made to the destruction of Jerusalem, and it is stated that this should take place on the seventeenth day of the fourth month. The capture of Jerusalem by the Babylonians took place on the ninth of this month (2 Kings xxv. 3), whereas, according to the Talmud

---

[1] We may compare with this a passage in a surviving fragment of the Apocryphal Ezekiel, where the fable of two guardians of a garden, one blind and one lame, is told to illustrate the necessity for the rejoining of body and soul for the judgement. The lame man mounted the back of the blind that they might steal the fruits, but each denied the theft when charged. Similarly in the judgement soul and body would each deny the responsibility for sin, but the restoration of their combination would ensure perfect justice, as in the fable where the blind man was compelled again to carry the lame that they might be scourged together. See M. R. James, in *Journal of Theological Studies*, xv, 1914, pp. 236 ff., and "The Lost Apocrypha of the Old Testament", 1920, pp. 64 ff.

[2] Cf. 1 Cor. xv. 35 ff.

[3] "The Biblical Antiquities of Philo", 1917, p. 58.

[4] *Loc. cit.*, p. 7. Cf. L. Gry (*Revue Biblique*, xlviii, 1939, pp. 344 f.), where the date is put early in the second century A.D.

[5] *Loc. cit.*, pp. 29 ff. Cf. Gry, *loc. cit.*, p. 344.

(Ta'anith 28b), Jerusalem was taken by Titus on the seventeenth.[1]

This work is not apocalyptic in form, and James thinks it is only an accident that has attached it to the name of Philo. It is a re-writing of history from Adam to David, and it only touches us here indirectly through its believed connexion with 2 Baruch. In iii. 10 it is said that when the world has run its course there will be a general resurrection of good and bad to judgement, when death will be abolished, and there will be a new heaven and a new earth. The latter will be an everlasting habitation of rich fruitfulness. Here there is nothing that is specially original, or that goes beyond what we have already met. In xix. 13, however, we find the curious idea that as the time of the end draws near, God, in His eagerness to raise the dead, will shorten the years. If the Apocalypse of Baruch is rightly dated after this work this passage may be the source of the idea of 2 Bar. xx. 1 : "Therefore, behold! the days come, and the times shall hasten more than those that went before, and the seasons shall speed beyond those that are past, and the years shall pass more quickly than those of to-day." The same idea, however, is found in the New Testament in Mark xiii. 20, and it may have been current in that age. Most of the connexions that have been noted between pseudo-Philo and 2 Baruch, however, concern points that do not lie within the range of our study.

The Ascension of Isaiah

The work which has come down to us under the title of the Ascension of Isaiah is believed by Charles to be the compilation of an editor who used three independent works, the Martyrdom of Isaiah, the Testament of Hezekiah, and the Vision of Isaiah.[2] Of these three, Charles thinks the first is

---

[1] Cf. H. Malter, "The Treatise Ta'anit of the Babylonian Talmud", 1928, p. 221.

[2] "The Ascension of Isaiah", 1900, pp. xxxvi ff. Cf. Box, in Charles and Box, "The Ascension of Isaiah", 1919, pp. 7 f. Dillmann ("Ascensio Isaiae", 1877, pp. ix–xiii; "Realencyclopädie für protestantische Theologie und Kirche", 2nd ed., xii, 1883, pp. 359 f.) had earlier held that a Jewish Martyrdom of

of Jewish origin, and the other two of Christian origin, and the date of all he puts in the first century A.D.[1] Burkitt, however, contests this view,[2] and regards the work as a unity throughout, speaking with a Christian voice, though it doubtless rests on traditions derived from Jewish sources. "I sometimes fancy," he says, "that the spirit of Beliar must be dwelling in some of my friends when they use the wooden saw to dissect the *Ascension of Isaiah*."

In its general structure, the Ascension of Isaiah resembles the Book of Daniel. The earlier chapters contain a story about Isaiah, and the later recount the vision of Isaiah, when he was transported to the seventh heaven. The story relates how Isaiah prophesied to Hezekiah that he would be sawn asunder by Manasseh (Asc. Isa. i). When, after the death of Hezekiah, Manasseh abandoned himself to evil courses, Isaiah withdrew to the mountains, but was betrayed by a Samaritan to Manasseh, who, under the influence of Beliar, arrested the prophet (Asc. Isa. ii f.). The reason for Beliar's hostility to Isaiah is said to have been the fact that Isaiah had prophesied of the coming of Christ and the establishment of the Christian Church, and also of the coming of Antichrist and the end of the world. The first part of the book ends

---

Isaiah had been combined with a Christian Vision of Isaiah by an author who composed ch. i, while some additions, including Charles's Testament of Hezekiah, were added later. E. Littmann (in "Jewish Encyclopedia", vi, 1907, p. 643) thinks Charles is convincing on the Testament of Hezekiah, but thinks Dillmann is right on ch. i. Cf. also Tisserant, "Ascension d'Isaïe", 1909, p. 59. J. A. Robinson (in Hastings' "Dictionary of the Bible", ii, 1899, p. 500) substantially follows Dillmann, but thinks that two hands only need be found in the book, and that a Christian author took the Jewish Martyrdom of Isaiah and composed the whole of the remainder. An excellent survey of the history of the criticism of the Ascension of Isaiah will be found in Tisserant, *op. cit.*, pp. 42 ff.

[1] J. Vernon Bartlet ("The Apostolic Age", 1900, pp. 521 ff.) would place the composition of iii. 13–iv. 21 (almost the whole of Charles's Testament of Hezekiah) during the years A.D. 64–8, and preferably in A.D. 65–6. G. Beer ("Realencyclopädie für protestantische Theologie und Kirche", 3rd ed., xvi, 1905, p. 261) would assign this section to the early second century A.D. at the earliest, while G. T. Stokes (in Smith and Wace, "Dictionary of Christian Biography", iii, 1882, p. 300) thought the book took its present shape at some time during the third century A.D.

[2] "Jewish and Christian Apocalypses", pp. 45 ff., 72 ff. Cf. James, "The Lost Apocrypha of the Old Testament", pp. 81 ff.; V. Burch, "The Literary Unity of the *Ascensio Isaiae*", in *Journal of Theological Studies*, xx, 1919, pp. 17 ff.

with an account of the sawing asunder of the prophet with a wooden saw (Asc. Isa. iii. 13–v).

It is the passage telling of the coming of Christ and of the end of the world which is attributed by Charles to the lost Testament of Hezekiah. This is clearly of Christian origin. It tells how the Beloved (which is a title for the Messiah peculiar to the Ascension of Isaiah, and found commonly throughout the whole)[1] should descend from the seventh heaven in the likeness of man, be crucified and buried, and rise again; how His disciples should teach all nations, but on the eve of His approach should be guilty of apostasy; how Beliar should then descend in the likeness of man, and should rule the world and persecute the Church. He should hold sway for three years and seven months and twenty-seven days,[2] when the Beloved should come again from the seventh heaven with the armies of the holy ones, and cast Beliar and his hosts into Gehenna, after which would take place the resurrection and the last judgement.

In this passage Antichrist is plainly declared to be the incarnation of Beliar, the ruler of this world. His identification with Nero is also clearly indicated. For he is described as a lawless king, the slayer of his mother, and the persecutor of the Church, into whose hands one of the Twelve Apostles shall be delivered, who shall set himself up as a god and be sacrificed to by all men (Asc. Isa. iv. 2 ff.).

The second part of the book relates the vision of Isaiah, in which he was taken up through the seven heavens[3] to the

---

[1] Cf. E. Tisserant, "Ascension d'Isaïe", 1909, pp. 8 ff.

[2] See Note E at the end of this chapter.

[3] The conception of the seven heavens is here quite different from that in 2 Enoch. Here the heavens are all places of glory, where the praises of God ascend, and each surpasses in glory the heaven that preceded it. In the lost Apocalypse of Zephaniah there was apparently a similar conception. For a fragment has survived in Clement of Alexandria (Stromata V. xi. 77; cf. ed. Stählin, in "Die griechischen Christlichen Schriftsteller der ersten drei Jahrhunderte", xv, 1907, p. 377) which reads: "And the spirit took me up and bore me to the fifth heaven, and I beheld angels that are called Lords, whose crown was set upon them in the Holy Spirit, and the throne of each of whom surpassed seven times the light of the sun as it shines, and they dwelt in temples of salvation, singing hymns to God." With this contrast the fifth heaven in the Slavonic Enoch.

highest heaven with its ineffable glory (Asc. Isa. vi ff.).
Here he was shown the books in which all human deeds are
recorded, and the garments and thrones and crowns laid up
for those who believe in the Cross of the Beloved (Asc. Isa. ix.
21 ff.). Then he saw the Lord go forth and descend through
the heaven to the earth, where He was born of Mary and
lived among men until He was crucified and buried, but
rose again and ascended through the heavens to sit down on
the right hand of God (Asc. Isa. x ff.).

Burkitt[1] notes the breach of the rule that apocalyptic
passages are silent about names in the mention of the names
of Joseph and Mary, and he thinks the solution of the difficulties which have been supposed to point to composite origin
is just that the author tried to serve two masters. In apocalyptic everything leads up to the last judgement and the
end of the world. But here this motif is crossed by another,
and specifically Christian motif, the representation of the incarnation as the supreme event of history. To this it may be
added that the position of the prophecy of the end of the
world in the earlier part of the book was probably artistically
designed to yield the impression that greater than the final
end of history is the supreme moment of history in whose light
all history must be judged.

The Apocalypse of Abraham

The Apocalypse of Abraham is a work which has been
preserved only in a Slavonic version. Box believes it to be
essentially a Jewish work, which has received some Christian
accretions.[2] It is to be dated after A.D. 70, and not later than
the early decades of the second century.

The first part of the book describes Abraham's conversion
from idolatry, his command to leave his father's house, and
the descent of fire to burn up that house as soon as he had
left it (Apoc. Abrah. i–viii). The second part contains the
apocalyptic vision of Abraham. He first offers sacrifice at
Horeb preparatory to the vision, after overcoming the temp-

[1] *Op. cit.*, pp. 45 ff.
[2] "The Apocalypse of Abraham", 1919, pp. x, xxi ff.

tation of Azazel, who tried to turn him from his purpose (Apoc. Abrah. ix ff.). Then Abraham is led by the angel Jaoel to heaven, where he has the vision of the divine throne (Apoc. Abrah. xv ff.). The description of this throne owes not a little to the Book of Ezekiel. God then speaks to Abraham, and unfolds to him the powers of heaven and promises him a seed as numerous as the stars (Apoc. Abrah. xix f.). He then explains to him the fall of man and its consequences for the race, and shows him the coming judgement in the destruction of the Temple (Apoc. Abrah. xxi ff.). This is due to the sin of idolatry on the part of Abraham's seed. When Abraham asks how long the judgement shall last he is told that God will be provoked by them through four generations of a hundred years each, and in the fourth there shall be misfortune among the heathen (Apoc. Abrah. xxviii f.). The duration of the age is then said to be twelve hours, where an hour appears to stand for a hundred years. It is supposed that the author is reckoning from the establishment of Jerusalem as the Holy City by David, and it is recalled that Josephus reckons the period from this event to the destruction of the Temple by Titus as eleven hundred and seventy-nine years.[1] If, then, the book was written shortly after this event, the author believed, like almost all the apocalyptists, that he stood near the end of the age. He is shown the ten plagues which shall befall the world before the age of righteousness dawns, and the punishment of the heathen, followed by the sound of the trumpet, when God's Elect comes with power, to gather His own together and to consume with fire those who have insulted them (Apoc. Abrah. xxix ff.).

Here it is of interest to note that Jaoel is the chief of the angels, corresponding to Michael in other texts, and Azazel is the chief of the evil spirits. The idea of twelve historical periods is interesting, though they are not separately characterized, and like the seventy weeks of the Book of Daniel, the number is probably chosen because it will serve the author's purpose as a symbolic approximation, to bring the climax

[1] "The Apocalypse of Abraham", 1919, p. 77.

to his own day. But he might have been expected to give some clearer indication than he does of the point from which he reckons. The Messiah figures as the Elect, but only as a name, and little is said about him or his work. There is no mention of the resurrection, and it is probable that the author's purpose was rather to indicate the imminence of the end, and its signs in the miseries that will befall men, than to describe its nature and consequences.

The Testament of Abraham

The Testament of Abraham, which is quite distinct from the Apocalypse of Abraham, is preserved in Greek in two recensions. James thinks it was written in the second century A.D. by a Christian writer who was acquainted with the Apocalypse of Peter.[1] Kohler, however, maintained that it is fundamentally a Jewish work, with Christian interpolations, and that it probably dates from the first century A.D.[2]

The longer form of the work recounts how Michael was sent to announce to Abraham his approaching death (Test. Abrah. i), but Abraham was reluctant to give up his soul, and asked that before he died he might be granted the boon of being shown the world and all created things (Test. Abrah. ii–ix). He was then conducted by Michael and shown the world in all its sin, and his indignation flamed forth, and he called down destruction on the sinners, until God intervened to interrupt the vision, lest all creatures should be destroyed (Test. Abrah. x). Abraham was then taken to the entrance to the first heaven, where he saw the two ways, one narrow and the other broad, with many souls being driven in through the broad gate, but few being borne through the narrow. At the parting of the ways was Adam, who rejoiced when the few were borne through, but who was in deep grief for the many (Test. Abrah. xi). Between the two gates of the two ways sat Abel enthroned, judging the souls and

---

[1] "The Testament of Abraham", 1892, pp. 23, 55.
[2] *Jewish Quarterly Review*, vii, 1895, pp. 581 ff.

weighing them in the balance. For the first judgement of man is by man, but at the Second Advent they shall be judged by the twelve tribes of Israel, while the third judgement shall be by God (Test. Abrah. xii f.). Abraham's pity was now stirred, and he interceded for those he had before cursed (Test. Abrah. xiv). He then returned to earth, but still refused to give up his soul (Test. Abrah. xv). God therefore summoned the angel of death and dispatched him for the soul of Abraham, but the patriarch still refused to give it up (Test. Abrah. xvi). Death refused to leave him, however, and finally put off the fairness and beauty with which he had decked himself, and showed himself in all his foulness and loathesomeness, so that all around Abraham died, and Abraham's spirit failed him (Test. Abrah. xvii). Still Abraham survived, however, and made intercession for all his servants, who were restored to life (Test. Abrah. xviii). Again Abraham refused to follow Death, and asked him to explain all his changing shapes. Death replied that for seven ages he would ravage the world (Test. Abrah. xix). Thereafter Abraham embraced the hand of Death, and his soul was borne away by Michael to Paradise (Test. Abrah. xx).

This apocalyptic work again has no background of crisis, and is couched throughout in terms of individual eschatology. The idea of a threefold judgement is interesting, and the second of these does not really fit in with the others, since it is a nationalistic judgement, inappropriate to the individual interest of the rest of the work. There is no Messiah and no Messianic kingdom, but we do find the idea of world ages, of which there are here seven, though they are in no way characterized. The figure of the angel of Death is also interesting, and the weighing of souls. In the main, however, this apocalypse stands apart from the others we have examined.

The Little Apocalypse of the Gospels

In the New Testament we find much eschatological teaching, associated with the range of ideas we have been considering, both on the lips of Jesus and throughout the literature.

Apart from the great final book of the Canon, however, we can look only at the passage often called the Little Apocalypse, found in Mark xiii and its parallels.[1] The study of the eschatological teaching of Paul and of the other writers of Epistles reveals how far the ideas of apocalyptic eschatology had permeated the Church, but since the Epistles can by no stretch be classed as apocalypses, they must here be left without consideration. The Little Apocalypse is different, however, in that we have here a formulated view of the end, rather than casual and piecemeal allusions to the end.

It lies outside our province to discuss how far this passage represents the teaching and outlook of our Lord, or how far we have here the later views of His followers attributed to Him, since a considerable literature has been devoted to this subject,[2] and much space would be required for its re-examination. We may note, however, that if it does not really represent the teaching of Jesus, then it shares the pseudonymous character of so much apocalyptic work, while if it does represent His teaching, we have here at last a clear breach with that tradition, but a breach in the sphere of oral teach-

---

[1] On the Little Apocalypse theory and its development see G. R. Beasley-Murray, "Jesus and the Future", 1954, pp. 1 ff., and on the relations between Mark xiii and other passages, see *ibid.*, pp. 226 ff. Cf. also *Expository Times*, lxiv, 1952–3, pp. 346 ff. See also C. E. B. Cranfield, in *Scottish Journal of Theology*, vi, 1953, pp. 189 ff., 287 ff., vii, 1954, pp. 284 ff.

[2] On the general question of the place of eschatology in the teaching of Jesus much has been written. Cf. A. Schweitzer, "The Quest of the Historical Jesus", Eng. trans., 2nd ed., 1922; E. von Dobschütz, "The Eschatology of the Gospels", 1910; E. W. Winstanley, "Jesus and the Future", 1913; W. Manson, "Christ's View of the Kingdom of God", 1918; L. Dougall and C. W. Emmet, "The Lord of Thought", 1922; G. Gloege, "Reich Gottes und Kirche im Neuen Testament", 1929; H. D. Wendland, "Die Eschatologie des Reiches Gottes bei Jesus", 1931; C. H. Dodd, "The Parables of the Kingdom", 3rd ed., 1936, and "The Apostolic Preaching and its Development", 1936; W. G. Kümmel, "Die Eschatologie der Evangelien", 1936; F. Holmström, "Das Eschatologische Denken der Gegenwart", German trans., 1936 (it is much to be regretted that no English edition of this important work has been published); J. Héring, "Le royaume de Dieu et sa venue", 1937; R. Otto, "The Kingdom of God and the Son of Man", Eng. trans., 1938; F. Busch, "Zum Verständnis der synoptischen Eschatologie", 1938; A. N. Wilder, "Eschatology and Ethics in the Teaching of Jesus", 1939; C. J. Cadoux, "The Historic Mission of Jesus", 1941. In the Bibliography at the end of this volume will be found the titles of a few of the many articles dealing with aspects of this question.

ing, which cannot well be pseudonymous, rather than in written teaching.[1]

It has been suggested that the Little Apocalypse was in circulation as a separate document before its incorporation in the Gospel of Mark. Whether so or not[2] is quite immaterial to our purpose. We are concerned only with the apocalyptic ideas and hopes expressed in the passage, whether they were first written down by Mark or by another, and whether they were actually expressed by Jesus or but attributed to Him. The passage contains references to the coming end of the age, with a description of the signs of that end, and a cryptic reference that would carry significance to the initiated, but not to others. Several of the features commonly found together in apocalyptic works are therefore found here.

Jesus is asked what shall be the sign of the destruction of the Temple (Mark xiii. 1–4), and replies by announcing that many shall arise claiming to be Himself and shall lead many astray (Mark xiii. 5 f.), that there shall be wars, earthquakes, and famines (Mark xiii. 7 f.), and that His followers shall be persecuted (Mark xiii. 9–13).

Then follows a cryptic reference to the "abomination of desolation". Here the phrase is taken from the Book of Daniel, where it stands in association with the approaching end of the age which the author expected. It is therefore to be presumed that the phrase is borrowed here in order to import similar associations. But whereas in the Book of Daniel it referred to the heathen altar and idol, or idols, which Antiochus set up in the Temple, it is here certainly applied to something quite other. Since the phrase is followed by the words "let him that readeth understand", it is clear that

---

[1] R. H. Lightfoot ("History and Interpretation in the Gospels", 1935, p. 124) notes that the discourse is secret, and finds this to indicate that we have here an effort on the part of the Church to apply the teaching of Jesus to its present urgent needs. Loisy ("L'Évangile selon Marc", 1912, pp. 366 f.) finds this secrecy to demonstrate that the discourse is not authentic, and so H. D. A. Major ("The Mission and Message of Jesus", 1937, pp. 158 f.). It may be noted that this secret or esoteric character is common to apocalyptic, and is not necessarily a mark of the inauthenticity of the contents of the chapter.

[2] See Note F at the end of this chapter.

the initiated reader is expected to understand what is meant. These words could hardly belong to the spoken discourse of our Lord, for they are addressed to a reader, and not to a hearer, and they imply that at the time when they were written the instructed reader might be expected to have the clue to their understanding.[1] It is commonly recalled that the Emperor Caligula ordered his statue to be placed in the Temple, though it was not actually placed there, owing to the death of the Emperor. It is often suggested that this was what was meant by the phrase "abomination of desolation" here. The order of Caligula was so similar to the action of Antiochus Epiphanes that the choice of the phrase would be well explained. Since the order was not carried out, however, it would be necessary to suppose that this whole verse was not part of the original discourse of our Lord, but was written by an author who believed it would be carried out, and would precipitate the fatal outbreak which had been so long brewing. It is significant, indeed, that Luke substitutes for this reference to the "abomination of desolation" the verse: "When ye see Jerusalem compassed about with armies, then know that her desolation is at hand" (Luke xxi. 20). This certainly looks as though Luke understood the reference, and knew it to be a mistaken one. He therefore reinterpreted, just as the author of Daniel had reinterpreted Jeremiah's seventy years, and the author of 4 Ezra had reinterpreted Daniel's fourth kingdom. The reasonable corollary of this would be that the whole verse, Mark xiii. 14, cannot be the utterance of Jesus, whatever may have been the case with the rest of the chapter, since we could hardly credit Him with the foreknowledge of Caligula's order, and at the same time

---

[1] J. Dean ("The Synoptic Gospels", 1938, p. 198) thinks these words did belong to the spoken discourse of our Lord, and that they have reference to what is written in the Book of Daniel. But Loisy is here right in observing that "that to which attention is to be paid is the prediction of Christ, and not the text of Daniel, which is not cited" ("L'Évangile selon Marc", 1912, pp. 374 f.), and J. Huby ("Évangile selon Saint Marc", 1938, p. 344) cites with approval Lagrange's observation ("Évangile selon Saint Marc", rev. ed., 1947, p. 341) that it is more natural to find here the Evangelist's advice to his readers than to ascribe them to the lips of our Lord.

with ignorance of the fact that the order would not be carried out.[1]

Resuming our review of the contents of the chapter, we find that it warns the faithful to flee in haste when the Temple should be desecrated by the "abomination of desolation", as unparalleled confusion and tribulation would follow (Mark xiii. 14–23). Natural portents would follow, and the sun would be darkened (Mark xiii. 24 f.), and the Son of Man would come in the clouds with hosts of angels to gather the faithful (Mark xiii. 26 f.). It is added that the events predicted would take place while the generation of those present still existed (Mark xiii. 30), but that neither men nor angels, nor even the Son, could know that hour beforehand (Mark xiii. 32).

It is apparent that this chapter deals with much more than the destruction of the Temple, with which it starts. The references to the heavenly portents and the coming of the Son of Man to gather the elect from every quarter show that it is thinking of the end of the age. Yet equally clearly it was thinking of something that would happen within a very few years. It seems to me unprofitable to dissect the chapter into two discourses, of which the one had reference to the fall of Jerusalem and the other to the end of the age,[2] though it may well be that it rests on utterances of our Lord made on different occasions. I think it mingled the two because it rested on the expectation that the end of the age was very

[1] M. Goguel ("The Life of Jesus", Eng. trans., 1933, p. 428) regards it simply as an apocalyptic idea which had become traditional under the influence of the text of Daniel. He holds the Lukan form to be original, and thinks the reference to the "abomination of desolation" is a substitution (*ibid.*, p. 139). A. Piganiol, on the contrary, regards the Markan form as decisive evidence for the dating of the Little Apocalypse in the year A.D. 40 (*Revue d'Histoire et de Philosophie Religieuses*, iv, 1924, pp. 245 ff.). C. C. Torrey would go further and use this reference to date the Gospel of Mark ("Documents of the Primitive Church", 1941, pp. 22 ff.). V. Taylor ("The Gospel according to St. Mark", 1952, pp. 511 f.) rejects the view that the reference is to Caligula's order, and finds the reference to be to the period of the Jewish War, A.D. 64–6 (cf. p. 31). S. G. F. Brandon (*New Testament Studies*, vii, 1960–1, pp. 134 ff.) thinks it reflects the situation at a slightly later date, A.D. 70. On the history of the interpretation of this verse, see G. R. Beasley-Murray, "A Commentary on Mark Thirteen", 1957, pp. 59 ff.

[2] See Note F at the end of this chapter.

nigh, and that the disaster towards which the Jews were manifestly heading would herald that end. That it was a mistaken expectation does not seem to be a sufficient reason to deny it to our Lord. For unlike the author of Daniel, who sought to indicate the time of the end very specifically, Jesus, according to this chapter itself, expressly disclaimed any exact knowledge of the time. That does not seem to me to be the sort of utterance that would be put into His mouth by another, and it bears the stamp of genuineness.[1] And where He confesses ignorance, there can be no irreverence in our accepting the confession. In so far as the chapter contains the utterance of Jesus, it may be understood to proclaim His certainty that a time of dire tribulation for Jerusalem lay in the not distant future, that a time of bitter persecution for His followers was before them, and that the glorious kingdom to which the Book of Daniel had looked forward was to come with divine power. He believed these things to be associated with one another, but expressly disclaimed any precise knowledge. The numerous attempts by His professed followers to attain precise knowledge seem to me to be evidence of serious disloyalty to Him, Who announced that the secrets they vainly try to fathom are reserved for God Himself. Where Jesus disclaimed knowledge, knowledge can be no spiritual boon to His followers.

In so far as He was speaking of the coming disaster for Jerusalem, of which He spoke on other occasions besides this, His word was based on profound spiritual principles, precisely as the word of the prophets had been. That blindness which showed itself on the spiritual side in the rejection of Him and of His message was a blindness which equally marked every side of the nation's life. For the welfare of men

[1] Beasley-Murray ("Commentary on Mark Thirteen", p. 11 n.) thinks the contents of the discourse as a whole have a high claim to authenticity, though he disclaims the idea that the chapter is precisely as Jesus uttered it. Similarly, C. E. B. Cranfield ("The Gospel according to St. Mark" [Camb. Greek Testament Commentary], 1959, p. 390) holds that the chapter records substantially the teaching of Christ. E. Stauffer ("New Testament Theology", Eng. trans., 1955, p. 344) brings Mark xiii into association with the Valedictions and Farewells in the Old Testament and related literature (cf. J. Munck, in "Aux Sources de la tradition chrétienne" [Goguel Festschrift], 1950, pp. 155 ff.).

and of nations springs only from spiritual sensitiveness to God's word and will. And therefore national disaster must follow the national rejection of God's messenger.

In so far as He was speaking of the end of the age, He took over elements of the widespread apocalyptic expectations, and like the apocalyptists, He made them the vehicle of a message of hope for His followers. And in that message, as we shall see, there lay a deep spiritual truth quite independent of the truth of the form in which it was cast. He also made them the vehicle of a summons to loyal vigilance: "Watch, therefore."

It is necessary to look at the conception of the Second Coming of Christ, which is apparent in this passage. Whence came this idea? If Jesus identified Himself with the Son of Man of Dan. vii. 13, interpreted in an individual sense, then the kingdom ought to have come with Him, and it is the faith of all His followers that He did establish the kingdom as a spiritual kingdom of those in whose hearts He rules.[1] Yet there are a number of passages in the Gospels which think of the coming of the Son of Man as a future event. But how can Jesus at once have identified Himself with the Son of Man of Dan. vii. 13 and thought of the coming of the Son of Man as still future?

It has already been said that T. W. Manson believes that on the lips of Jesus the term "Son of Man" at first symbolized the kingdom of God, and that the individualizing of the concept and its identification with Him is the outcome of His ministry. I am not able to accept this view, though I think it is in part correct. Dr. Wheeler Robinson has applied the concept of corporate personality most fruitfully to a number of Old Testament problems,[2] and I think it holds

---

[1] It is common to-day to speak of the "rule of God", or some such phrase, instead of the "kingdom of God". The term probably includes the ideas of both the rule and the realm of God, but the realm not as geographically conceived, but rather as the collective body of those who acknowledge the rule. As such it is, of course, to be distinguished from the Church. Goguel describes it as "the new order which will be established when the present order comes to an end" ("The Life of Jesus", 1933, p. 312).

[2] Cf. "The Hebrew Conception of Corporate Personality", in "Werden und Wesen des Alten Testaments" (ed. J. Hempel), 1936, pp. 49 ff.

the clue to this one also. The Hebrew could pass from the individual to the community to which he belonged, or which he represented, and from the community to the individual in whom it was focused, much more easily than we do. The concept of the Son of Man was, in my view, originally a collective one, which then became individualized in thought in the person of Him who should be its leader and representative, and who should supremely in Himself express its mission.[1] As a Jew familiar with this characteristic of Hebrew thinking, Jesus could both think of Himself as the Son of Man in this sense and at the same time think of the Son of Man as a figure for the kingdom which He represented.[2] He was the Son of Man who had come to bring in the Son of Man, who had come to inaugurate the enduring kingdom of the saints. But from the moment that He realized that He was also the Suffering Servant, and that these two hitherto quite separate concepts were fused in Him, He knew that in His earthly ministry He could not represent in Himself the consummation of the hope of Dan. vii. He had come to inaugurate the kingdom by suffering, but that its consummation would be glorious, and that it would be charged with authority and power, He could not but be assured, without abandoning the whole Son of Man concept altogether. Hence its establishment in His suffering must be followed by its consummation in glory.

It would take us too far here to examine all the passages which speak of this future coming of the Son of Man. They are, however, the passages where the collective understanding of the phrase is attended with the least difficulty, and in one case where Matthew has "the Son of Man", Mark has "the kingdom of God". It is a passage which shows that Jesus expected this consummation of the coming of the kingdom in the near future, within the lifetime of some of those who were then with Him. "Verily I say unto you, There be some of them who stand here, which shall in no

[1] For a careful study of all the "Son of Man" sayings in the Gospels, cf. H. B. Sharman, "Son of Man and Kingdom of God", 1943.
[2] Cf. C. J. Cadoux, "The Historic Mission of Jesus", 1941, p. 100.

wise taste of death till they see the Son of Man coming in his kingdom" (Matt. xvi. 28), or "till they see the kingdom of God come with power" (Mark ix. 1). But the preceding verse, in both Mark and Matthew, makes clear reference to the coming of the Son of Man in glory, and Matthew's substitution of "the Son of Man" in the second verse is not an alteration of the meaning, but merely the repetition of the synonymous phrase which Mark has already used in the · previous verse. For Mark has perceived that the Son of Man here meant the kingdom of God. So, too, in the passage in the Little Apocalypse, which speaks of the coming of the Son of Man in clouds with great power and glory, it is probable that the Son of Man is primarily a symbol for the coming kingdom in its consummation.

I cannot feel that it is exclusively such a symbol, however, even here. For when Jesus realized that it was by the way of suffering that He should establish the kingdom, He also believed that His mission would not end in suffering, but that death should be followed by resurrection. In the Fourth Gospel He is represented as teaching that His spiritual presence would continue to be with His disciples (John xiv. 18 ff., xv. 4 ff.), so that He would not be withdrawn from the sphere of human action. Already in Matthew we find a similar thought in the final verse of the Gospel, where Jesus says: "I am with you alway, even unto the end of the world" (Matt. xxviii. 20). In one sense, therefore, He would not need to come again to the world, since He would not leave it. But if Jesus believed, as I cannot doubt that He did, that in Himself He expressed the mission of the Son of Man to inaugurate the kingdom, and that He would rise from the dead and continue to exercise a living and present influence in the world, directing the kingdom by His spirit throughout the course of its establishment, He could only believe that in the consummation of the kingdom in glory He would still figure as its representative and head. The concept of the Second Coming is one which was born of the inner logic, or rather dynamic, of His consciousness of His vocation. It meant that He who fulfilled the promise of Dan. vii. 13 also passed on the hope of its fulfilment to His followers, to carry on the eschatological hope He came to fulfil. The apparent inconsistency is not really due to want of logic, but to fluidity of concept.[1]

The Book of Revelation

In the Book of Revelation we have a great apocalypse once more, which far surpasses the whole range of pseudonymous works which stand between the Book of Daniel and itself. It did not easily secure for itself canonicity in the New Testament, and with the exception of a few notable passages, canonicity has failed to preserve it from neglect. For apart from these few passages, it is probably the least read book in the New Testament. Yet it was by a sound instinct that it was included in the Canon.[2]

Its date and authorship have been much discussed, and there is never likely to be anything like agreement about them. It has been traditionally ascribed to John the son of Zebedee, to whom also the Fourth Gospel is ascribed. There are still those who defend the ascription, while others deny a common authorship to the two works, and hence deny one or both to the son of Zebedee. The book itself merely claims to have been written by one whose name was John, living in the isle of Patmos. Whether he was the son of Zebedee or not, there is no reason to deny that its author was named John. The book is therefore not pseudonymous. Here is its first notable breach with the tradition of apocalyptic writings, and it shows that at last we have an author who is worthy to stand beside the author of the book of Daniel.

It has been suggested above that the pseudonymity of the

---

[1] See Note G at the end of this chapter.

[2] This view is not shared by C. H. Dodd, who observes of this book that its "excessive emphasis on the future has the effect of relegating to a secondary place just those elements in the original Gospel which are most distinctive of Christianity. . . . Under the influence of this revived Jewish eschatology, Christianity was in danger of falling back into the position of the earlier apocalyptists. . . . In its conception of the character of God and His attitude to man the book falls below the level, not only of the teaching of Jesus, but of the best parts of the Old Testament" ("The Apostolic Preaching and its Developments", 1936, pp. 87 ff.).

Book of Daniel grew out of the genesis of the book. The author began by telling stories about Daniel, and then put his visions into the mouth of Daniel to proclaim a common authorship. Subsequent imitators copied this feature as of the essence of apocalyptic. John does not. For, like the Book of Daniel, his work has a more natural genesis. He does not begin by telling stories about an ancient worthy, and so he has no need to cast his visions in the form of visions of another. He begins by writing letters to the Churches he knows well, and whose life he wishes to guide. He therefore has no need to write as other than himself. He is not afraid to be original in the form in which he casts his apocalyptic message, any more than the author of the Book of Daniel was. And because he does not attribute his work to an ancient worthy, he has no need to bridge the gulf between the past and the present by history in the form of prophecy, as the prelude to his predictions of the future.

These predictions are of the apocalyptic order, and it is not to be surprised at that many of the ideas that figure in other apocalyptic works have their counterparts here. He took over much that belonged to the field in which he worked, and used it for his purpose. For his purpose was urgent and practical, as the author of the Book of Daniel's purpose had been. He lived in the days of sore trial, days that he believed to be fraught with great issues for the world, and he wrote to exhort men to be faithful and to fortify them with hope.

Charles believes in the fundamental unity of this work, and declares that that unity is "immeasurably greater than in any of the great Jewish apocalypses of an earlier or contemporary date".[1] He finds many dislocations and interpolations in it, however, and holds that the author died before he

---

[1] "Critical Commentary on the Revelation of St. John", i, 1920, p. lxxxvii. So, too, E. Lohmeyer, "Die Offenbarung des Johannes", 1926, pp. 181 f. Contrast P. Wendland, "Die urchristlichen Literaturformen", 2nd ed., 1912, p. 382; and B. W. Bacon, in *Harvard Theological Review*, xxiii, 1930, pp. 240 f.: "If there is one feature of the controversy which can be called a matter of common consent for all competent scholars of modern times, it is the agreement that the work is highly composite."

completed his work, and that the editor who completed it was an arch-heretic, who betrays a depth of stupidity all but incomprehensible, and matched only by his ignorance.[1] This view has not commended itself to others, and in our brief review of the contents and teaching of the book it will be left out of account. For our purpose is to look at the ideas and hopes which the book expresses or fosters, and to let it rather speak for itself than to impose any theory upon it.

After a short prologue, the seer opens with the letters to the seven Churches of Asia, which he was commanded by the Lord, who appeared unto him as the Son of Man in splendour, to write to them. The letters are addressed to the angels of the Churches, rather than directly to the Churches. By this is probably meant the guardian spirits of the Churches. The purpose of the letters was to tell them the things which were and the things which were to come. They are couched in symbolic language, and they describe the spiritual condition of the Churches, and the judgement pronounced on them (Rev. i–iii). The contrast between the severe judgements passed on the Churches here and the conception of the Church in the rest of the book as the persecuted community of the saints has often been noted. But as E. F. Scott observes: "In the later portion of the book the Church is regarded simply as the Church, the people of Christ over against the heathen Empire. In these introductory chapters the Church is contrasted, not with the surrounding world, but with its own ideal. It must be a Church in reality as well as in name, or in the dreadful trial that is coming it will break down."[2]

Then follows the prophecy of the things that should come to pass in the future. The seer is transported to Heaven, where he sees the throne of God, and in the right hand of God the book of the divine secrets, sealed with seven seals,

---

[1] *Op. cit.*, i, p. liii. This theory is rejected by Lohmeyer, *op. cit.*, p. 164. Cf. also the comment of Burkitt (*Proceedings of the British Academy*, xvii, 1931, p. 443), who cites this as an example of Charles's efforts "to apply strict logic to works whose writers were governed rather by hope and enthusiasm than by reason and consistency".

[2] "The Book of Revelation", 4th ed., 1941, p. 61.

which none was worthy to open until the Lamb that had been slain and restored to life came forward and was acclaimed as worthy (Rev. iv f.). Into the imagery of this scene much that was derived from the Old Testament enters, and much that was doubtless derived from other sources. Many of the elements have been traced back to a mythological origin, but it is more important to appreciate the spirit and purpose of the author than to trace the origins of his materials, origins of which he was probably himself much less aware than his learned modern students. What he is really concerned to set forth is the glory of God and the unique honour and worth of Christ, the Lamb that was slain.[1]

As the Lamb opens the first four seals, four horsemen symbolizing their contents appear. The first is a conqueror, the second releases strife, the third brings famine, and the fourth death. The opening of the fifth seal brings the cry of the martyrs, and the sixth earthquakes and celestial portents and widespread terror. Here, however, a Remnant is preserved, consisting of a hundred and forty-four thousand elect Jews, and a multitude that no man could number, representing the Gentile converts to Christianity. The opening of the seventh seal brings a great silence in Heaven for the space of half an hour (Rev. vi. 1–viii. 1). Of the many interpretations of the seals I think Charles offers the most natural.[2] It is that here we have the traditional apocalyptic expectation of a series of woes that shall precede the end, but here based on the Lukan form of the Little Apocalypse of the Gospels (Luke xxi). There we read that there shall be wars and tumults, nation rising against nation and kingdom against kingdom, earthquakes, famines, and pestilences, followed by terror and signs from Heaven. It is added that before these things there shall be persecution for the elect. It will be seen that if persecution is placed after pestilence, in accordance with this

---

[1] Cf. C. Brütsch ("L'Apocalypse de Jésus-Christ", 3rd ed., 1942, p. 15): "Dès les premiers versets, nous sommes fixés sur le contenu du livre; sa perspective maîtresse s'impose d'emblée à notre regard: il s'agit de la 'révélation de Jésus-Christ'. Ce qui est vrai de toute la Bible, l'est en particulier du dernier de ses écrits: Jésus-Christ nous y est révélé."

[2] "Critical Commentary on the Revelation of St. John", i, p. 158.

intimation that it belongs higher up, the list exactly corresponds save for the earthquakes of Luke xxi. 11, which are separated from the other natural portents. There is even the same curious duplication of war at the beginning, where the conqueror of the first seal followed by the warfare of the second corresponds to the wars and tumults followed by nation rising against nation.

The action now seems to pause, and instead of the great *dénouement* that we are led to expect on the opening of the seventh seal, a fresh series of woes is opened up. And at the end of this series of seven the same thing happens. When the reader is keyed up to expectation a third series of seven woes opens out. It has been much discussed whether these are parallel series of woes or successive. So far as the form of the vision goes they are clearly successive. But that is probably part of the artistry of the writer. Just as when one is ascending a mountain the summit appears to be close, only to give place to a further height beyond, itself perhaps to disclose another when we approach it, so the author of this apocalypse presents these three successive series of woes, each promising to lead to the final scene of the drama, but serving only to hold the interest and to prevent the journey from dragging. Moreover, the sense of the tremendousness of the final scene, when we reach it, is increased by the triple series of woes that have preceded it. The duplication of Pharaoh's dream added to the impressiveness of its warning (Gen. xli. 32), and the presentation of a series of visions in the Book of Daniel, all culminating in a common point of history, similarly added weight to the impression created. That here the woes are successive in the form of the story, but parallel in significance, will not trouble anyone who recalls the inconcinnity of his own dreams, and who remembers that this is presented in the form of a vision.

The second series of woes is marked by the blowing of seven angelic trumpets. As the angels blow the trumpets the successive disasters fall upon the earth. The disasters here are not identical with those of the first series, since the author wishes to add variety to his pictures. But they are largely the same in substance, and the change is mainly of order and presentation. "We cannot but feel that John is hard put to it," says Scott, "to introduce variety into his dismal picture. He pretty well exhausts himself in the first series, where he tells, in splendid, imaginative language, of war, civil dissension, famine, plague, persecution, earthquake. In the second and third series we have little more than a repetition of these standard types of calamity."[1] Before the seventh trumpet was sounded, an angel appeared to assure the seer that the sounding of the seventh trumpet would herald the end, and the seer was made to eat a book. Then there is a fresh interlude, in which John saw two witnesses fighting against the Beast, and perishing in Jerusalem, where they lay unburied for three and a half years, when they were restored to life and taken up to Heaven. These two witnesses had prophesied for twelve hundred and sixty days, or three and a half years of thirty-day months. The period of three and a half years goes back through many apocalyptic works to the Book of Daniel, and it had become part of the stock of apocalyptic expectation. Here we have half a week of witness, followed by half a week of dishonour, in preparation for the resurrection to honour. It is probable that other elements of this picture were taken over from other sources, and their precise symbolism can never be known with any certainty. At the end of this interlude the seventh trumpet was sounded, and the Kingdom of Christ, that should endure for ever, began (Rev. viii. 2–xi. 18). Instead of the glories of that kingdom being described, however, we are plunged at once, after a momentary glimpse, into fresh afflictions.

The Ark of the Covenant appears in the heavenly Temple, and a woman in travail, threatened by a seven-headed Dragon. The woman brings forth a child, destined to rule all nations, whom the Dragon wished to devour, but who was carried to Heaven to the Throne of God. There followed war in Heaven between Michael and the Dragon, until the Dragon was expelled from Heaven and cast down to the earth. Here he persecuted the woman, who had already gone

[1] "The Book of Revelation", p. 67.

into the wilderness and found a place of refuge for twelve hundred and sixty days—again the three and a half years (Rev. xi. 19–xii. 17). It is probable that here John is working with some old mythological material, though he is not in the slightest interested in the significance it had in its original form. The child almost certainly represents Christ, but the picture is symbolical and therefore does not depict His birth from Mary, but rather represents Him as the child of the eternal cause of Truth. The enmity of the Dragon in Heaven and the persecution on earth suggest that behind all the human adversaries of that cause lie transcendental spiritual powers of evil.

There now arises from the sea a Beast with seven heads and ten horns, corresponding to the Dragon that appeared in Heaven, and the Dragon gave his authority to the Beast. The Beast had a mouth speaking great things and blasphemies, and he had authority to continue for forty-two months —three and a half years once more—during which he should make war on the saints. A second beast arose from the land, and persuaded men to worship the first Beast, and put on them the mark of the Beast, or the number of his name. The number was six hundred and sixty-six.[1] Over against the Beast stood the Lamb on Mount Zion, with the hundred and forty-four thousand first-fruits unto God and the Lamb (Rev. xiii–xiv. 6). The Dragon against whom Michael fought in Heaven was the demonic Antichrist, corresponding to the Beliar of the earlier works. The Beast, to whom the Dragon

[1] C. Ryder Smith's ingenious and skilful study of "The Three 'Woes' of the Apocalypse" (*London Quarterly and Holborn Review*, January 1942, pp. 16–33) deserves to be mentioned, and especially for its interpretation of the numbers of the book. He suggests that they form a carefully integrated chronological scheme, dating from 588 B.C., on the basis of the formula 2 days = 1 year, of which he finds a hint in the book. In the case of the number of the Beast, however, he finds this to stand both for Nero and for a date. But here he exceptionally uses the formula 1 day = 1 year, and finds a hint of this in the statement that it is the number of a man (Rev. xiii. 18), *i.e.* by normal human reckoning. While there is much that is attractive in this view, it seems unnecessary to credit the author with careful chronological calculations, for which his conditions on the isle of Patmos are not likely to have provided him with materials, when the numbers can be more simply explained by their occurrence in the Book of Daniel, with the exception of the number of the Beast, which was determined by the writer's idea as to who was the Beast.

hands over its authority and power, is the earthly Antichrist, the Incarnation of the other, and it corresponds to the Little Horn of Daniel's visions, a king who persecutes the saints. Like the Little Horn of the Book of Daniel, the Beast has a mouth speaking great things and blasphemies, and worship is offered to it. For him that hath understanding the clue to the identification of the Beast is given in its number. This is perhaps a numerical cipher for Nero, since the numerical value of the letters of Nero Caesar, when written in Hebrew letters, with the name spelt in the Greek way, Neron, is 666.[1] There are, however, many other interpretations of the number, and no certainty is possible.[2]

Three angels now appear to make proclamation, announcing the hour of judgement, heralding the fall of Babylon, and pronouncing doom on all who worshipped the Beast. Then a white cloud appears, seated on which is one like a Son of Man, signalizing the hour of doom (Rev. xiv. 6–20). But again the judgement tarries, and the scene melts into a fresh series of woes. Seven angels appear, corresponding to the seven angels with trumpets of the earlier passage. This time they bear seven bowls, containing seven plagues which they pour out over the earth, and as they pour them the martyred faithful sing praises to God. After the sixth had been poured out the nations gathered together to Armageddon to war.

---

[1] Some manuscripts have the number 616, and it is commonly held that this reflects the spelling of the name in the Latin way, Nero. But C. C. Torrey ("Documents of the Primitive Church", 1941, p. 226 n.) declares that there is no support in known usage for this spelling, and finds the number 666 to point to Nero, and the number 616 to point to Caligula.

[2] Cf. F. C. Porter (in Hastings' "Dictionary of the Bible", iv, 1902, p. 258b): "The number does not prove, and can hardly be said to give substantial support to, the identification of the beast with Nero." E. B. Allo ("Saint Jean: l'Apocalypse", 1921, p. 194) regards the identification with Gaius Caesar, if the number is 616, or with Nero Caesar, if it is 666, as the only likely suggestions; but he declares the whole attempt to identify the Beast by this number to be arid conjecture (*ibid.*, p. 214). Lohmeyer ("Die Offenbarung des Johannes", 1926, p. 116) holds the number 666 to be the triangular number of 36 (*i.e.* the sum of all the integers from 1 to 36), while 36 is itself the triangular number of 8. He then connects the number of the Beast with "the eighth" in Rev. xvii. 11. E. Mireaux ("La Reine Bérénice", 1951, pp. 244 f.) suggests that the number 666 is the sum of the initials of the first ten Roman emperors in the Greek spelling of their names, and argues that the book was composed in A.D. 70.

The pouring out of the seventh bowl heralded the end of Babylon (Rev. xv f.). That Babylon stands for Rome becomes increasingly clear as the action proceeds. Just as the author of the Book of Daniel had used Nebuchadnezzar as a lay figure when he wanted to say things that really had relevance to Antiochus, so John speaks of Babylon when he is really thinking of Rome.

The fall of Rome is now described in greater detail. For this the scene once more changes, and a woman clad in scarlet appears upon the Beast. The woman is the Great Harlot, Babylon the Great, and the Beast's heads and horns are now interpreted to show that the destruction of the Beast and of Babylon the Great, to be announced immediately afterwards, was associated with an eighth head or king, who was and is not. Then the saints are exhorted to rejoice, and the destruction of Babylon is symbolized by the casting of a millstone into the sea. Thereupon the angelic hosts rejoiced and broke forth into song (Rev. xvi. 1–xix. 10). The Word of God, seated on a white horse, now appears and destroys the two Beasts, the one that was worshipped and the one that persuaded men to worship it (Rev. xix. 11–21). Here the Beast is not an individual incarnation of Antichrist, but represents the imperial power of Rome, a collective Antichrist, if you will, in the line of the Caesars, culminating in the eighth king. This is not without its parallel in the Book of Daniel. For there the fourth beast represented the fourth kingdom, which was then represented by the Little Horn, symbolizing a king in whom its iniquity culminated, and the one who exercised the *imperium* of the beast at the time of the culmination of the vision. So here the eighth king is but a horn of the Beast; yet he is the Beast itself, for in him its character and authority inhere at the time now to be described. But Nero was not the eighth of the Caesars, and if the common dating of the book in the last decade of the first century is correct, Nero had been dead for some time. Many writers bring in the expectation that was current at the time that Nero would return, and this may lie behind the phrase, "he was and is not and shall come" (Rev. xvii. 8). To John it would doubtless seem particularly appropriate that on the one side should be the Lamb that was slain and raised again, and on the other the incarnation of iniquity who similarly would be raised, but to meet his doom, and to bring doom upon Rome in which he ruled and the whole imperial line which he represented.

And now comes the millennium, when Satan lies bound for a thousand years, and Christ and His saints reign, after the first resurrection, which is only for the saints. After the thousand years Satan is loosed for a fresh attack on the saints, but only to be devoured by fire and cast into the eternal lake of fire (Rev. xx. 1–10). Then comes the general resurrection and the last judgement, followed by the renewal of the heavens and the earth (Rev. xx. 11–xxi. 8). Finally, the new Jerusalem, antithetic to Babylon the Great, is described in all its radiance and glory, and the book is closed with the solemn assurance that the time is at hand when its predictions will be fulfilled (Rev. xxi. 9–xxii. 20).

Many of the elements we have found in so many of the apocalyptic works are found here. The demonic Antichrist and his human incarnation we have already noted. The Messiah appears as the Lamb, or as the child of the travailing woman, and He is everywhere identified with Jesus. But He is more than a human Messiah. He died and rose again, and now He has inherited unparalleled power and dominion and glory, so that He surpasses the angels and the archangels, and shares the glory of God Himself.

Repeatedly are the dire troubles that will herald the end of the age described, and it is clear that the writer believed that he was living in that age of trouble, and looked forward to the swiftly approaching deliverance. It is to be a time of persecution for the saints, such as was depicted in that first apocalypse of the Book of Daniel, and the writer is primarily interested in that persecution whereby the Beast will show all his beastliness. But he does not throw over all the other ideas which we have found in many writers. The world that persecutes the Church curses also itself with strife, and finds all kinds of plagues loosed upon it. Moreover, the cosmic significance of the attack on the saints is expressed in happenings in the world of Nature, where fresh ills are poured on men.

The enduring kingdom and the resurrection figure here. But the treatment is peculiar. The idea of a temporary kingdom, lasting for a thousand years, which we have found suggested in the Slavonic Enoch, is combined with the idea of an everlasting kingdom, while the idea of a kingdom on earth is combined with that of a kingdom in the New Jerusalem, or in a new heaven and a new earth. Both ideas had been found earlier, but here they are combined to yield first a temporary earthly kingdom, and then after an interval of renewed Satanic activity the everlasting kingdom in the New Jerusalem. This made it possible for the idea of a resurrection of the righteous only and the idea of a general resurrection to be combined. The great final judgement and the destruction of all evil belongs to this as to almost all of the other apocalypses.

But though these and other ideas that belong to the common stock of apocalyptic were taken up and used, they were worked into a design that is *sui generis*, and worked in with a skill that is surpassing. There are many obscurities, and the scenes melt one into another in a manner that often bewilders us. But there are also passages whose majesty and music can be recognized by those who have little knowledge of the book as a whole, and lyric passages recurring from time to time to lift the reader by their nobility from the darkness of the woes and the sufferings, and to save him from being lost in the bizarre detail and forgetting that this apocalypse is first and foremost a vision of the glory of Christ, and of the eternal triumph over all the forces of evil which He is destined to achieve. With a great apocalypse in the Book of Daniel our review began, and with a great apocalypse in the Book of Revelation it ends. It is by no accident that the one has been incorporated in the canon of the Old Testament and the other in that of the New. For they stand out far above all those others that lie between. Nevertheless, they, too, had had a part to play. For by their study we can trace the growth of ideas, and understand something of the apocalyptic background of the ministry of John the Baptist and of Jesus, and of the writers of the New Testament.

NOTE C. THE FIGURE OF TAXO IN THE ASSUMPTION OF MOSES

The identification of the figure of Taxo has provided the most vexed question associated with the Assumption of Moses. As has been stated above, Charles identified him with the Eleazar of 2 Macc. vi. 18 ff. To this view Burkitt brought support[1] by the suggestion that in the name Taxo we have a cipher for Eleazar. The identification is effected by supposing a final letter to have been lost from the name, and by substituting the following letter of the alphabet for each letter in the then assumed Hebrew form of the word. Naturally Charles welcomed this suggestion,[2] and it has also been adopted by Hölscher,[3] but transferred to another Eleazar, who was contemporary with Bar-Cochba in the second century A.D. On quite other grounds, as I have indicated above, it seems impossible to place the book late enough for Hölscher's identification to be acceptable, while my difficulty about the suggestion of Charles is that the Maccabaean Eleazar seems hardly a sufficiently outstanding character to have been given this exaggerated significance so long after his time.[4] For he would be the only person whose precise name was indicated in all the survey of history in this book. If it was desired to indicate him with precision his actual name could not be given, as that would be contrary to the practice of apocalyptic. For names of people who were not born at the time of the putative author of the work are not given. Where persons are indicated, it is either by a

---

[1] In Hastings' "Dictionary of the Bible", iii, 1900, p. 449b.

[2] In "Apocrypha and Pseudepigrapha", ii, p. 421. In his earlier work, "The Assumption of Moses", 1897, he had already identified Taxo with Eleazar, but had not equated the names.

[3] *Zeitschrift für die neutestamentliche Wissenschaft*, xvii, 1916, pp. 108 ff., 149 ff.

[4] Cf. Hölscher, *ibid.*, p. 118: "What possible interest could that obscure Eleazar of a long past age have for the apocalyptist?"

symbolic figure, such as an animal or a horn of an animal, or by some numerical or other cipher. But the resort to a cipher is elsewhere reserved for a contemporary figure, whom it would be dangerous to indicate openly, but who could be identified with certainty by those who were given the key to the cipher.

Lattey[1] follows the view of Hausrath,[2] that Taxo is to be equated with Shiloh, of Gen. xlix. 10, and that the reference is to the passage "until Shiloh come". The equation is effected by supposing that Taxo is a mistake for Takmo, and that when this word is written in Hebrew each letter stands for the preceding letter of the alphabet. It is unfortunate that it is again necessary to emend the word before it will serve the purpose to which it is to be put. For while the change is not in itself graphically difficult, and not one to which any exception could be taken, if there were any evidence in its favour, it is always a doubtful policy to base a theory on a wholly unsupported conjectural emendation. For there is nothing whatever, except the assumed cipher, to suggest Shiloh.

Lattey believes that Taxo stands for the Messiah, but that he is a suffering Messiah, and that the author supposed that Taxo's death and the death of his sons by fasting would bring in the Messianic age. This seems to me to be highly improbable, and its sole support is the assumed equation of Taxo and Shiloh. The plene writing of the word "Shiloh" in Hebrew in Gen. xlix. 10 at so early a date is essential to the theory, and it has all the available evidence squarely against it. The Samaritan text is against it, and the renderings of the ancient versions show that they did not have it before their translators. The versions show that it was not read as a proper name at all, and it nowhere figures as a personal proper name of the Messiah until much later. It is therefore an assumption that the original Hebrew of the Assumption of Moses read "Takmo"; an assumption that this was a cryptogram for Shiloh; an assumption that the

---

[1] *Catholic Biblical Quarterly*, January 1942, pp. 17 f.
[2] "Neutestamentliche Zeitgeschichte", iv, 1877, p. 77 n.

Hebrew text of Gen. xlix. 10 read this word plene at that time; and an assumption that it was already understood as a title of the Messiah. It is further an assumption that the Suffering Servant of Isa. liii had been brought into association with any Messianic title before the ministry of Christ.[1] For none of these assumptions is any evidence available.

Moreover, the proposed view is in radical disagreement with the conception of the Suffering Servant, whereby it is explained. For Lattey says, "we have here a voluntary death for Israel, of the kind which has come to be known as a hunger-strike, a death so voluntary that it must surely be reprobated as a suicide. . . . Evidently the writer looks upon it as heroic, and it is to bring about the final consummation."[2] But the death of the Suffering Servant of Isa. liii is anything but suicide. I am not persuaded, however, that suicide is in mind here. What Taxo appears to me to mean is to take refuge in the caves, rather than be disloyal to the will of God, even though that may bring the risk of death, whether from starvation or from other cause. He does not passively yield himself to martyrdom, but flees to the caves, though the hope they offer is but slight.

Other considerations seem to me to be fatal to this theory of the identification of Taxo. The reference to his seven sons suggests that he was a real person, already existing, and not an ideal figure. Nowhere else do we read of the sons of the Messiah. Nor can I see why anyone should resort to a cryptogram for Shiloh. Even supposing the evidence for the existence of that name as a personal designation at so early a date were unexceptionable, Shiloh is itself so cryptic a name for the Messiah that there is still no agreement as to why it should have been chosen in Gen. xlix. 10. To resort to a cryptogram for what is already cryptic seems a gratuitous performance. Moreover, I find nothing in the text to indicate

---

[1] This assumption has been made by others, but without any evidence. It is rejected by J. Héring, in *Revue d'Histoire et de Philosophie Religieuses*, xviii, 1938, pp. 419 ff. Cf. Volz, "Eschatologie der jüdischen Gemeinde im neutest. Zeitalter", 1934, p. 238: "Isa. liii was first brought into association with the Messiah at a later date." In "The Servant of the Lord", 1952, pp. 61 ff., I examine this question at length.   [2] *Loc. cit.*, p. 17.

that the death of Taxo and his sons would effect the coming of the kingdom of God.[1] It would be followed by the coming of the kingdom, which would avenge their innocent death. But there is nothing in that to associate Taxo either with the Messiah or with the Suffering Servant. The one was expected to establish the kingdom by His strength, and the other to serve and save by His vicarious suffering. Taxo does neither. His contemplated death but cries out to Heaven for vengeance.[2] It may also be noted that the author of the Assumption of Moses supposed that Israel would find some special satisfaction in contemplating the sufferings of her foes in Gehenna after the establishment of the kingdom. This is a strange comment on the idea that he brought Isa. liii into his conception of the means of establishment of the kingdom. For nothing could be in greater contrast to the spirit and message of that chapter.

It may be added that there is a passage in Josephus which tells of one curiously like Taxo, who lived in the days of Herod. "Now there was one old man who was caught within one of these caves, with seven children and a wife: these prayed him to give them leave to go out, and yield themselves up to the enemy; but he stood at the cave's mouth, and always slew that child of his who went out, till he had destroyed them every one, and after that he slew his wife, and cast their dead bodies down the precipice, and himself after them, and so underwent death rather than slavery."[3] There is nothing here to explain why such a person should be supposed to be doing anything of world significance, and there is therefore no reason to identify him with Taxo.[4] On

[1] Cf. Lagrange, "Le Judaïsme avant J.-C.", p. 240: "The times are hard, and men are impotent. There is nothing to do but to await the intervention of God. And Taxo will play no part in that."

[2] E. de Faye ("Les apocalypses juives", 1892, p. 72) thinks that Taxo is without doubt the elect people, the incorruptible seed. He finds the text to be less incorruptible, however, and declares the name Taxo to be a corrupt reading.

[3] "Antiquities", xiv, 429 (XIV, xv, 5), trans. of Whiston.

[4] Cf. "Wars", i, 312 f. (I, xvi, 4). Since the issue of the first edition I find that Klausner at one time held that these passages in Josephus give the clue to the interpretation of the figure of Taxo ("Jesus of Nazareth", Eng. trans. by H. Danby, p. 143 n.). But this view he later repudiated for the view that *tks'* is a

the other hand, it is not clear from the Assumption of Moses why the death of Taxo and his sons should signalize the moment for the establishment of the kingdom.

A further effort to solve this puzzle has been made by C. C. Torrey,[1] who by *gematria* equates Taxo with the Aramaic form of "The Hasmonaean", *i.e.* Mattathias.[2] In a different way Kaminetsky reached the same conclusion.[3] But whereas Kaminetsky thought Taxo rests on a misunderstanding of the word *tksh* (read as a proper name instead of as a verb = his name thou shalt conceal), Torrey rests his on the numerical summation of the values of the letters of "The Hasmonaean" and of the assumed Hebrew form, *ṭqśw*, of the word transliterated Taxo. Kaminetsky offers no special reason why the name of Mattathias should be concealed, and only justifies his equation by saying that all that is written here refers to him. Torrey's case has therefore a strong advantage over his in that it offers a clearer point of connexion, and it has an equally strong advantage over the views of Hausrath and Burkitt in that it involves no emendation of the assumed form which was transliterated Taxo. It should be noted, however, that no two letters of Kaminetsky's *tksh* and Torrey's *ṭqśw* are alike.[4]

To the objection that Mattathias had but five sons, whereas Taxo had seven, Torrey opposes the suggestion that the reference is not to Mattathias' actual sons, but to the seven Hasmonaean rulers from Judas Maccabaeus to Antigonus. The difficulty here is that it would be somewhat artificial for Mattathias to exhort Antigonus to flee into a cave to escape

---

scribal error for *mty'*, by which one of the early Ḥasidim was certainly meant ("Ha-ra'yon ham-Meshiḥi be-Yiśrael", 1927, p. 204). This would appear to be an alternative way of reaching the connexion with Mattathias (see below), but one that assumes that every letter save one has been wrongly transmitted.

[1] "'Taxo' in the Assumption of Moses", in *Journal of Biblical Literature*, lxii, 1943, pp. 1–7. Cf. my note, "The Figure of 'Taxo' in the Assumption of Moses", *ibid.*, lxiv, 1945, pp. 141–4, and Torrey, "'Taxo' Once More", *ibid.*, pp. 395–7.

[2] So also R. H. Pfeiffer, "History of New Testament Times", 1949, p. 80 n.

[3] *Hash-Shiloaḥ*, xv, 1905, p. 47.

[4] G. Kuhn (*Zeitschrift für die alttestamentliche Wissenschaft*, N.F. ii, 1925, p. 129) thinks that Taxo represents Hebrew *ṭqśw*, but suggests that this was a metathesis for *qwśṭ*, which means "truth".

the persecution of Antiochus Epiphanes (Ass. Mos. ix. 6). Moreover, it is then quite irrelevant for Torrey to observe that "chapter ix is occupied solely with the refusal of Taxo and his sons to disobey the commands of God even under the severest persecution".[1]

Further, there is no suggestion that Taxo and his sons raised the standard of revolt, and Charles thinks that the author of the Assumption of Moses deliberately left the family of Mattathias without mention, because he disapproved of the Maccabaean rising.[2] His ideal was, "Let us die rather than transgress." To this Torrey replies that this was precisely the attitude of Mattathias at the outset. He does not explain the relevance of this ideal, not to Mattathias at first merely, but to the whole Hasmonaean dynasty—the supposed sons of Taxo.

Again, the Hasmonaean line is commonly believed to be referred to in Ass. Mos. vi. 1, but mentioned for dishonour. Here Torrey agrees, but finds the terms of censure so comparatively mild that it may be dismissed. It is doubtful if the writer would have thought that a charge of working iniquity in the Holy of Holies was a mild one. To anyone who believed that death was preferable to any transgression against the law of God, this supreme sin would hardly be a trivial matter.

Nor is it clear why Mattathias could not be referred to as unmistakably as Nebuchadnezzar and Daniel and others who figure in this book. He could not be referred to by name, since he was of later age than the putative author, but a cipher is usually reserved for persons whom it would be dangerous to refer to openly. To this Torrey replies that to have indicated Mattathias clearly, such as by referring to his five sons instead of the mysterious seven, would have been to fix the interpretation as Mattathias for all time, whereas the intention was to indicate not so much the man himself as what he represented. This evades the issue, since by Torrey's hypothesis this was indicated by the choice of the number of

[1] *Journal of Biblical Literature*, lxiv, 1945, p. 396.
[2] "Apocrypha and Pseudepigrapha", ii, 1913, p. 420.

"sons" rather than by the name Taxo, and the assumed necessity for a cipher[1] is not apparent.

S. Mowinckel has argued[2] that Taxo is the Latin form of the Greek *Taxōn*,[3] which corresponds to the *Meḥōḳēḳ* who figures in the Zadokite Work. There the *Meḥōḳēḳ* is identified with the "searcher of the Law",[4] who is elsewhere identified with the "star",[5] who appears to have been reorganizer of the sect from which the Zadokite Work came. Mowinckel therefore suggests that Taxo was the one "who established the right order within the congregation of the Covenanters", and whom the members of the sect had to obey until the Teacher of Righteousness should return.[6] M. Delcor has raised some objections to this view,[7] which, despite its attractiveness, I am not able to accept. The Zadokite Work was written within forty years of the death of the Teacher of Righteousness, which fell most probably in the second century B.C.[8] It is therefore improbable that at the date when the Assumption of Moses was written its author should have thought of the Messianic age immediately following the death of Taxo, who must almost certainly have died long before the work was composed.[9]

The figure remains completely obscure, therefore. It is

---

[1] *Journal of Biblical Literature*, lxiv, 1945, p. 395.

[2] "Congress Volume. Copenhagen, 1953" (Supplements to *Vetus Testamentum*, i), 1953, pp. 88 ff. Cf. also C. Clemen, in Kautzsch, "Apokryphen und Pseudepigraphen", ii, 1900, p. 326.

[3] G. Kuhn (*Zeitschrift für die alttestamentliche Wissenschaft*, N.F. ii, 1925, p. 125) had earlier pronounced the equation with Greek *Taxōn* improbable. So more recently A. S. van der Woude ("Die messianischen Vorstellungen der Gemeinde von Qumrân", 1957, p. 86), who notes, as Kuhn had earlier done, that we should have expected *tassōn* and not *taxōn*.

[4] Zadokite Work, viii. 5.

[5] Zadokite Work, ix. 8.

[6] *Loc. cit.*, p. 93. It is improbable, indeed, that there is any thought of the return of the Teacher; cf. *Bulletin of the John Rylands Library*, xliv, 1961–2, pp. 125 f., 145 f.

[7] *Revue Biblique*, lxii, 1955, pp. 60 ff.

[8] See above, pp. 87 f.

[9] S. Zeitlin (*Jewish Quarterly Review*, xxxviii, 1947–8, pp. 4 ff.) proposes the view that Taxo is the latinized form of the Greek *Toxon*, which represents the Hebrew *Ḳesheth*, or "Bow". He then identifies Taxo with Rabbi Joshua, who opposed the revolt led by Bar Cochba. This view seems to me to have little probability.

probable that he was an actual person, contemporary with the writer, whom it would have been dangerous to indicate more openly. This suggests that he was a well-known person, and the significance attached to his death would independently suggest this. Yet no contemporary figure in the age when the book is believed to have been written, who would fulfil these conditions, is known. Possibly in the circles for which the book was written exaggerated significance was attached to one who created no ripple on the surface of history.

NOTE D. THE UNITY OF 4 EZRA AND 2 BARUCH

The unity of the Ezra Apocalypse was first challenged by Kabisch,[1] who found five separate works collected together. He has been followed by Charles[2] and Box,[3] who have, however, modified his view in some respects. The five works found by Kabisch are: (1) a Salathiel apocalypse; (2) an Ezra apocalypse; (3) the Eagle Vision; (4) the Son of Man Vision; and (5) an Ezra fragment. These are assigned to various dates, but all falling within the first century A.D., except the Son of Man Vision, which is placed in the first century B.C.

As early as 1895, M. R. James expressed his doubts on the subject of this dissection,[4] and more recently has definitely rejected it.[5] Meanwhile, a whole series of scholars had rejected the view, including Clemen,[6] Lagrange,[7] F. C. Porter,[8]

[1] "Das vierte Buch Esra auf seine Quellen untersucht", 1889. So, too, E. de Faye, "Les apocalypses juives", 1892, pp. 155 ff.

[2] "Critical History of the Doctrine of a Future Life", p. 338.

[3] "The Ezra-Apocalypse", 1912, pp. xxi ff., and in Charles's "Apocrypha and Pseudepigrapha", ii, p. 551. Cf. R. C. Dentan, "The Apocrypha, Bridge of the Testaments", 1954, pp. 93 ff.; F. V. Filson, "Which Books Belong to the Bible?" 1957, pp. 75 f.; B. M. Metzger, "An Introduction to the Apocrypha", 1957, pp. 22 f.

[4] In Bensly and James, "The Fourth Book of Ezra", p. lxxxix.

[5] *Journal of Theological Studies*, xviii, 1917, pp. 167 ff., xix, 1918, pp. 347 ff.; "Lost Apocrypha of the Old Testament", 1920, pp. 79 f.

[6] *Theologische Studien und Kritiken*, lxxi, 1898, pp. 237 ff.

[7] *Revue Biblique*, xiv (N.S. ii), 1905, pp. 486 ff. So, too, L. Vaganay, "Le problème eschatologique dans le iv⁰ livre d'Esdras", 1906, pp. 7 ff.

[8] "The Messages of the Apocalyptical Writers", 1905, p. 336.

Sanday,[1] and Burkitt,[2] and more recently it has been rejected by Violet[3] and Gry.[4] The weight of opinion is therefore strongly against the theory, but its acceptance by Charles and Box means that it figures in the works principally used by the English reader. Oesterley is persuaded by James to eliminate the Salathiel apocalypse, but follows Charles and Box in maintaining the book to be composite.[5] Torrey, however, retains a Salathiel apocalypse, which he dates before A.D. 70, and an Ezra apocalypse in chapter xiv, which he dates in the time of Domitian.[6]

James found some evidence on which to challenge the whole basis of the view at the one point where it claims an objective piece of evidence, viz. the occurrence of the name Salathiel in 2 Esdr. iii. 1: "I, Salathiel, who am also Esdras." He shows that there is evidence to distinguish the Ezra of the Apocalypse from the Ezra of the Book of Ezra of the Hebrew Canon,[7] and concludes: "The Apocalypse of Salathiel, the centre of all the theories of dissection, is a ghost-book: conjured up by Kabisch in 1889, it has hovered about us long enough. I never liked the look of it, and I earnestly hope that it may now be permitted to vanish." [8]

The unity of the Apocalypse of Baruch was also first denied by Kabisch,[9] who is again followed by Charles.[10] Charles

[1] Preface to Box's "Ezra-Apocalypse", pp. 5 ff.

[2] "Jewish and Christian Apocalypses", 1914, pp. 41 f. Cf. also *Proceedings of the British Academy*, xvii, 1931, p. 443.

[3] "Die Apokalypsen des Esra und des Baruch", 1924, pp. xlii ff. So, too, Keulers, "Die eschatologische Lehre des vierten Esrabuches", 1922, pp. 41 ff.

[4] "Les dires prophétiques d'Esdras", i, 1938, pp. xciv ff.

[5] "II Esdras", 1933, p. xv.

[6] "The Apocryphal Literature", 1945, pp. 116 ff.

[7] Cf. *Journal of Theological Studies*, xviii, 1917, p. 168: "The author of 4 Esdras has consciously invented an earlier Ezra, one who never returned to Jerusalem, and was taken up to heaven when his work was finished: impossible, therefore, to be identified with the historical Ezra. But to this creature of his imagination he has transferred one act which was, rather vaguely, attributed to the historical Ezra, namely, the restoration of the Scriptures, which he has transfigured into a miracle."   [8] *Ibid.*, xix, 1918, p. 349.

[9] "Die Quellen der Apokalypse Baruchs", in *Jahrbücher für protestantische Theologie*, xviii, 1892, pp. 66 ff. (The date of this article is commonly given incorrectly as 1891. So Charles, "Apocalypse of Baruch", 1896, p. xxxix; in Hastings' "Dictionary of the Bible", i, 1898, p. 250b; in "Encyclopaedia Biblica", i, 1899, col. 217; in "Apocrypha and Pseudepigrapha", ii, 1913, p.

then places part of the work before the destruction of Jerusalem in A.D. 70, and the final redaction as late as A.D. 130. This dissection is once more rejected by several of the scholars who maintain the unity of 4 Ezra, including Clemen,[1] Lagrange,[2] James,[3] and Violet.[4] Violet believes that the disagreements within the book are due to the fact that the author used various oral or written sources in the preparation of his book, but that it is essentially the compilation of a single hand. Similarly, James says: "I find it impossible to accept the scheme of the dissection of Baruch as set forth by Dr. Charles. In this case, as in that of Esdras, the inability to allow for slight inconsistencies consequent upon the weaving together of disparate strands of apocalyptic tradition has been the snare of over-ingenious critics."[5]

It may be added that Violet would place the composition of the book early in the second century A.D.,[6] while Volz assigns it to a date *circa* A.D. 90.[7]

In general, I share the scepticism with which these dissection hypotheses are viewed. Not alone in the case of these two books, but throughout the apocalyptic literature, there is far too ready a disposition to resort to dissection whenever some minor inconsistency is found. If Charles could hold, as has been noted above, that an author could not have written in Aramaic in the Maccabaean age (when discussing the Ethiopic Enoch), and that an author must have written in

---

480; Oesterley, in Charles's "Apocalypse of Baruch", 1918, p. x n.; Frey, in Pirot's "Supplément", i, 1928, col. 423.)

[10] "The Apocalypse of Baruch", 1896, pp. liii ff.

[1] *Theologische Studien und Kritiken*, lxxi, 1898, pp. 227 ff.

[2] *Revue Biblique*, xiv (N.S. ii), 1905, pp. 501 ff.

[3] *Journal of Theological Studies*, xvi, 1915, p. 405.

[4] "Die Apokalypsen des Esra und des Baruch", 1924, pp. lxxiii f.

[5] *Journal of Theological Studies*, *loc. cit.* Cf. Burkitt ("Jewish and Christian Apocalypses", p. 41): "So far as the Apocalypse of Baruch is concerned, I really do not see why it should be regarded as composite." Cf. Oesterley, Introduction to Charles, "The Apocalypse of Baruch", 1918, p. xii.

[6] *Op. cit.*, p. xci. Cf. Gry, in *Revue Biblique*, xlviii, 1939, pp. 345 ff.

[7] "Die Eschatologie der jüdischen Gemeinde", p. 40. A. M. le Hir ("Études Biblique", i, 1869, pp. 173 ff.) held that the book in its present form dates from A.D. 218, but that it rested on an older Jewish work of the last quarter of the first century A.D.

Aramaic in the Maccabaean age (when discussing the Book of Daniel), it ought not to be held impossible for less scientific writers to be guilty of inconsistency!

NOTE E. THE DURATION OF ANTICHRIST'S REIGN IN THE ASCENSION OF ISAIAH

It has been noted above that Charles believes that part of the Ascension of Isaiah consists of an extract from the lost Testament of Hezekiah. This view rests on the duration assigned to Antichrist's reign in the Ascension of Isaiah, where a period of three years and seven months and twenty-seven days is indicated.

George Cedrenus[1] records that in the Testament of Hezekiah Isaiah says that Antichrist will rule for three years and seven months, which is twelve hundred and ninety days, and after Antichrist is cast into Tartarus Christ will come and there will be a resurrection and general judgement. It is because this so closely resembles some points in one section of the Ascension of Isaiah that it is held to be its source.

It is curious, however, that the three years and seven months are reckoned as twelve hundred and ninety days, reckoning thirty days to the month, whereas in the Ascension of Isaiah the period is a different one. It is defined as three years and seven months and twenty-seven days, which, in our present text, are reckoned to total three hundred and thirty-two days. It is probable that "one thousand" has accidentally fallen out before this,[2] and it has been conjectured that the "thirty-two" is an error for "thirty-five", since, according to the Julian reckoning, the period amounts

---

[1] Cf. Migne, "Patrologia Graeca", cxxi, 1894, col. 152. In the English translation of Beer's article (see above, p. 124 n. 1) given in "The New Schaff–Herzog Encyclopedia of Religious Knowledge", ix, 1911, p. 341a, Cedrenus is twice erroneously said to refer here to a Testament of Ezekiel, where the original German edition has Hezekiah.

[2] J. Vernon Bartlet ("The Apostolic Age", 1900, p. 524) thinks the reference is to the period from the Neronian martyrdoms in A.D. 64 and the death of Nero in A.D. 68, and suggests that the reading of two MSS, 3,032 days, may be a final effort to save the credit of this prophecy.

to thirteen hundred and thirty-five days.[1] Since both reckonings of the Ascension of Isaiah differ from those of the lost Testament of Hezekiah, it is difficult to see how they provide evidence of a common source. Moreover, in the passage from Cedrenus the coming of Christ is placed after the destruction of Beliar, whereas in the Ascension of Isaiah it is placed before it.

So far as the reckoning of the period is concerned, there is no need to look farther than the Book of Daniel to provide the source of both. For in Dan. xii. 11 we find the number twelve hundred and ninety, or three years and seven months of thirty-day months,[2] while in Dan. xii. 12 we have thirteen hundred and thirty-five days, or three years and seven months and twenty-seven days in the Julian Calendar.[3]

The scanty evidence from George Cedrenus about the Testament of Hezekiah can only indicate that it is other than our present Ascension of Isaiah.

NOTE F. THE SOURCE AND UNITY OF THE LITTLE APOCALYPSE OF THE GOSPELS

It is much disputed whether the Little Apocalypse was composed by Mark, or taken over by him as a document already in circulation separately, and whether it expresses ideas which were really given currency by Jesus or but attributed to Him by His followers. It is also disputed whether it is a unity or a combination of at least two separate utterances. These are all questions for the New Testament scholars to settle, and as they scarcely affect our purpose they cannot be fully examined here.[4]

[1] See Charles, "The Ascension of Isaiah", pp. 28, 32 f.
[2] Probably in the Book of Daniel it stood for three and a half years, with an intercalary month in one of the years.
[3] Cf. E. Tisserant, "Ascension d'Isaïe", 1909, pp. 120f.
[4] On this chapter see especially G. R. Beasley-Murray, "Jesus and the Future", 1954, and "Commentary on Mark Thirteen", 1957. V. Taylor ("The Gospel according to St. Mark", 1952, p. 637) holds that Mark or an earlier compiler formed groups of sayings of Jesus into the Apocalyptic discourse, adding editorial phrases and extracts from his sayings source. R. H. Lightfoot ("The Gospel Message of St. Mark", 1950, pp. 48 ff.) notes parallels between

Schmiedel[1] says: "In contents the passage is quite alien from Jesus' teaching as recorded elsewhere, whilst on the other hand it is closely related to other apocalypses. It will, accordingly, not be unsafe to assume that an apocalypse which originally had a separate existence has here been put into the mouth of Jesus and mixed up with utterances that actually came from Him."[2] Similarly, R. H. Charles[3] pronounces quite definitely that this is a Christian adaptation of an originally Jewish work, and that it is not derived from Christ. Burkitt,[4] on the other hand, says: "I regard Mark xiii. 3–37 as a literary composition, the literary composition of the Evangelist. In it he has put together Sayings of Jesus which he had about the future, just as in iv. 2–32 he has put together his store of Galilean Parables." Or again:[5] "I do not think that Mark xiii. 3–37, or the portions of it which are often called the Little Apocalypse, ever had a separate literary existence before incorporation in the Gospel of Mark. Some of the single Sayings may be genuine utterances of Jesus belonging to other occasions, others may be Sayings never really said by Jesus."

That the passage contains utterances of Jesus, though not necessarily all spoken on a single occasion, I see no reason to doubt, though it is probable that there has been some expansion. C. H. Dodd[6] observes that: "A critical analysis

---

Mark xiii and Mark's Passion narrative, and suggests that in the Passion the chapter had its first fulfilment (p. 54).

[1] In Cheyne and Black, "Encyclopaedia Biblica", ii, 1901, col. 1857.

[2] Cf. F. C. Grant, "The Earliest Gospel", 1943, p. 249: "This apocalyptic element is certainly present in the Gospels, and it was present in the Gospel tradition; but it probably came in at a point early in the history of the tradition, and it grew stronger in some circles as time passed."

[3] "Critical History of the Doctrine of a Future Life", p. 384. Cf. W. G. Kümmel, "Die Eschatologie der Evangelien", 1936, pp. 7 f. E. W. Winstanley ("Jesus and the Future", 1913, pp. 205 ff.), while not pronouncing this section unauthentic, refrains from using it as representing Christ's teaching.

[4] "The History of Christianity in the Light of Modern Knowledge", 1929, p. 245.

[5] *Ibid.* Cf. T. W. Manson, "The Teaching of Jesus", p. 260, and contrast what Burkitt had earlier written in "The Gospel History and Its Transmission", 1906, pp. 66 ff.

[6] In Manson's "Companion to the Bible", 1939, p. 374.

of the Gospels suggests that during the formation of the tradition it was just the eschatological elements in it that suffered most expansion and development."

As to the unity of the chapter, several scholars divide it into two sources, of which one dealt with the fall of Jerusalem and the other with the end of the age.[1] It is surprising with what regularity apocalyptic writings are divided out among a variety of authors, and always on the same ground of some inconcinnity of ideas. It seems wiser to recognize that the strictly logical integration of the elements into a whole is not characteristic of apocalyptic, and is not to be sought there. McCown[2] notes that the same logical inconsistency is a feature of Egyptian apocalyptic. "Speaking generally," says Burkitt,[3] "it may be said that the division of Apocalypses into their original conjectured constituents is an extremely delicate task, for it assumes that these anticipations, these dreams of the future, will be self-consistent. A certain degree of consistency we must indeed expect. . . . But his pictures of the future will not always harmonize in detail." "While any one unit of apocalyptic vision," says Wilder,[4] "will form a consistent if sometimes bizarre picture, an apocalyptic writing may include numerous inconsistent separate pictures."

There is, therefore, no need to analyse this chapter to find different hands at work in it, though, as has been said above, it may owe its present form to the Evangelist, who brought together material spoken on more than one occasion. Goguel observes:[5] "The artificial character of the connexion between the announcement of the destruction of the Temple and the eschatological discourse does not prove that of the two sections one must necessarily be non-authentic. They may both be authentic, but they may have been linked together by an editor."

[1] So Charles, *op. cit.*, pp. 379 ff., and very many others. With this contrast F. Busch, "Zum Verständnis der synoptischen Eschatologie", 1938, pp. 38 ff.
[2] *Harvard Theological Review*, xviii, 1925, p. 379.
[3] "Jewish and Christian Apocalypses", p. 40.
[4] "Eschatology and Ethics in the Teaching of Jesus", 1939, p. 15.
[5] "Life of Jesus", Eng. trans., 1933, p. 426.

I find no reason to deny that most of the material of this chapter consists of genuine utterances of Jesus, and if we had these utterances in their original setting the transitions might be less baffling. Even the linking together of the fall of Jerusalem and the end of the age may be due to Him, who expressly disclaimed omniscience on the matter.[1]

NOTE G. THE SECOND ADVENT

It will be seen from what has been written above that I do not regard the belief in the Second Advent as a delusion of primitive Christianity, but as something which is inherent in the fundamental Christian beliefs. I would deprecate all attempts to determine when it is to take place, or to define its manner, but it seems to me eminently reasonable to believe that if the Kingdom of God is ever to be realized on earth Christ will have the manifestly supreme place in it.

Since the first edition of this book was published I have had access to O. Cullmann's little book on "The Return of Christ, according to the New Testament",[2] which presents a closely similar point of view. Here it is argued that while any attempt to date the Second Advent is futile and wrong,[3] the hope of that Advent is integral to New Testament thought. It is not something that can be dropped without affecting anything but itself, but something that is directly related to the message of the Cross and the Resurrection.[4] To Greek thought, with its cyclic conception of Time, it is alien, but to the Hebraic and Christian conception of Time, which is linear, it is closely related. The Kingdom of God is not merely something supra-terrestrial, but something that is to

[1] C. C. Torrey ("Documents of the Primitive Church", 1941, p. 17) says that "no scientific basis exists for supposing Mark xiii to have been expanded by interpolation after it left the hands of the Evangelist, nor for regarding the great discourse as anything else than an original unity. . . . Every portion of this material is needed in its present place; no word of it could be omitted."

[2] "Le retour du Christ, espérance de l'Église, selon le Nouveau Testament", 1943.

[3] "L'essentiel de l'espérance n'est pas le calcul de la date, mais bien plutôt la certitude que Christ viendra dans la gloire achever son œuvre à la fin des temps" (ibid., p. 33; cf. p. 22). [4] Ibid., pp. 19 f.

be realized on earth as the crown and climax of the redemption that stands between Creation and this re-creation of heaven and earth. And therefore Christ will return to earth.[1] Cullmann deprecates any excessive emphasis on the Second Advent, or lifting of it out of relation to the faith and love to which it must be intimately related if it is to accord with the New Testament teaching; but he insists that "to reject this hope is to mutilate the New Testament message of Salvation".[2] Like all Christian belief, it is not merely speculative, but practical. All the details of the imagery of the Book of Revelation are of less moment than the great essence of the hope,[3] which, if rightly understood, and understood as the author of Acts i. 6 ff. understood it, is a powerful motive for world-wide witness.[4]

This view of Cullmann's is in marked contrast to that of T. F. Glasson,[5] who ascribes the rise of the belief in the Second Advent to the Early Church, and eliminates it wholly from the teaching of Jesus. That Glasson is uncritical of what appears to support his thesis has been indicated elsewhere in the present volume. At the same time he is hypercritical of all that stands in its way. Thus, anything in the Gospels which has relation to a Day of Judgement is treated as secondary, while anything that does not appear to envisage a Day of Judgement is accepted without question as genuinely the teaching of Jesus. Glasson does not ask how far we could regard the Gospels as valid evidence for any aspect of the teaching of Jesus, if they are so completely unreliable for all the eschatological teaching attributed to Him, but if his thesis is sound it would seem that it were wiser to profess a complete scepticism as to what He taught and to cease to be interested in the teaching of Jesus.[6]

Glasson accepts Matt. xxvi. 64 as a genuine saying of our Lord's, but argues that it has no relation to the Second

---

[1] Op. cit., p. 18.   [2] Ibid., pp. 12 f.   [3] Ibid., p. 30.

[4] Ibid., p. 34. He adds: "Il ne faut pas questionner sur la date, mais regarder au présent où le Saint-Esprit pousse l'Église à annoncer sans trêve ni cesse l'Évangile du salut."   [5] "The Second Advent", 1945.

[6] Cf. J. Lowe's review of Glasson, in Journal of Theological Studies, xlvii, 1946, pp. 80 ff.

Advent by basing its interpretation on his own interpretation of Dan. vii. 13. This, in its turn, takes quite inadequate account of the context (see above), and is made to rest on 1 En. xiv by the expedient of the uncritical acceptance of Charles's self-inconsistent views on the date and original language of the Book of Daniel and of 1 En. vi–xxxvi. The whole structure stands, therefore, on an insufficient basis, and on a quite arbitrary exegesis.

CHAPTER FOUR

The Enduring Message of Apocalyptic

NOW THAT we have traced something of the history of apocalyptic from its roots that lie far back in the past through the series of apocalyptic writings that span the period from the issue of the Book of Daniel to the writing of the Book of Revelation, it remains for us to look more closely at some of the fundamental ideas that recur in so many of them, and to ask what meaning or message they can have for ages other than their own, and in particular for ours. As a study in the history of ideas, the study of these books may be of fascinating interest. Such a study, however, can make but a limited appeal to men, and unless there is in it all some abiding message, it is idle to expect men to undertake it. The type of student who has always shown intense interest in the apocalypses of the Old and New Testaments has always believed that they were relevant to his own day and generation, in the sense that their prophecies were about to culminate in the events soon to take place. Unless some deeper relevance can be shown, there would seem to be no alternative but to abandon these books to such students, and to advise all who are impatient with such use to continue to ignore them. At the outset of these lectures I proclaimed my conviction that there is a deeper relevance, and that behind them lie profound spiritual principles which are true for every generation. It is my hope that I can justify that conviction.

In our review of the works we have found a recurring idea that history can be divided into a number of periods or ages. Sometimes the number appears as four, and it then corresponds to the great empires that were within the writer's knowledge, which he assumed would be the only such empires history would witness. Sometimes the number is seven, or ten, or twelve, when it seems to correspond to periods of history each with a special inner quality or character, rather than to the series of national empires. In neither case is there anything noteworthy in this itself. For it is undeniable that the world has seen a succession of imperial Powers, and that history can be conveniently divided up into periods in which each has been successively the major Power. It is also undeniable that the *Zeitgeist* of human civilization has varied from age to age, and that history can be viewed from this point of view. In these apocalypses, however, there is more than the recognition that these things have, as a matter of fact, been. There is also the persuasion that they were predetermined, and that the number selected for the periods was one that could not be exceeded. Four world empires, and only four could there be; so many kinds of age and so many only could there be. In this there is nothing of abiding value. For history has rolled on, and new empires have arisen to perplex those interpreters who have believed that the number four was indeed final; and successive ages have continued to unfold new varieties of *Zeitgeist*.

Of more lasting validity, however, is the belief that lies behind all this that God is in control of history. He is not an indifferent spectator of human affairs, but to man He ever says: "Thus far shalt thou go, and no farther." Nothing that is born of man is eternal. His empires rise and seem unshakeably established, only to fall and give rise to others. He may give vent to his spirit, now in this direction and now in that, to impose a character upon his age, but it will run its course and give place to another. But the apocalyptists believed that this was not an aimless and endless futility. Over it all was God, Who was directing it all to—

> "*one far-off divine event,*
> *To which the whole creation moves.*"

They did not believe that God was indifferent to the world He had made; nor did they think He was impotent to take a hand in its course. They would have smiled at the idea so widespread in our day that God is of all beings the most helpless. Few, indeed, would formulate their faith in those words, but many would appear to cherish their substance. For they believe that man is vastly powerful to influence the course of the world by his acts, or to launch ideas that will change the course of history, while God is shut outside the circle of history, a mere spectator, and powerless to intervene. The apocalyptists believed in God, and believed that He had some purpose for the world He had made, and that His power was equal to its achievement. Their faith goes beyond the faith in the divine control of history, indeed. It is a faith in the divine initiative in history for the attainment of its final goal.[1] Such a belief is fundamental to the Christian view of God and the world. For the whole doctrine of the Incarnation proclaims our belief that God was active in human history in the person of Jesus Christ to achieve His great and gracious purpose.

Long before the rise of the apocalyptists, the prophets had proclaimed their belief in the divine control of history, and in the divine initiative in history. Often they spoke as though nations were but puppets in the hands of God to do His will, and frequently they talked of the events of history as the acts of God. This did not mean, however, that they had a purely deterministic view of man or of history. They were able to hold within the unity of a single idea the certainty that men and nations were themselves responsible for their acts, and the certainty that without their knowing it they were serving divine purposes. For the prophets were not troubled with our modern dilemmas. When they declared that Assyria and Babylon were God's instruments to punish Israel, in order to bring her to the sense of her sin against Him who had treated her with such unfailing graciousness, they did not approve of the acts of Assyria and Babylon. They believed

---

[1] T. W. Manson ("Aux Sources de la tradition chrétienne" [Goguel Fest-schrift], 1950, p. 142) observes that though the fact that the "forecasts" of apocalyptic are *vaticinia ex eventu* robs their accuracy of any evidential value for the providential ordering of the universe, it leaves them quite unaffected as evidence for the intensity with which the belief in such providential ordering was held.

that Israel was receiving the just reward of her folly, and that she herself was the final cause of her own suffering. Viewed as God's act, her chastisement was deserved; but viewed as man's act, it carried fresh condemnation on those who executed it. For they who executed the divine will on Israel were not regarded as God's servants, but as arrogant perpetrators of their own evil purposes.[1]

In this there is no inconsistency, and no injustice. Our pseudo-logical minds are inclined to ask how it can be just to condemn those who are believed to be the instruments of God's will. But that is because we fail to see the situation as a whole, and abstract certain elements, to base on them our false conclusions. If men were merely puppets, themselves irresponsible for their acts, it were unjust to offer praise or blame for those acts. But if they are essentially their acts, springing out of the good or evil purposes of their hearts, though also used by the inscrutable wisdom of God to further His purposes, men are rightly praised or blamed for them. The ruthless aggression of Assyria and Babylon was not the act of Powers consecrated to the will of God. It was the expression of their own lust for power. Their harsh treatment of Israel was not the expression of their obedience to the will of God. It was the thing they delighted to do.[2] For when God uses men and nations to perform His will He does not compel them to their course of action, or destroy their freedom. He but uses their action, freely chosen for themselves, to perform His purpose. The divine activity in history

[1] Cf. Isa. x. 5 ff. G. B. Gray ("Critical and Exegetical Commentary on Isaiah", i, 1912, p. 196) comments: "Assyria, who was being used by Yahweh to punish His disobedient people, had arrogantly attributed all its success to its own power, not discerning that it was a mere instrument in Yahweh's hands; therefore it must be destroyed." Later Gray suggests that the condemnation of Assyria is because it exceeds its commission, but I find no suggestion of this in the passage. Such a view is in complete conflict with verse 15, indeed, where Assyria is declared to be as powerless to go beyond the purpose of God as the axe or the saw to go beyond the purpose of the workman who uses them. The passage in no sense contrasts God's commission and Assyria's performance. It but emphasizes that though Assyria is the instrument of God's will, it is in complete ignorance of the fact.

[2] Cf. Isa. x. 7: "Howbeit he meaneth not so, neither doth his heart think so; but it is in his heart to destroy, and to cut off nations not a few."

does not override human freedom. It but uses it to serve the divine will. The event of history can be looked at merely from the human side, and read in terms of moral purpose and the exercise of physical and material forces; or it can be viewed in terms of the divine purpose it serves. "Crucify Him; crucify Him," shouted men whose very words fill us with horror. And yet we, who regard the response to that cry as the climax of human sin, regard it also as God's remedy for sin. We are not inconsistent. And the prophets were not inconsistent.

But we must return from this digression to note that whereas the prophets believed in the divine initiative and control in all history, the apocalyptists seem to reserve it for the great final act of history. I do not think this is quite fair to them, however. Their supreme interest is in the great final act of history, and they wish to set that act, in all its uniqueness, in sharp relief against all the history that has preceded it. I do not think they would have denied the hand of God in all history, for they certainly did not repudiate the teaching of the prophets. But they looked at all the course of human history merely from the human side, as the record of human lust for power and oppression and ruthlessness, until they came to the final *dénouement* of history, which was regarded solely and uniquely as the act of God.

Again, let us remind ourselves that if God is in all history, there are moments of history in which He may be found in special, or unique, degree. It belongs to our Christian faith that He was uniquely in the Incarnation. That Incarnation may be set over against all other divine manifestations in history, yet few of us would deny those other manifestations.

The apocalyptists looked for the unique divine initiative at the end of history, when God would not use human freedom to achieve His purpose in an act which could be regarded from the human side as man's, but when He would Himself act in a way as solely His own as His act in creation had been. To this act there would be no human side, for it would not be the act of a man. Hence, for the apocalyptists to have emphasized the divine hand in all history would have obscured the uniqueness of this expected act of God.

I find nothing inherently unreasonable in this faith of the apocalyptists. Unless we believe in the eternity of human history in our world, we must expect that somehow, some-when, the course of history will come to an end. We can look for it to peter out, or we can look for the world to be snuffed out ignominiously. But if we believe that it is God's world, and that He created it with some purpose, we must find some way of translating the faith of the apocalyptists that that purpose will be achieved. The ending of the round of human struggle and intrigue and strife must see the realization of the divine goal of it all, if goal there has been. And it must appear as God's goal, for His it has been from the beginning. We may not share the apocalyptists' ideas as to how or when this will be. But there seems abiding worth in their faith that God whose hand we may find in all history will supremely reveal Himself in the goal of history, will, indeed, so reveal Himself then that all other revelation of His working in human affairs will pale into insignificance beside it.

Turning to another of the persistent ideas of the apocalyptists, we observe that they looked for the end of the world to be preceded by a time of unprecedented suffering, and by the domination of evil. For the righteous they predicted bitter persecution, and for the world at large widespread disasters, and all the suffering that human tyranny can bring. Even Nature herself would be disturbed, and would bring fresh ills upon men by her unwonted behaviour. Often we have found, in some form or other, the conception of a great monster of evil as the leader or oppressor of the world in this evil age, and the idea that the world is to be handed over to his misrule for the time being. This Antichrist idea we have found in various forms. Sometimes it is a human figure, sometimes a superhuman demon, and sometimes an in-carnate demon. But it is always the embodiment of all that opposes the will of God. In the superhuman sphere there is the conception of fallen angels, whose fall is greater than the fall of man, since they were created for so much higher a destiny, now ranged against God and thwarting His will and corrupting His creation. At their head is Beliar, or Satan, or Mastema, or Azazel, as their leader is variously called, ranging himself against God and rivalling His dignity. In the human sphere, whether regarded as a mere man or as the incarnation of this demonic spirit, we have the figure of a powerful king or ruler, subduing men beneath his evil sway, filled with the sense of his own importance, setting himself up to be equal with God, claiming divine honours, and trampling on the saints. The writer may have Antiochus Epiphanes or Nero in mind, or he may think more vaguely of one who shall incarnate in himself all that is hateful and blasphemous. But the outlines of the figure are fundamentally the same.

Some of the works we have examined were written apparently in times of peace, when the writer could work out in calm detachment his anticipation of the end of things. But more often it would seem that he was living in an evil age, and believed it to be the final fling of evil. He depicted the conditions he saw around him, but in a cosmic setting, viewed not merely as a local affair, but as something of universal significance, and accompanied by supernatural signs as the fitting expression of his sense of its importance. He saw the sufferings through which he was living as the clash, not of men, but of principles, and therefore of spiritual beings, of God and Beliar. Few of us can see our own days, or even our own little affairs, in perspective, and we need not scorn these writers because they had an exaggerated sense of the importance of the events through which they were living. They believed that they were engaged in a final struggle, that they were suffering the last great persecution, and that never before had evil been so evil, and never again could it so raise its head, for its final destruction was nigh.

It is easy for us to see that they were mistaken, and that their prophecies were unfulfilled. That is why other writers re-applied their message to their own day in the successive apocalyptic works. It is also why interpreters all down the years have read a succession of new meanings into their words, to impose the conditions of their own day upon the prophecies. Especially has this been the case in times of trouble and widespread calamity, when men, with an exaggerated perspective of their own day, precisely like that of the apocalyptists, have believed that the prophecies had their own day in mind, and not the day of their authors. For times of evil and of persecution have been renewed again and again in the world, and neither Antiochus nor Nero has proved the last cruel oppressor to have a mouth speaking great things and blasphemies, or to measure himself against the Most High and claim divine honours. Antichrists, of substantially the same pattern, have been numerous, and in our own day there are not wanting those who find that Hitler fits the description. Of his lust for power, his published programme and his whole career alike bear witness; of his persecution of the Church in Germany and Norway, wherever it refuses to hand its soul into his keeping, there is no want of evidence; of his desire to dethrone God and to substitute the German spirit, or its embodiment in himself, as the object of men's worship, his leading agents have left no doubt; of the universal suffering into which he has cast the world, we are all acutely conscious. It is not therefore surprising that to some Hitler appears to be Antichrist, and his name is made to yield the number of the Beast. He is even read into Dan. xi, and found to be the contemptible person to whom the honour of the kingdom had not been given (Dan. xi. 21), who had no regard for the gods of his fathers nor the desire of women (Dan. xi. 37).

Yet where for more than two thousand years a hope has proved illusory, we should beware of embracing it afresh. The writers of these books were mistaken in their hopes of imminent deliverance; their interpreters who believed the consummation was imminent in their day have proved mistaken; and they who bring the same principles and the same hopes afresh to the prophecies will prove equally mistaken.[1]

[1] I have retained these paragraphs unchanged from the first edition. Comment is superfluous.

Beneath the mistaken hopes, however, we can see a sound instinct, and more that is fundamentally true than all that is false. What brings sorrow and disaster to the world is Beliar and his incarnations, and all who suffer persecution because of their loyalty to the will and way of God are doing something of vast significance. Their suffering is something that touches more than their own little lives, and the exaggerated perspective that turns it into something of universal significance is not wholly mistaken. For by their very suffering their little lives are linked to the eternal will and purpose of God. The demonic Beliar stands for a persistent force of evil, not in any one man alone, but behind all evil men, incarnate in them in varying degrees. The human Antichrist stands, alas! for the recurring Antichrists the world has seen. For the upsurge of sin in the human heart is fundamentally the same in all ages, and leads to the same sorts of character. The common sins that are in all our hearts, and all around us, are very much what they were in ancient days. And the rarer forms of sin in the overweening pride and ambition of men who attain power, but who lack humility, are also very much the same in the hearts of those who harbour them. Hence, just as the lustful and the violent of one generation much resemble the lustful and the violent of another, so the Antichrist of one generation resembles the Antichrist of another, for he has the same spirit of Beliar in him.

Does this mean that we accept the dualism of these writers, and conceive of a demonic court set over against God's court? Traditional Christian theology has not shrunk from such dualism, if dualism it really is, for it has taken over Satan as the prince of evil, and Milton's demonic court would have more than satisfied all the apocalyptists. But to-day we are very susceptible about the suggestion of dualism. We are much too philosophical to tolerate such an idea. We must have as our ultimate a unity, and any suggestion of dualism seems to us to threaten the validity of our monotheism. Both philosophically and theologically we are eager to avoid it.

We do not object to a logical correlation of ideas. We

cannot think of one side of a sheet of paper without another, or one end of a finite straight line without another; we cannot think of light that is not the negation of darkness, or of a good that is without its logical opposite evil. When we say that God is good, we mean that in Him is no evil; when we say that He is light, we mean that in Him is no darkness. In that sense the idea of evil is logically involved in the affirmation of the goodness of God. But this is far other than affirming that evil is co-eternal with the goodness of God, or that from all eternity to all eternity it must be embodied in a personal being standing over against God. In that sense neither the apocalyptists nor Christian theologians have been dualists.[1]

But goodness and evil are personal terms. Abstractions have no independent existence. And goodness and evil are not impersonal entities, floating around somewhere in space. They inhere in persons and only in persons. Goodness alone is eternal, for God is good, and He alone exists from eternity. Its logical correlate, evil, came into existence in the first evil being who opposed the will of God,[2] and it continues in evil persons so long as evil persons continue to be. There is here nothing to threaten monotheism, or our philosophic desire for ultimate unity.

Is there no meaning, then, in many of our forms of speech? We talk of an evil spirit coming over a man, or of an evil spirit being in the air. In countless ways we conceive of evil as coming upon a man from without, where there is no direct contact with another evil man. Is it all meaningless, or do we, after all, mean that there is such a thing as impersonal evil, evil in the abstract, in the form of some impersonal influence, floating around us in space?

Here I think we can find some help from the Hebrew conception of corporate personality. The Hebrew never thought of a man as merely an individual. He was also part of a

---

[1] Cf. Volz ("Eschatologie der jüdischen Gemeinde", p. 87): "Dualism is not developed in Judaism, as in Parsism, to a greater sharpness."

[2] This leaves quite open the question whether the first evil being was human or not.

larger whole, consisting not merely of the other contemporary members of the group to which he belonged, but embracing those who had gone before, into the inheritance of whose spirit his generation had come, and those who would come after, who were equally bound up in this living social unity. This corporate unity, transcending as it did his individuality, might function through him, so that he might be its organ and its representative. "The whole group," says Wheeler Robinson,[1] "including its past, present and future members, might function as a single individual through any one of those members conceived as representative of it." Or again, "The group possesses a consciousness which is distributed amongst its individual members and does not exist simply as a figure of speech or as an ideal."[2]

We recognize this in some circumstances. A group of people by some subtle influence that is generated in their association may act in a way that no one of them would alone have chosen. I do not mean that their action may represent a compromise between the extremes that some of them may desire. I mean that their common action may exceed in meanness, or cowardice, or injustice, or cruelty, anything that any of them would alone have been guilty of. Nor is it necessary to collect men together in one place at one time for this subtle influence to operate. We are all in large measure the creatures of our age, reflecting the *Zeitgeist* of our day. And that *Zeitgeist* is not something that exists outside all living individuals, nor merely in a large number of separate individuals. It inheres in the totality of the whole, and is operative in greater or lesser measure in each. It characterizes our day, yet it is not born of our day alone. It is generated in the stream of life that binds the former generations to ours; or rather, it is a continuous living

[1] "Werden und Wesen des alten Testaments" (ed. J. Hempel), 1936, p. 49.
[2] *Ibid.*, p. 52. Cf. A. R. Johnson, "The One and the Many in the Israelite Conception of God", 1942, p. 12: "The social unit or kin-group, however widely conceived, is a single *nephesh* or 'person'—albeit what H. Wheeler Robinson has designated a 'corporate personality'." The same writer later speaks of "an oscillation in the mind of the writer according as he thinks of the social unit in question as an association of individuals or as a corporate personality" (p. 15).

development, and it is as artificial to separate it wholly from the *Zeitgeist* of the past generation as it would be to treat manhood and youth as two quite separate states. In their distinctness they are bound together by the unity of a single life.

I think this may help us to give some meaning to Beliar. Originally Beliar is the personification of the idea of evil, treated then as a superhuman entity, the fount of all evil. But the personification of an idea is not a real person and, as has been said, evil inheres in real persons and in real persons alone. But if we are more than separate individuals, if we are members of a wider whole that embraces the past as well as the present, that gathers into the stream of its life each one of us and that operates through us, then a potent force of evil may be in the stream of that life, derived from individuals, but transcending individuals, though found in varying degrees in individuals. And Beliar may stand for that totality of evil beings, not alone of our day but of all days, maintaining from age to age and from generation to generation the evil which is found in the unceasing stream of evil men, the evil which is incarnated in greater or lesser measure in them all, yet which in the whole is heightened beyond any of its individual manifestations. In all our sin we are not merely ourselves sinning. We are contributing something to the vitality of Beliar, and adding the weight of our evil personality to the force of evil found in that stream that gathers men into itself and operates through them.[1] And in all our sin we are the incarnations of Beliar. And by the

[1] It should be clear that I do not regard Beliar as a figure comparable with God. He is not a single individual, standing outside sinful men as the instigator and fount of their evil, so that it is conceivable that all other evil beings, save Beliar alone, might cease to be. For in their ceasing Beliar would cease. For Beliar is the incarnate evil of the whole in each, functioning through individuals, who are also knit together in a deep unity. I neither accept the hypostatization of an idea which has given us the personal devil of traditional theology, nor the purely individual view of evil to which the rejection of that hypostatization has commonly given rise in modern times. Man has sociality as well as individuality, and receives an inheritance from past and present, and Beliar may serve to remind us of that sociality on its evil side. On its good side that sociality is co-operation with the God who is its source. For there is no good that does not issue from God.

same token, when we endure the persecution of Beliar because of our loyalty to the will of God, we are partakers in the divine enterprise of the battle with Beliar.

The apocalyptists, therefore, with sound instinct unfolded the meaning of tribulation. To the persecuted saints they brought courage and inspiration, and the exhilaration of a sense of mission. To others they declared that their miseries were the inevitable fruit of yielding themselves to the dominion of Beliar. They were miseries that contained no seed of hope, and to endure which no spring of reasoned courage could be found. That is a message which is still relevant to men, whatever the measure of the miseries of the age in which they live. When suffering is widespread, and oppression is rife, it reminds men that Beliar is powerful because they have made him so; and when careless ease abounds it warns men that if they enthrone Beliar by their indifference to the will of God, he will soon manifest the character of his rule and beat them with scorpions. For Antichrist is thrown up by the age that worships Beliar.

It is a common idea that the apocalyptists were pessimists. This is quite untrue. They did not believe in the power of the evil present to generate the longed-for morrow. But that was not because they were pessimists, but because they were realists. They would have had no use for our modern myth of progress, and they certainly would not have accepted the widespread modern idea of moral and spiritual evolution. They believed that evil is evil, and that of itself it could beget nothing but evil. But they did not believe that evil could not give place to good. On the contrary, they affirmed with confidence that the best was yet to be, and that it would be a best surpassing all that the mind of man could conceive. It would not arise of itself, however. It would have its source in God, and when evil gave place to good it would be because God swept evil away and established good. That is not pessimism, but optimism, and it is optimism that is surely grounded, because it is grounded in the heart of God Himself. Their despair of the world that was living without God was coupled with the lively hope that all things work together for good to them that love God.[1] Their spring of hope was in God alone. That was not the mark of their blindness, but of their clear-sightedness. Their faith was more surely based than the shallow faith we have known in our modern age. They knew nothing of the idea that man would steadily work his way upward on the stepping-stones of his sins to the goal of his being. They believed he could rise only by the power of God. Their faith contemplated a more glorious goal for the world than its modern counterpart. But to this we must return in a moment.

Let it be observed that their faith in God was born of their experience of God. The unseen world was very real to them, and they could contemplate its glories as vividly as they could contemplate the sufferings of the seen world around them, because God was so real to them in their experience. That superb faith which they displayed was not the pathetic attachment to an idea. It was faith in the living God, who came to them in the crucible of their affliction. The author of the Book of Daniel expressed it in his story of the three youths in the fire. There they were joined by a fourth, who was like unto a Son of God, a divine Being. That story symbolizes the experience of men who were suffering torments and death, and who were conscious that God was with them in their sufferings, sustaining them not so much with the hopes of a glorious future as with the radiance of His presence. The hope of the glorious future was but the corollary of that presence.[2] So again John is sure of the final triumph of the saints because of his living experience of the Lamb. He sees in his vision not merely the unfolding of events. At the very outset of his book he tells of his vision of Christ in all His glory, and later he sees more than once the glory of the throne of God and the Lamb receiving the adoring praises of angels. To him these visions were

[1] Cf. M. Goguel ("The Life of Jesus", Eng. trans., 1933, p. 312): "In the expectation of the Kingdom of God there is a combination of pessimism and optimism: pessimism because the present world is hopelessly evil, and optimism because this condition is not destined to last for ever."

[2] Cf. E. C. Hoskyns (*Theology*, xiv, 1927, p. 251): "Christianity was primarily a possession, and only consequently and secondarily a hope."

supremely real, and God and Christ were not mere words, but vital realities of his own experience. He did not trust right somehow to win the day; he trusted the God he had known and the Christ whom all heaven adored.

There is here something of abiding value. We may not share the apocalyptists' faith that that glorious future is about to break upon us, or that it will come in one swift moment. But we may share their conviction that it will come only by the power of God, and that it is only for the saints. For so long as evil is in the world, the will of God cannot be perfectly done, and the world of our ideals cannot dawn. So long as evil men are in the world, Beliar is in the world, striving with God for the power and the dominion thereof. And the goal to which we look can come only when Beliar is no more. Moreover, we can be sustained in our faith by our experience of the presence of God. For it is of the essence of our Christian faith that He will share our way with us, and enrich us with His fellowship. We may prove our faith in that experience, that that experience may become the ground of all our faith.

The goal is described as a kingdom. It is unlike all other kingdoms, however, for it is the kingdom of God. Sometimes it is thought of as a kingdom here on earth, sometimes as on a new earth, that is transformed into a fitting home for it, sometimes as in heaven.[1] Sometimes it is thought of as a kingdom of God administered through the saints; sometimes as administered through a great personal leader who in Himself embodies its spirit, by whatever title that leader may be described. Sometimes the kingdom is thought of as a temporary one,[2] be it for four hundred years or for a thousand, while at others it is thought of as one that shall endure so long as time shall last. Sometimes there is no thought of any but those who are living at the time when it is established,

---

[1] Cf., however, N. Messel, "Die Einheitlichkeit der jüdischen Eschatologie", 1915, pp. 72 ff., where it is argued that the kingdom is uniformly thought of as an earthly one.

[2] See a most valuable article by J. W. Bailey (*Journal of Biblical Literature*, liii, 1934, pp. 170 ff.) on "The Temporary Messianic Reign in the Literature of Early Judaism".

while at others there is the thought of the righteous dead who are raised to share its glories. And in the Book of Revelation, as we have seen, many of these apparently alternative ideas are synthesized to yield a temporary millennium, followed by an everlasting kingdom. But through all these varying forms the great thing is that it is to be the kingdom of God.

The apocalyptists were not dreamers of Utopia. The world of which they thought was not built of the unsubstantial stuff of their own ideas. It was the kingdom of God. It was not the place where all the clever things they could think of would be given reality; it was the place where the will of God would be perfectly done.

Here again is something of abiding message, and to no age more relevant than our own. We are continually regaled with plans of reconstruction, and we fondly imagine that if we get ideal schemes for the post-war world we shall be well on the way to the millennium. I do not underestimate the importance of sound schemes. But our ideal schemes may strike against many hard and grim realities and be torn to shreds, if we forget what the apocalyptists have told us. The ideal world is the kingdom of God, and it is for the saints of the Most High. Our schemes of reconstruction are couched almost wholly in economic terms, and we make the capital mistake of supposing that an economic paradise would be the millennium.[1] We forget that "a man's life consisteth not in the abundance of the things which he possesseth" (Luke xii. 15). For years we have worshipped the false gods of comfort, and we plan to worship them more lavishly in future. But if our reconstruction is to carry us to any satisfying goal, it must be first and foremost a spiritual reconstruction. If it merely embodies the ingenuity of man it will contain no seed of enduring hope; but if it embodies the will of God it will contain such seed.

That God has a will for our world is almost axiomatic.

[1] Cf. F. C. Burkitt ("Cambridge Biblical Essays", 1909, pp. 208 f.): "The Gospel is the great protest against the modern view that the really important thing is to be comfortable. . . . If we have learnt the Gospel message, we shall at least escape the error of imagining that universal comfort and the Kingdom of God are synonymous."

For He could hardly have created a world without any plan or purpose for it. And if God has a will for our world it surely far surpasses what any of us can think out for ourselves, and it is worth our while to seek to know it and to establish it. But God cannot reveal His will to men who will not walk in His way, or who will not receive His spirit. For it is only by the illumination of that spirit that His will can be known; and it is only by men who walk in His way that His will can be established. That is why the kingdom of God is only for the saints of the Most High. It is not by any arbitrary or selfish decree that it is so limited, but by an inescapable necessity. So long as there are men who reject the spirit and will of God, so long the opposition to Him continues in the world, and so long His will cannot be perfectly done, and His glorious purpose cannot be perfectly attained. Therefore it is that the measure of our success in our reconstruction must be the measure of our spiritual rebirth, the measure of our walk with God, the measure of our obedience to His will. All our dreams of Utopia must end in disappointment and dis-illusionment unless they recognize that a perfect world must be a world of perfect men, and perfect schemes can be im-plemented only by perfect men. Let us by all means fashion our schemes, but let us at the same time be insistent on the necessity for men who desire their realization to turn to God in humble obedience, to become the saints of the Most High by their eager desire to know and to do His will, and by their utter loyalty to Him.

Yet the apocalyptists did not for a moment imagine that the kingdom of God would be established by human means. It could be established only by a divine act. It would be a stone cut without hands that would become the mountain, or one like unto a Son of Man coming on the clouds of heaven. Sometimes it was thought of as the direct exercise of the power of God, and sometimes as the exercise of that power through the divinely commissioned individual, whether a human Messiah raised up by God, or a superhuman Being sent down from heaven, or the Lamb that was slain coming down to receive His kingdom. To the apocalyptists evil is not so much self-destroyed as destroyed by God. It brings upon its perpetrators and all who support it the widespread ills of the pre-millennial era. But its destruction and abolition can only be God's act. It cannot cure itself, and the deepest tragedy of evil is that through the very ills it brings on men it breeds itself anew. All the bitterness it brings to men cannot turn them from it, for sin is not cleansed by sin.

This view of the tragedy of evil was born of a sound instinct. It was also born of the sense that all sin is fundamentally and primarily sin against God. The triumph over sin must therefore be His. While, therefore, the apocalyptists fostered and stimulated the spirit of loyalty to the will of God in days when that loyalty brought grievous suffering, they did not imagine that that loyalty would itself bring in the kingdom. Nevertheless, they did foster that loyalty. It might seem that their attitude was "Save yourselves from this crooked and untoward generation. You cannot save the world, but by your loyalty you can save yourselves, and inherit the kingdom." Yet that would be quite alien to their thought. For the saints were not saved by their loyalty, but by God, and they inherited the kingdom not because their loyalty gave it to them, but because God bestowed it on them.

This emphasis on the divine initiative might seem calculated to kill all human initiative. For how could one do anything to help bring in the kingdom, if it were wholly God's act? Yet the apocalyptists fostered loyalty, comforted and encouraged the loyal, and believed they were doing the will of God in so doing. For they were not governed by an arid logic. For the paradox of grace is that the act which is wholly God's may yet be wrought through man. When they encouraged loyalty it was not the selfish interest of the loyal that they had in mind. It was just that they believed loyalty was well-pleasing to God, and was serving the purpose of God. When Shadrach, Meshach, and Abed-nego purposed loyalty they did not cheer themselves with the thought of some reward that should be theirs. They desired to be loyal because loyalty was supremely good in itself. They faced the possibility that God might abandon them. Yet would they not abandon Him. The loyal by their loyalty linked themselves to the purpose of God, and while their loyalty could not of itself, merely as their act, bring in the kingdom, it could be given a place by God in His own divine act of deliverance.

Now this again seems to me to be of abiding validity. Few of us look for the sudden sweeping away of human iniquity, and the establishment of the kingdom of God in a moment, and many are inclined to smile at the simplicity of the apocalyptists. I am bound to say their hope seems to me more reasonable than the widespread expectation to-day that a man-made Utopia is just round the corner. Yet after so many centuries of disappointed hopes that the kingdom of God is about to burst upon the world, it is hard for us to cherish that immediate hope. Yet we may still share the inner core of the faith of the apocalyptists. We may believe that the kingdom will come more gradually than they supposed, and yet no less strongly than they we may believe that it must be brought in by God's act. We may find no satisfaction in a merely evolutionary view of the advent of the kingdom, in the sense that forces innate in man will gradually lift him to its establishment. Yet we may cherish the faith that they who commit themselves in loyalty to God, and yield themselves to be the instruments of His purpose, may be given a place in His purpose. If by their service the kingdom is brought a little nearer, it is not because that service springs out of their own hearts, but because it is directed by God. For God Himself is the spring of their thought and act. Or, to put it in New Testament terms, "It is no longer I that live, but Christ liveth in me" (Gal. ii. 20).

We may therefore rightly seek, not alone to give such loyalty ourselves, but to spread its spirit. When William Carey proposed the establishment of a mission to spread the gospel in heathen lands he was rebuked by one of the company, who observed: "When God pleases to convert the heathen, He'll do it without consulting you or me."[1] That

[1] Cf. S. P. Carey, "William Carey", 1923, p. 50. Cf. the parody, caustically

184

was quite other than the spirit of the apocalyptists. The kingdom of God is a world in which the will of God is perfectly done. And whoso desires that world must by the same token seek to further the performance of the will of God in himself and in others. And he who desires a world of men who are consumed with the spirit of loyalty to God must seek to be himself loyal, and to spread the spirit of loyalty.[1] He will give himself no halo, but will confess that he is but an unprofitable servant, who has done no more than his barest duty. And he will not suppose that there is virtue in his service because he has rendered it, but because God willed it and accepted it.

In most of the apocalypses there is a sense of urgency. The time is short, and the kingdom is at hand. Yet a little while and the day of suffering will be over, and the grand day to which all history has been tending will dawn. It is perhaps hard for us to recover that note of urgency, if we believe that the coming of the kingdom is more gradual than apocalyptists supposed. For still to-day the kingdom seems very far off. Yet if our desire for the kingdom of God is intense, our loyalty will be passionate, and our sense of the urgency of the call to spread the spirit of loyalty will not be lacking. For the sense of urgency may be born of our perception of the dire need of the world that is without God; it may also be born of our perception of the great purpose of God. When we have some glimpse of the world that God designs, the world in which His will is perfectly done, and when we perceive that all human sin wounds Him more deeply than it curses man, we cannot be idle spectators. We commit ourselves to His purposes to be their instrument, and rejoice to

---

representing Barthianism, quoted by J. K. Mozley (*Journal of Theological Studies*, xl, 1939, p. 337):

> "*Sit down, O men of God,*
> *His Kingdom He will bring*
> *Whenever it may please His will;*
> *You cannot do a thing!*"

[1] Cf. Dan. xii. 3: "They that turn many to righteousness (shall shine) as the stars for ever and ever."

be used by Him to the utmost degree that He is willing to use us.

Of the dire need of the world to-day we are all conscious, and all the talk of reconstruction is the testimony to the yearning of men for a better order. If we share that yearning, and at the same time realize that only the kingdom of God can satisfy our need, and that it is only for the saints of the Most High, the very intensity of our yearning will bring back the lost sense of urgency in the service of the kingdom.

For we need not share the apocalyptists' belief that evil can be eliminated only when all evil men are destroyed. They looked for the sudden sweeping away of all evil men, who would be consumed by the breath of the mouth of God's Anointed, or overwhelmed in swift calamity poured out upon them by God. But while evil can never of itself give birth to good, God is able to transform evil men into good men. He is able not alone to redeem human society, but to redeem individual men. The apocalyptists were so absorbed in the thought of the redemption of society that they were less concerned with the redemption of the individuals it comprised. And yet their very endeavours to keep alive and deepen and spread the spirit of loyalty shows that they were not wholly without thought for the individual. We may try to keep both individuals and society clearly before our eyes, and desire to be God's instruments for the redemption of both. And we may believe that the furtherance of each side of the divine purpose will advance the other.

It may be that some are so evil that only destruction can be their portion. But we who have experience of the grace of God in our own hearts will not readily cease to testify of the wonder of that grace, and of the glory of the divine will, and will cherish the hope that the grace of God will win them to the acceptance of His will, and will transmute the base metal of the Beliar-possessed personality into the gold of the divinely possessed heart. Redemption is wholly of God. Yet its treasure is not forced on men, but must be freely received.

Nor have we yet noted the enduring ethical and spiritual principles of conduct on which the apocalyptists insisted.

The author of the Book of Daniel, in his stories and in his visions, declared profound and enduring truths. In his story of the youths who refused the King's food that offended their conscience, and thrived on the simple fare to which they reduced themselves, he proclaimed that obedience to the will of God is the way of man's truest welfare. In his story of the three youths who refused to bow down to the King's idol, and who displayed so noble a trust in God and so superb a loyalty to Him, even though He should fail them, and again in his story of Daniel electing to be cast into the den of lions rather than fail to prostrate himself before God, he proclaimed that the supreme duty of man is to obey God, at whatever cost. In the stories all these were delivered from the burning fiery furnace and from the lions, but in real life many, alas, were not delivered. Yet even for them the story of the youths in the fire is not without meaning. For they were not alone delivered from the fire. Before that deliverance they experienced the presence of One like unto a Son of God beside them in the fire. There is an abiding message to men here, that they who suffer for their loyalty to the will of God are not abandoned by God, but are sustained in their very suffering by Him who shares it with them. In the story of Nebuchadnezzar's madness the author proclaimed that they who exalt themselves shall be brought low, and that all the glory of man is subject to the hand of God. In the story of Belshazzar's feast there lies a warning against sacrilege, and an affirmation of the instability of all authority that does not derive from God. And in the visions he declares repeatedly that all that is not of God is doomed to destruction, and every power that elevates itself against God shall be broken.

So we could go on through all the apocalyptic literature to find deep and enduring principles of moral, social, and religious worth set forth openly or implicitly again and again. They are not all on the same level. Some are more nationalistic in their outlook, and some record the destruction of the wicked with an exultation that is not to be commended. Some, like the Book of Jubilees, put the outer rites of the law on a level with the inner principles of godly living, though even there it is to be remembered that the author's veneration of the rites rests on a spiritual principle. It is because God wills them and orders them that they are to be observed, and not because of any virtue they have in themselves. For throughout all their work the apocalyptists proclaim this great principle, that the will of God is the first law for man, and that in doing that will is his highest welfare. A man lives not primarily unto himself, or unto his neighbour, but unto God. He must not count himself to be dear unto himself, but must love God with a love that knows no limits and shrinks from no sacrifice.

And in the great Book of Revelation we find it nobly declared that the material force of man must yield to the power of God, that the martyred saints are not unheeded of the God they serve, and that all that is not of God must perish. Throughout the whole there is an implicit call to loyalty to the Lamb, and the sense that that loyalty is the only enduring good of man. In the letters to the Seven Churches there is an open summons to pure living, to warm zeal in faithful service, and to a loyalty that shall not shrink from any sacrifice. The vision of life and service that John holds before the Church is worthy to inspire the Church of every age, and his sense of the futility of all opposition to the will of God has enduring meaning.

Nor can we forget that it is to the apocalyptists that we owe our hope of the Hereafter. Granted that there had been preparations for that hope in the earlier writings of the Old Testament, and in foreign thought, it is here that we find it developed in Judaism, to be passed on to the Christian Church. It varies in its form in the different works, as we have seen. Sometimes it is thought of as a resurrection of the righteous only; sometimes as a resurrection of the notably righteous, and the notably wicked; and sometimes as a general resurrection of all. Sometimes it is a resurrection to life on earth, and sometimes a resurrection with a transformed body to life on a new earth, and sometimes a resurrection to a purely spiritual bliss in Heaven, or its counterpart of suffering.[1] But through all these forms is the firm assurance of the writers that they who are loyal to the will of God shall not be excluded from the life of the kingdom of God. They shall live, because the abiding God is the spring of their life, and they shall live in ineffable joy because they shall live with God. Whether on earth or in heaven they shall be where God's will alone is done, and therein lies the secret of their joy. "They shall hunger no more," said the angel to John, "neither thirst any more, neither shall the sun light on them nor any heat, for the Lamb which is in the midst of the throne shall feed them and shall lead them unto living fountains of water, and God shall wipe away all tears from their eyes" (Rev. vii. 16 f.).

Finally, we may note that the apocalyptists all look forward to a great Assize at the end of history, when men and nations shall be judged at the bar of God. All must one day render an account of their actions and receive the due recompense of their deeds from the hand of God. This has been taken over into all Christian thought, so that it is found even where there is least interest in apocalyptic. Yet it was in the apocalyptic writings that this idea took root and developed, and from apocalyptic it passed over into Christian thought in general.

Again, there is no uniformity of idea as to precisely when in the scheme of things this Judgement will take place, but there is a deep conviction that because man lives unto God, unto God he must render account. To keep alive this sense that life is charged with responsibility, and that we are responsible unto God, is to render a lasting service to men. In our age the thought of the Judgement has receded far into the background, and there is a widespread idea that what we do with our lives is of little moment. Sometimes we pervert the belief in the love of God into an excuse for ignoring our duty to Him. We set love and justice over against one another, and imagine that a God of love can have no use for justice, and therefore there can be no

[1] Cf. J.-B. Frey, "La vie de l'au-delà dans les conceptions juives au temps de Jésus-Christ", in *Biblica*, xiii, 1932, pp. 129 ff.

Judgement. I cannot but feel that this is to our infinite loss and a foolish delusion.

That God is harsh and vindictive is, of course, unthinkable, but that God is just is one of the most elementary of the prophetic messages of the Old Testament. If the thought of the Last Judgement rested on a sense that God is arbitrary it would be rightly rejected. But it rests on the idea that that Judgement is inevitable, because it is born of an inner necessity. It is not that God decides whom He will admit and whom He will reject from the joys of His kingdom; it is rather that He recognizes who has entered and who has refused to enter His kingdom. For the Judgement that He passes is fundamentally the judgement we have already passed on ourselves. That is why it is an absolute, and an inescapable judgement. He who will not order his life by the will of God cannot belong to the kingdom, not because God will not admit him, but because admission to the kingdom is a matter of the spirit, and he will have none of that spirit. Just because we picture the bliss of the kingdom in physical and material images, we suppose that in the Hereafter all men will desire that bliss, and a loving God will not have the heart to deny them their desire. And we tacitly assume that God will set His seal on what is a purely selfish desire of men. The bliss of the kingdom is the joy of doing the will of God. It is the antithesis of selfish desire. Paul could say, "I would that I were accursed for my brethren's sake" (Rom. ix. 3), and in that utterance he experienced a foretaste of the bliss of the kingdom. When the apocalyptists described the kingdom as a comfortable place they were merely trying to describe the indescribable. But they made it clear that they envisaged the kingdom as a kingdom of God —that is, the divine rule in men's hearts, so that His will and His alone is supreme. They did not suppose that men who do not now realize that to do the will of God is itself the supreme joy of man will realize it hereafter; for the self that stands in the judgement will be the self developed in life. And the judgement is fundamentally that the kind of self a man has elected to be is the kind of self that he must be. "He that is unjust, let him be unjust still; and he which is filthy, let him be filthy still; and he that is righteous, let him be righteous still; and he that is holy, let him be holy still" (Rev. xxii. 11). In this there is nothing arbitrary. It is but the corollary of the love that endowed man with moral freedom to choose for himself the kind of self he would be.

The evil are excluded from the kingdom because they who will not enter cannot be within it. If they have chosen to oppose the will of God, and to reject His influence from their hearts, they can have no place in a world in which His will alone is done. Sometimes they are thought of as suffering eternal torments, but at others they are thought of as destroyed, and ceasing to be. And unless we are to commit ourselves to an eternal dualism, the latter would seem to be inevitable. Only that which is worthy to live, that which is of God, can ultimately live, and if He is to be all and in all, then all that is alien to His will must cease to be.

The apocalyptists were never severely logical, however, and perhaps they may warn us not to think or press one side of truth to its logical ultimate, and exalt it to be the whole of truth. After all, this assumes that men are wholly good or wholly bad. That is an assumption unwarranted by experience. The process of judgement will be more complex than our tidy little minds can realize. It is wiser for us, therefore, here as elsewhere in our study of the apocalyptists, to avoid pressing the details, and to cherish only the great principles that underlie them, and simply to realize that the self that we have elected to be will one day stand revealed to us in the light of the presence of God, and that man's supreme bliss, both in this life and the Hereafter, is in doing God's will. Nothing higher or holier, or more worthy of man that was made in the image of God, can be conceived.

Not wholly irrelevant to our modern world, then, is the study of apocalyptic. If we come to it with literalistic minds it may be a peril to us, but if we read these works in the light of the times from which they issued, and find an abiding message in the deep spiritual principles on which they rest, instead of concentrating on the symbols and dreams in which those principles were dressed, they may have much to say to us. Nevertheless, they do not contain the whole of truth. We have to think not alone of the end of the age, and the manifestation of God's hand in catastrophe, but of other aspects of truth. The apocalyptists said little of God as Father, and we should not have learned from them that the home provides a more fitting setting for our thoughts of Him than the court. That Jesus accepted much of the apocalyptic thought seems to me hardly to be denied. But with it He combined much else.[1] The very idea of the kingdom of God, so deeply embedded in His thought, came from the apocalyptists. But He also said much that is formally inconsistent with their ideas.[2] He spake the Parable of the Leaven, and emphasized the yearning love of God for sinners; and whereas the apocalyptists only looked longingly for the day of deliverance from tribulation and vengeance upon their tormentors, He taught His disciples to pray for their tormentors. In the rich complex of His thought there is much that is non-apocalyptic, and the elements mutually modified one another. His Messiahship was not what men were looking for, because it was compounded with the thought of the Suffering Servant. And similarly His thought of the kingdom of God was modified by association with other ideas, so that there fell from Him all but the spiritual essence

[1] Cf. E. F. Scott ("The Kingdom and the Messiah", 1911, p. 91): "Down even to details the conventional features of the apocalyptic hope appear in His (*i.e.* Christ's) teaching. But while He thus accepted the idea of the kingdom as He found it, He employed it only as a framework for His own original message. The speculative problems on which the thought of Enoch, Baruch, and 4th Esdras is mainly centred have little interest to Him. He refuses to assign a date to the final consummation or to solve any of the riddles concerning the nature of the future life. . . . Adopting though He does the current eschatological ideas, He is at no pains to combine them in a consistent picture."

[2] Cf. E. F. Scott (*Journal of Biblical Literature*, xli, 1922, p. 139): "It may fairly be argued that although Jesus fell in with the apocalyptic outlook his thought was an inward contradiction to it, and that not a few of the difficulties which have been brought to light by the modern enquiry are due to this cause. The two outstanding features of apocalyptic thought are that the Kingdom lies in the future, and that it will come suddenly by the immediate act of God. . . . These fundamental beliefs of apocalyptic were both foreign to the mind of Jesus." This seems to me much to overstate the antithesis. To the apocalyptists the Kingdom lies wholly in the future; but to Jesus it is both in the present and in the future. It is both an experience and a hope.

of the hope of the apocalyptists. He looked less for the over-throw by force from without of the kingdoms of the world than for their transformation from within by the spread of the spirit of willing obedience to the will of God. In all our recognition of our debt to the apocalyptists, therefore, let us not exaggerate our debt, or forget that we see them most in perspective when we see them in the light of Christ's teaching as a whole.

Bibliography

It is impossible to note more than a selection from the enormous literature on the subjects treated. The appended list includes representative writings of the principal varieties of standpoint on all the chief matters discussed. A number of further references to works consulted on special points will be found in the footnotes throughout the book. Books to which I have been unable to get access are marked with an asterisk.

(1) *Historical Background*

E. BARKER, From Alexander to Constantine, 1956, Oxford.

J. VERNON BARTLET, The Apostolic Age, 1900, Edinburgh.

E. R. BEVAN, The House of Seleucus, 2 vols., 1902, London.

—— Jerusalem under the High Priests, 1904, London.

—— A History of Egypt under the Ptolemaic Dynasty, 1927, London.

E. BICKERMANN, Der Gott der Makkabäer, 1937, Berlin.

A. BOUCHÉ-LECLERCQ, Histoire des Lagides, 4 vols., 1903–7, Paris.

—— Histoire des Séleucides, 2 vols., 1913–14, Paris.

Cambridge Ancient History (edited by J. B. Bury, S. A. Cook, F. E. Adcock, M. P. Charlesworth), vols. vi–xi, 1927–36, Cambridge.

H. GRAETZ, Geschichte der Juden, 11 vols. in 13, 1900, Leipzig.

J. MORGENSTERN, "Jerusalem—485 B.C.", in *Hebrew Union College Annual*, xxvii, 1956, pp. 101–79; xxviii, 1957, pp. 15–47; xxxi, 1960, pp. 1–29, Cincinnati.

W. O. E. OESTERLEY, History of Israel, ii, 1932, Oxford.

R. H. PFEIFFER, History of New Testament Times, 1949, New York.

G. RICCIOTTI, Storia d'Israele, ii, 1934, Turin; French trans. by P. Auvray, Histoire d'Israël, ii, 1939, Paris; Eng. trans. by C. della Penta and R. T. A. Murphy, The History of Israel, ii, 1955, Milwaukee.

H. W. ROBINSON, The History of Israel: its Facts and Factors, 1938, London.

H. H. ROWLEY, "Nehemiah's Mission and its Background", in *Bulletin of the John Rylands Library*, xxxvii, 1954–5, pp. 528–61, Manchester.

—— "Hezekiah's Rebellion and Reform", in *Bulletin of the John Rylands Library*, xliv, 1961–2, pp. 395–431, Manchester.

A. SCHLATTER, Geschichte Israels von Alexander dem Grossen bis Hadrian, 3rd ed., 1925, Stuttgart.

E. SCHÜRER, History of the Jewish People in the Time of Jesus Christ, Eng. trans. by J. Macpherson, S. Taylor, and P. Christie, 5 vols., 1890, Edinburgh.

—— Geschichte des jüdischen Volkes, 4th ed., 3 vols., 1901–9, Leipzig.

L. SEINECKE, Geschichte des Volkes Israel, 2 vols., 1876–84, Göttingen.

J. N. SCHOFIELD, The Historical Background of the Bible, 1938, London.

B. STADE, Geschichte des Volkes Israel, 2 vols., 1888–9, Berlin.

J. WELLHAUSEN, Prolegomena to the History of Israel, Eng. trans. by J. S. Black and A. Menzies, 1885, Edinburgh.

(2) *General Works on the Religion and Literature of Judaism in the Period*

W. F. ALBRIGHT, From the Stone Age to Christianity, 1940, Baltimore.

N. BENTWICH, Hellenism, 1919, Philadelphia.

J. BONSIRVEN, Le judaïsme palestinien, 2 vols., 1934, Paris.

—— La Bible apocryphe, 1953, Paris.

W. BOUSSET, Die Religion des Judentums im späthellenis-tischen Zeitalter, 2nd ed., 1906, Berlin; 3rd ed., revised by H. Gressmann, 1926, Tübingen.

G. H. BOX, "The Historical and Religious Backgrounds of the Early Christian Movement", in The Abingdon Bible Commentary, 1921, pp. 839–52, London.

L. H. BROCKINGTON, A Critical Introduction to the Apocrypha, 1961, London.

A. CAUSSE, Les "pauvres" d'Israël, 1922, Strasbourg.

—— Israël et la vision de l'humanité, 1924, Strasbourg.

—— Les dispersés d'Israël, 1929, Paris.

—— Du groupe ethnique à la communauté religieuse, 1938, Paris.

R. H. CHARLES, Religious Development between the Old and the New Testaments, 1914, London.

R. C. DENTAN, The Apocrypha, Bridge of the Testaments, 1954, Greenwich, Conn.

W. EICHRODT, Theologie des Alten Testaments, 3 vols., 1933–9, Leipzig; Eng. trans. of vol. i by J. Baker, Theology of the Old Testament, 1961, London.

O. EISSFELDT, Einleitung in das Alte Testament, unter Einschluss der Apokryphen und Pseudepigraphen, 1934, 2nd ed., 1956, Tübingen.

W. FAIRWEATHER, The Background of the Gospels, 1920, Edinburgh.

F. V. FILSON, Which Books belong to the Bible?, 1957, Philadelphia.

L. FINKELSTEIN, The Pharisees, 2 vols., 1938, Philadelphia.

C. GUIGNEBERT, The Jewish World in the time of Jesus, Eng. trans. by S. H. Hooke, 1939, London.

A. HARNACK, Geschichte der neutestamentlichen Litteratur bis Eusebius, 2 vols., 1893–1904, Leipzig.

A. G. HEBERT, The Throne of David, 1941, London.

R. T. HERFORD, Talmud and Apocrypha, 1933, London.

G. HÖLSCHER, Geschichte der israelitischen und jüdischen Religion, 1922, Giessen.

A. KUENEN, The Religion of Israel, Eng. trans. by A. H. May, 3 vols., 1882–3, London.

M.-J. LAGRANGE, Le judaïsme avant Jésus-Christ, 1931, Paris.

A. LODS, The Prophets and the Rise of Judaism, Eng. trans. by S. H. Hooke, 1937, London.

A. LODS, Histoire de la littérature hébraïque et juive, 1950, Paris.

J. MEINHOLD, Einführung in das Alte Testament, 3rd ed., 1932, Giessen.

B. M. METZGER, An Introduction to the Apocrypha, 1957, New York.

E. MEYER, Entstehung des Judentums, 1896, Halle.

—— Ursprung und Anfänge des Christentums, 3 vols., 1921–3, Stuttgart.

G. F. MOORE, Judaism in the First Centuries of the Christian Era, 3 vols., 1927–30, Cambridge, Mass.

W. O. E. OESTERLEY, The Books of the Apocrypha: their Origin, Teaching and Contents, 3rd imp., 1916, London.

—— An Introduction to the Books of the Apocrypha, 1935, London.

—— The Jews and Judaism during the Greek Period, 1941, London.

—— ed. by, The Age of Transition, 1937, London.

—— and G. H. Box, The Religion and Worship of the Synagogue, 1911, London.

R. H. PFEIFFER, Introduction to the Old Testament, 1941, New York.

H. H. ROWLEY, The Faith of Israel, 1956, London.

D. S. RUSSELL, Between the Testaments, 1960, London.

C. STEUERNAGEL, Lehrbuch der Einleitung in das Alte Testament mit einem Anhang über die Apokryphen und Pseudepigraphen, 1921, Tübingen.

A. WEISER, Introduction to the Old Testament, Eng. trans. by D. M. Barton, 1961, London.

(3) *General Works on Apocalyptic Literature and Eschatology*

H. T. ANDREWS, "The Message of Jewish Apocalyptic for Modern Times", in *The Expositor*, 8th series, xiv, 1917, pp. 58–71, London.

—— "Apocalyptic Literature", in Peake's Commentary on the Bible, 1920, pp. 431–5, London.

W. BALDENSPERGER, Das Selbstbewusstsein Jesu im Lichte

der messianschen Hoffnungen seiner Zeit, 2nd ed., 1892, Strasbourg; 3rd ed., as Die messianisch-apokalyptischen Hoffnungen des Judenthums, 1903, Strasbourg.

M. A. BEEK, Inleiding in de Joodse apocalyptiek van het Ouden Nieuwtestamentisch tijdvak, 1950, Haarlem.

G. BEER, "Pseudepigraphen des Alten Testaments", in Herzog-Hauck, "Realencyclopädie für protestantische Theologie und Kirche", 3rd ed., xvi, 1905, pp. 229–65, Leipzig.

G. R. BERRY, "The Apocalyptic Literature of the Old Testament", in *Journal of Biblical Literature*, lxii, 1943, pp. 9–16, Philadelphia.

J. BLOCH, On the Apocalyptic in Judaism (*Jewish Quarterly Review*, Monograph Series, ii), 1952, Philadelphia.

C. A. BRIGGS, Messianic Prophecy, 1886, Edinburgh.

F. C. BURKITT, Jewish and Christian Apocalypses, 1914, London.

R. H. CHARLES, "Eschatology of the Apocryphal and Apocalyptic Literature", in Hastings' Dictionary of the Bible, i, 1898, pp. 741–9, Edinburgh.

—— "Apocalyptic Literature", in Cheyne and Black's Encyclopaedia Biblica, i, 1899, cols. 213–50, London.

—— "Eschatology", *ibid.*, ii, 1901, cols. 1335–90,

—— A Critical History of the Doctrine of a Future Life, 1913, London.

—— ed. by, The Apocrypha and Pseudepigrapha of the Old Testament, 2 vols., 1913, Oxford.

A. B. DAVIDSON, "Eschatology", in Hastings' Dictionary of the Bible, i, 1898, pp. 734–41, Edinburgh.

W. J. DEANE, Pseudepigrapha, 1891, Edinburgh.

L. DENNEFELD, "Messianisme", in Dictionnaire de Théologie Catholique, x, Part 2, 1929, cols. 1404–1568, Paris.

J. DRUMMOND, The Jewish Messiah, 1877, London.

A. H. EDELKOORT, Die Christus-verwachting in het Oude Testament, 1941, Wageningen.

E. DE FAYE, Les apocalypses juives, 1892, Paris.

W. J. FERRAR, From Daniel to St. John the Divine, 1930, London.

J.-B. FREY, "La Révélation d'après les conceptions juives au temps de Jésus-Christ", in *Revue Biblique*, N.S. xiii, 1916, pp. 472–540, Paris.

—— "Apocalyptique", in Pirot's Supplément au Dictionnaire de la Bible, i, 1928, cols. 326–54, Paris.

—— "Apocryphes de l'Ancien Testament", *ibid.*, cols. 354–459.

—— "Le conflit entre le messianisme de Jésus et le messianisme des juifs de son temps", in *Biblica*, xiv, 1933, pp. 133–49, 269–93, Rome.

O. F. FRITZSCHE, Libri Apocryphi Veteris Testamenti graece, 1871, Leipzig.

S. B. FROST, Old Testament Apocalyptic, its origin and growth, 1952, London.

L. E. FULLER, "The Literature of the Intertestamental Period", in The Abingdon Bible Commentary, 1929, pp. 187–99, London.

—— "Religious Development of the Intertestamental Period", *ibid.*, pp. 200–13.

A. VON GALL, ΒΑΣΙΛΕΙΑ ΤΟΥ ΘΕΟΥ, eine religionsgeschichtliche Studie zur vorkirchlichen Eschatologie, 1926, Heidelberg.

J. GIBLET, "Prophétisme et attente d'un messie prophète dans l'Ancien judaïsme", in L'Attente du Messie (Recherches Bibliques), 1954, pp. 85–130, Paris.

T. F. GLASSON, Greek Influence in Jewish Eschatology, 1961, London.

G. S. GOODSPEED, Israel's Messianic Hope to the Time of Jesus, 1900, New York.

P. GRELOT, "Le Messie dans les Apocryphes de l'Ancien Testament", in La Venue du Messie (Recherches Bibliques, vi), 1962, pp. 19–50, Paris.

H. GRESSMANN, Der Ursprung der israelitischen-jüdischen Eschatologie, 1905, Göttingen.

—— Der Messias, 1929, Göttingen.

—— I. Elbogen, J. Bergmann, etc., Entwicklungsstufen der jüdischen Religion, 1927, Giessen.

H. GUNKEL, Schöpfung und Chaos in Urzeit und Endzeit, 1895, Göttingen.

A. HILGENFELD, Die jüdische Apokalyptik in ihrer geschicht-lichen Entwickelung, 1857, Jena.

—— Messias Judaeorum, 1869, Leipzig.

G. HÖLSCHER, "Problèmes de la littérature apocalyptique juive", in Revue d'Histoire et de Philosophie Religieuses, ix, 1929, pp. 101–14, Strasbourg.

H. M. HUGHES, The Ethics of Jewish Apocryphal Literature, n.d., London.

J. KAUFMANN, "Apokalyptik", in Encyclopaedia Judaica, ii, 1928, cols. 1142–54, Berlin.

E. KAUTZSCH, ed. by, Apokryphen und Pseudepigraphen des Alten Testaments, 2 vols., 1900, Tübingen.

J. KLAUSNER, Ha-ra'yon ham-Meshiḥi be-Yiśrael (= The Messianic Idea in Israel), 1927, Jerusalem.

K. KOHLER, "Eschatology", in Jewish Encyclopedia, v, 1903, pp. 209–18, New York.

E. KÖNIG, Die Messianischen Weissagungen des Alten Testaments, 1923, Stuttgart.

M.-J. LAGRANGE, Le messianisme chez les juifs, 1909, Paris.

J. A. MACCULLOCH, "Eschatology", in Hastings' Encyclo-paedia of Religion and Ethics, v, 1912, pp. 373–91, Edinburgh.

J. E. MCFADYEN, "Israel's Messianic Hope", in the Abingdon Bible Commentary, 1929, pp. 177–86, London.

E. MANGENOT, "Apocalypses apocryphes", in Dictionnaire de Théologie Catholique, i, 1903, cols. 1479–98, Paris.

N. MESSEL, Die Einheitlichkeit der jüdischen Eschatologie (Beihefte zur Zeitschrift für die alttestamentliche Wissen-schaft, Nr. 30), 1915, Giessen.

S. MOWINCKEL, He that Cometh, Eng. trans. by G. W. Ander-son, 1956, Oxford.

W. O. E. OESTERLEY, The Evolution of the Messianic Idea, 1908, London.

—— Immortality and the Unseen World, 1921, London.

O. PLÖGER, Theokratie und Eschatologie, 1959, Neukirchen.

F. C. PORTER, The Messages of the Apocalyptical Writers, 1905, London.

E. RIEHM, Messianic Prophecy, 1891, Edinburgh.

P. RIESSLER, Altjüdischen Schrifttum ausserhalb der Bibel, 1927, Augsburg.

F. SCHWALLY, Das Leben nach dem Tode, 1892, Giessen.

V. H. STANTON, The Jewish and Christian Messiah, 1886, Edinburgh.

E. F. SUTCLIFFE, The Old Testament and the Future Life, 1946, London.

C. C. TORREY, "Apocalypse", in Jewish Encyclopedia, i, 1901, pp. 669–74, New York.

—— The Apocryphal Literature, 1945, New Haven.

B. VAWTER, "Apocalyptic: its relation to Prophecy", in Catholic Biblical Quarterly, xxii, 1960, pp. 33–46, Washington.

P. VOLZ, Jüdische Eschatologie von Daniel bis Akiba, 1903, Tübingen.

—— Die Eschatologie der jüdischen Gemeinde im neutestamentlichen Zeitalter, 1934, Tübingen. (Second edition of preceding work.)

A. C. WELCH, Visions of the End, 1922, London.

J. WELLHAUSEN, "Zur apokalyptischen Literatur", in Skizzen und Vorarbeiten, vi, 1899, pp. 215–49, Berlin.

H. J. WICKS, The Doctrine of God in the Jewish Apocryphal and Apocalyptic Literature, 1915, London.

A. N. WILDER, "The Nature of Jewish Eschatology", in Journal of Biblical Literature, l, 1931, pp. 201–6, New Haven.

(4) *General Works Dealing with New Testament Eschatology*

B. W. BACON, "The Son of Man in the Usage of Jesus", in Journal of Biblical Literature, xli, 1922, pp. 143–82, New Haven.

G. R. BEASLEY-MURRAY, Jesus and the Future, 1954, London.

M. BLACK, "Servant of the Lord and Son of Man", Scottish Journal of Theology, vi, 1953, pp. 1–11, Edinburgh.

R. BULTMANN, Jesus and the Word, Eng. trans. by L. P. Smith and E. Huntress, 1935, London.

F. C. BURKITT, "The Eschatological Idea in the Gospel", in Cambridge Biblical Essays (ed. by H. B. Swete), 1909, pp. 195–213, London.

F. BUSCH, Zum Verständnis der synoptischen Eschatologie: Markus 13 neu untersucht, 1938, Gütersloh.

C. J. CADOUX, The Historic Mission of Jesus, 1941, London.

J. Y. CAMPBELL, "The Kingdom of God Has Come", in *Expository Times*, xlviii, 1936–7, pp. 91–4, Edinburgh.

S. J. CASE, "The Alleged Messianic Consciousness of Jesus", in *Journal of Biblical Literature*, xlvi, 1927, pp. 1–19, New Haven.

K. W. CLARK, "Realized Eschatology", *ibid.*, lix, 1940, pp. 367–83, Philadephia.

C. T. CRAIG, "Realized Eschatology", *ibid.*, lvi, 1937, pp. 17–26, Philadelphia.

J. M. CREED, "The Heavenly Man", in *Journal of Theological Studies*, xxvi, 1925, pp. 113–36, Oxford.

—— "The Kingdom of God Has Come", in *Expository Times*, xlviii, 1936–7, pp. 184 f., Edinburgh.

O. CULLMANN, "La pensée eschatologique d'après un livre récent", in *Revue d'Histoire et de Philosophie Religieuses*, xviii, 1938, pp. 347–55, Strasbourg. (Examination of Holmström, see below.)

—— Le retour de Christ, espérance de l'Eglise, selon le Nouveau Testament, 1943, Neuchâtel.

E. VON DOBSCHÜTZ, The Eschatology of the Gospels, 1910, London.

C. H. DODD, "The This-Worldly Kingdom of God in our Lord's Teaching", in *Theology*, xiv, 1927, pp. 258–60, London.

—— The Parables of the Kingdom, 3rd ed., 1936, London.

—— The Apostolic Preaching and its Developments, 1936, London.

—— "The Kingdom of God Has Come", in *Expository Times*, xlviii, 1936–7, pp. 138–42, Edinburgh.

L. DOUGALL and C. W. EMMET, The Lord of Thought, 1922, London.

P. FIEBIG, Der Menschensohn, 1901, Tübingen.

R. N. FLEW, "Jesus and the Kingdom of God", in *Expository Times*, xlvi, 1934–5, pp. 214–18, Edinburgh.

T. F. GLASSON, The Second Advent, 1945, London.

G. GLOEGE, Das Reich Gottes im Neuen Testament, 1928, Borna-Leipzig.

—— Reich Gottes und Kirche im Neuen Testament (Neutestamentliche Forschungen, 2 Reihe, iv), 1929, Gütersloh.

M. GOGUEL, "La vie et la pensée de Jésus", in *Revue d'Histoire et de Philosophie Religieuses*, v, 1925, pp. 509–39, Strasbourg.

—— The Life of Jesus, Eng. trans. by O. Wyon, 1933, London.

F. C. GRANT, The Earliest Gospel, 1943, New York.

J. HÉRING, Le royaume de Dieu et sa venue d'après Jésus et Saint Paul, 1937, Paris.

—— "Messie juif et messie chrétien", in *Revue d'Histoire et de Philosophie Religieuses*, xviii, 1938, pp. 419–31, Strasbourg.

F. HOLMSTRÖM, Das eschatologische Denken der Gegenwart, German trans. from the Swedish by H. Kruska, 1936, Gütersloh.

H. HOLZINGER, "Zur Menschensohnfrage", in Beiträge zur alttestamentlichen Wissenschaft (Budde Festschrift, Beihefte zur *Zeitschrift für die alttestamentliche Wissenschaft*, Nr. 34), 1920, pp. 102–6, Giessen.

E. C. HOSKYNS, "The Other-Worldly Kingdom of God in the New Testament", in *Theology*, xiv, 1937, pp. 249–55, London.

H. L. JACKSON, The Eschatology of Jesus, 1913, London.

G. KITTEL, "The This-Worldly Kingdom of God in our Lord's Teaching", in *Theology*, xiv, 1927, pp. 260–2, London.

C. H. KRAELING, Anthropos and Son of Man, 1927, New York.

W. G. KÜMMEL, Die Eschatologie der Evangelien (Offprint from Theologische Blätter, 1936, Nr. 9–10), 1936, Leipzig.

H. LIETZMANN, Der Menschensohn, 1896, Leipzig.

R. H. LIGHTFOOT, History and Interpretation in the Gospels, 1935, London.

C. C. MCCOWN, "The Eschatology of Jesus Reconsidered", in *Journal of Religion*, xvi, 1936, pp. 30–46, Chicago.

T. W. MANSON, The Teaching of Jesus, 2nd ed., 1935, Cambridge.

W. MANSON, Christ's View of the Kingdom of God, 1918, London.

S. MATHEWS, The Messianic Hope in the New Testament, 1906, Chicago.

J. MOFFATT, The Theology of the Gospels, 1912, London.

S. MOWINCKEL, "Ophavet til den senjødiske forestilling om Menneskesønnen", in *Norsk Teologisk Tidsskrift*, 1944, pp. 189–244, Oslo.

J. MUNCK, "Discours d'adieu dans le Nouveau Testament", in Aux Sources de la tradition chrétienne (Goguel Festschrift), 1950, pp. 155–70, Neuchâtel and Paris.

R. OTTO, The Kingdom of God and the Son of Man, Eng. trans. by F. V. Filson and Bertram Lee Woolf, 1938, London.

P. PARKER, "The Meaning of 'Son of Man'", in *Journal of Biblical Literature*, lx, 1941, pp. 151–7, Philadelphia.

A. S. PEAKE, "The Messiah and the Son of Man", in The Servant of Yahweh, 1931, pp. 194–237, Manchester (reprinted from *Bulletin of the John Rylands Library*, viii, 1924).

K. L. SCHMIDT, "The Other-Worldly Kingdom of God in our Lord's Teaching", in *Theology*, xiv, 1927, pp. 255–8, London.

—— "Jesus Christus", in Die Religion in Geschichte und Gegenwart (ed. Gunkel and Zscharnack), 2nd ed., iii, 1929, cols. 110–51, Tübingen.

A. SCHWEITZER, The Quest of the Historical Jesus, Eng. trans. by W. Montgomery, 2nd ed., 1922, London.

E. F. SCOTT, The Kingdom and the Messiah, 1911, Edinburgh.

H. B. SHARMAN, Son of Man and the Kingdom of God, 1943, New York.

W. STAERK, Soter, 1933, Gütersloh.

—— Die Erlösererwartung in den östlichen Religionen, 1938, Stuttgart.

E. STAUFFER, New Testament Theology, Eng. trans. by J. Marsh, 1955, London.

C. C. TORREY, Documents of the Primitive Church, 1941, New York.

H. D. WENDLAND, Die Eschatologie des Reiches Gottes bei Jesus, 1931, Gütersloh.

A. N. WILDER, Eschatology and Ethics in the Teaching of Jesus, 1939, New York.

E. W. WINSTANLEY, Jesus and the Future, 1913, Edinburgh.

(5) *Works on Separate Books or on Special Points*

J. G. AALDERS, Gog en Magog en Ezechiël, 1951, Kampen.

F.-M. ABEL, Les Livres des Maccabées (Études Bibliques), 1949, Paris.

E. B. ALLO, Saint Jean: l'Apocalypse (Études Bibliques), 1921, Paris.

—— "Apocalypse", in Pirot's Supplément au Dictionnaire de la Bible, i, 1928, cols. 306–25, Paris.

C. ALEXANDER, ΧΡΗΣΜΟΙ ΣΙΒΥΛΛΙΑΚΟΙ, 2 vols., 1841–56, Paris.

C. P. VAN ANDEL, De Struktuur van de Henoch-Traditie en het Nieuwe Testament, 1955, Utrecht.

R. AUGÉ, Ezequiel (Montserrat Bible), 1955, Montserrat.

P. AUVRAY, Ézéchiel (Bible de Jérusalem), 2nd ed., 1957, Paris.

B. W. BACON, "The Authoress of Revelation—a Conjecture", in *Harvard Theological Review*, xxiii, 1930, pp. 235–50, Cambridge, Mass.

J. W. BAILEY, "The Temporary Messianic Reign in the Literature of Early Judaism", in *Journal of Biblical Literature*, liii, 1934, pp. 170–87, Philadelphia.

W. E. BARNES, "Fresh Light on Maccabaean Times", in *Journal of Theological Studies*, xii, 1911, pp. 301–3, Oxford.

H. N. BATE, Sibylline Oracles, Books III–V, 1918, London.

G. R. BEASLEY-MURRAY, "The Two Messiahs in the Testaments of the Twelve Patriarchs", in *Journal of Theological Studies*, xlviii, 1947, pp. 1–12, Oxford.

—— "The Rise and Fall of the Little Apocalypse Theory", in *Expository Times*, lxiv, 1952–3, pp. 346–9, Edinburgh.

G. R. BEASLEY-MURRAY, A Commentary on Mark Thirteen, 1957, London.

R. L. BENSLY, The Fourth Book of Ezra (Texts and Studies, III, ii), with Introduction by M. R. James, 1895, Cambridge.

A. BENTZEN, Daniel (in O. Eissfeldt's Handbuch zum Alten Testament), 1937, Tübingen.

G. R. BERRY, "The Date of Ezekiel xxxviii. 1–xxxix. 20", in *Journal of Biblical Literature*, xli, 1922, pp. 224–32, New Haven.

A. BERTHOLET, "The pre-Christian Belief in the Resurrection of the Body", in *American Journal of Theology*, xx, 1916, pp. 1–30, Chicago.

A. A. BEVAN, A Short Commentary on Daniel, 1892, Cambridge.

H. BÉVENOT, Die beiden Makkabäerbücher (Bonner Bibel), 1931, Bonn.

E. J. BICKERMAN, "The Date of the Testaments of the Twelve Patriarchs", in *Journal of Biblical Literature*, lxix, 1950, pp. 245–60, Philadelphia.

P. BILLERBECK, "Diese Welt, die Tage des Messias und die zukünftige Welt", Excursus 29 in H. L. Strack and P. Billerbeck, Kommentar zum Neuen Testament, iv, 1928, pp. 799–976, Munich.

—— "Vorzeichen und Berechnung der Tage des Messias", Excursus 30, *ibid.*, pp. 977–1015.

M. BLACK, "The Messiah in the Testament of Levi xviii", in *Expository Times*, lx, 1948–9, pp. 321 f., lxi, 1949–50, pp. 157 f.

J. S. BLACK, *see* W. Fairweather.

J. H. BÖHMER, "Wer ist Gog von Magog?" in *Zeitschrift für wissenschaftliche Theologie*, xl, 1897, pp. 321–55, Leipzig.

—— Reich Gottes und Menschensohn im Buche Daniel, 1899, Leipzig.

—— Der alttestamentliche Unterbau des Reiches Gottes, 1902, Leipzig.

E. BÖKLEN, Die Verwandtschaft der jüdisch-christlichen mit der parsischen Eschatologie, 1902, Göttingen.

F. BOHN, "Die Bedeutung des Buches der Jubiläen", in *Theologische Studien und Kritiken*, lxxiii, 1900, pp. 167–84, Gotha.

G. N. BONWETSCH, Die Bücher der Geheimnisse Henochs (Texte und Untersuchungen, xliv, Heft 2), 1922, Leipzig.

A. VAN DEN BORN, "Le pays du Magog", in *Oudtestamentische Studiën*, x, 1954, pp. 197–201, Leiden.

A. BOUCHÉ-LECLERCQ, "Les oracles sibyllins", in *Revue de l'Histoire des Religions*, vii, 1883, pp. 236–48; viii, 1883, pp. 619–34; ix, 1884, pp. 220–33, Paris.

W. BOUSSET, The Antichrist Legend, Eng. trans. by A. H. Keane, 1896, London.

—— "Antichrist", in Encyclopaedia Biblica, i, 1899, cols. 177–83, London.

—— "The Apocalypse", *ibid.*, i, cols. 194–212.

—— "Die Testamente der Zwölf Patriarchen", in *Zeitschrift für die neutestamentliche Wissenschaft*, i, 1900, pp. 141–75, 187–209, 344–6, Giessen.

—— "Antichrist", in Hastings' Encyclopaedia of Religion and Ethics, i, 1908, pp. 578–81, Edinburgh.

G. H. BOX, The Ezra-Apocalypse, 1912, London.

—— The Apocalypse of Abraham, 1927, London.

—— The Testament of Abraham, 1927, London.

S. G. F. BRANDON, "The Date of the Markan Gospel", in *New Testament Studies*, vii, 1960–1, pp. 126–41, Cambridge.

F.-M. BRAUN, "Les Testaments des XII Patriarches et le problème de leur origine", in *Revue Biblique*, lxvii, 1960, pp. 516–49, Paris.

B. BRINKMANN, "Die Lehre von der Parusie beim hl. Paulus in ihrem Verhältnis zu den Anschauungen des Buches Henoch", in *Biblica*, xiii, 1932, pp. 315–34, 418–34, Rome.

E. BRUSTON, "Ézéchiel", in La Bible du Centenaire, ii, 1947, pp. 594–706, Paris.

C. BRÜTSCH, L'Apocalypse de Jésus-Christ, 3rd ed., 1942, Geneva.

A. BÜCHLER, "Studies in the Book of Jubilees", in *Revue des Études juives*, lxxxii, 1926, pp. 253–74, Paris.

V. BURCH, "The Literary Unity of the Ascensio Isaiae", in *Journal of Theological Studies*, xx, 1919, pp. 17–23, Oxford.

D. BUZY, "Antéchrist", in Pirot's Supplément au Dictionnaire de la Bible, i, 1928, cols. 297–305, Paris.

*G. W. CARTER, Zoroastrianism and Judaism, 1918, Boston.

S. J. CASE, "Gentile Forms of Millennial Hope", in *The Biblical World*, N.S. l, 1917, pp. 67–85, Chicago.

—— The Revelation of John: a Historical Interpretation, 1919, Chicago.

A. CAUSSE, Der Ursprung der jüdischen Lehre von der Auferstehung, 1908, Cahors.

—— "Le mythe de la nouvelle Jérusalem du Deutéro-Esaïe à la IIIᵉ Sibylle", in *Revue d'Histoire et de Philosophie Religieuses*, xviii, 1938, pp. 377–414, Strasbourg.

R. H. CHARLES, The Apocalypse of Baruch, 1896, London.

—— The Assumption of Moses, 1897, London.

—— The Ascension of Isaiah, 1900, London.

—— The Book of Jubilees, 1902, London.

—— "The Testaments of the XII Patriarchs", in Hastings' Dictionary of the Bible, iv, 1902, pp. 721–5, Edinburgh.

—— The Testaments of the Twelve Patriarchs, 1908, London.

—— The Greek Versions of the Testaments of the Twelve Patriarchs, 1908 (reprinted in 1960), Oxford.

—— "The Testaments of the XII Patriarchs in relation to the New Testament", in *The Expositor*, 7th series, vii, 1909, pp. 111–18, London.

—— The Book of Enoch, 2nd ed., 1912, Oxford.

—— The Book of Jubilees, with an Introduction by G. H. Box, 1917, London.

—— The Testaments of the Twelve Patriarchs, with an Introduction by W. O. E. Oesterley, 1917, London.

—— The Apocalypse of Baruch, with an Introduction by W. O. E. Oesterley, 1918, London.

—— The Ascension of Isaiah, with an Introduction by G. H. Box, 1919, London.

R. H. CHARLES, A Critical and Exegetical Commentary on the Revelation of St. John, 2 vols., 1920, Edinburgh.

——Lectures on the Apocalypse, 1922, London.

—— The Book of Enoch, with an Introduction by W. O. E. Oesterley, 1925, London.

—— A Critical and Exegetical Commentary on the Book of Daniel, 1929, Oxford.

—— and A. Cowley, "An Early Source of the Testaments of the Patriarchs", in *Jewish Quarterly Review*, xix, 1906–7, pp. 566–83, London.

——, *see also* W. R. Morfill.

T. K. CHEYNE, "Hezekiah", in Encyclopaedia Biblica, ii, 1901, cols. 2058–60, London.

C. CLEMEN, "Die Zusammensetzung des Buches Henoch, der Apokalypse des Baruch, und des vierten Buches Esra", in *Theologische Studien und Kritiken*, lxxi, 1898, pp. 211–46, Gotha.

G. A. COOKE, Ezekiel (International Critical Commentary), 1936, Edinburgh.

W. COSSMANN, Die Entwicklung der Gerichtsgedanken bei den alttestamentlichen Propheten (Beihefte zur *Zeitschrift für die alttestamentliche Wissenschaft*, Nr. 29), 1915, Giessen.

A. COWLEY, *see* R. H. Charles.

C. E. B. CRANFIELD, "St. Mark 13", in *Scottish Journal of Theology*, vi, 1953, pp. 189–196, 287–303, vii, 1954, pp. 284–303, Edinburgh.

—— The Gospel according to St. Mark (Cambridge Greek Testament Commentary), 1959, Cambridge.

G. DAHL, "Crisis in Ezekiel Research", in Quantulacumque (Kirsopp Lake Festschrift), 1937, pp. 265–84, London.

J. DEAN, The Synoptic Gospels (in The Westminster Version of the Sacred Scriptures), 1938, London.

P. (E.) DHORME, "Les Traditions babyloniennes sur les origines", in *Revue Biblique*, N.S. xvi, 1919, pp. 350–71, Paris.

A. DILLMANN, Das Buch Henoch, 1853, Leipzig.

—— Ascensio Isaiae, aethiopice et latine, 1877, Leipzig.

—— "Pseudepigraphen des Alten Testaments", in J. J. Herzog, Real-encyclopädie für protestantische Theologie und Kirche", 2nd ed., edited by G. L. Plitt, xii, 1883, pp. 341–67, Leipzig.

S. R. DRIVER, The Book of Daniel (Cambridge Bible), 1922, Cambridge.

H. L. ELLISON, "Gog and Magog", in The New Bible Dictionary, ed. by J. D. Douglas, 1962, p. 480, London.

R. EPPEL, Le Piétisme juif dans les Testaments des douze Patriarches, 1930, Paris.

H. EWALD, Abhandlung über Entstehung, Inhalt und Werth der sibyllischen Bücher, 1858, Göttingen.

W. FAIRWEATHER and J. S. Black, The First Book of Maccabees (Cambridge Bible), 1908 ed., Cambridge.

W. J. FERRAR, The Assumption of Moses, 1918, London.

L. FINKELSTEIN, "The Date of the Book of Jubilees", in *Harvard Theological Review*, xxxvi, 1943, pp. 19–24, Cambridge, Mass.

J. FLEMMING and L. R. Radermacher, Das Buch Henoch (Die griechischen Christlichen Schriftsteller der ersten drei Jahrhunderte), 1901, Leipzig.

G. FOHRER, Die Hauptprobleme des Buches Ezechiel, 1952, Berlin.

J.-B. FREY, "La vie de l'au-delà dans les conceptions juives au temps de Jésus-Christ", in *Biblica*, xiii, 1932, pp. 120–68, Rome.

O. VON GEBHARDT, Die Psalmen Salomo's (Texte und Untersuchungen, xiii, Heft 2), 1895, Leipzig.

J. GEFFCKEN, Die Oracula Sibyllina (Die griechischen Christlichen Schriftsteller der ersten drei Jahrhunderte), 1902, Leipzig.

—— Komposition und Entstehungszeit der Oracula Sibyllina (Texte und Untersuchungen, N.F. viii, Heft 1), 1902, Leipzig.

A. GILBY, *see* R. Grosseteste.

P. GRELOT, "Notes sur le Testament araméen de Lévi", in *Revue Biblique*, lxiii, 1956, pp. 391–406, Paris.

—— "La Légende d'Hénoch dans les Apocryphes et dans la Bible, Origine et signification", in *Recherches de Science religieuse*, xlvi, 1958, pp. 5–62, 181–210, Paris.

W. GRONKOWSKI, Le Messianisme d'Ézéchiel, 1930, Paris.

R. GROSSETESTE, The Testament of the Twelve Patriarchs, the sons of Jacob, Translated out of Greek into Latin by Robert Grosthead, sometime Bishop of Lincoln, and now Englished (by A. Gilby), 1716, London.

L. GRY, "Le Roi-Messie dans Hénoch (parties anciennes)", in Le Muséon, N.S. vi, 1905, pp. 129–39, Louvain.

—— Le Messie des Psaumes de Salomon", ibid., vii, 1906, pp. 231–48.

—— "Le messianisme des Paraboles d'Hénoch", ibid., ix, 1908, pp. 318–67.

—— "Quand furent composées les Paraboles d'Hénoch?" ibid., x, 1909, pp. 103–41.

—— "Le messianisme des Paraboles d'Hénoch et la théologie juive contemporaine", ibid., x, 1909, pp. 143–54.

—— *Les Paraboles d'Hénoch et leur messianisme, 1910, Paris.

—— Les dires prophétiques d'Esdras, 2 vols., 1938, Paris.

—— "La date de le fin des temps, selon les révélations ou les calculs du pseudo-Philon et de Baruch", in Revue Biblique, xlviii, 1939, pp. 337–56, Paris.

C. GUTBERLET, Das erste Buch der Machabäer, 1920, Münster i. W.

J. HERRMANN, Ezechiel (Kommentar zum Alten Testament), 1924, Leipzig and Erlangen.

A. J. B. HIGGINS, "Priest and Messiah", in Vetus Testamentum, iii, 1953, pp. 321–36, Leiden.

A. M. LE HIR, Études Bibliques, 2 vols., 1869, Paris.

J. C. K. HOFMANN, "Über die Entstehungszeit des Buches Henoch", in Zeitschrift der deutschen morgenländischen Gesellschaft, vi, 1852, pp. 87–91, Leipzig.

G. HÖLSCHER, "Über die Entstehungszeit der Himmelfahrt Moses", in Zeitschrift für die neutestamentliche Wissenschaft, xvii, 1916, pp. 108–27, 149–58, Giessen.

J. HUBY, Évangile selon Saint Marc, 1938, Paris.

M. R. JAMES, The Testament of Abraham (Texts and Studies II, ii), 1892, Cambridge.

M. R. JAMES, Apocrypha Anecdota (Texts and Studies, II, iii, and V, i), 1892, 1897, Cambridge.

—— "The Apocryphal Ezekiel", in *Journal of Theological Studies*, xv, 1914, pp. 236–43, Oxford.

—— "Notes on Apocrypha: i. Pseudo-Philo and Baruch", *ibid.*, xvi, 1915, pp. 403–5.

—— "Ego Salathiel qui et Esdras", *ibid.*, xviii, 1917, pp. 167–9.

—— "Salathiel qui et Esdras", *ibid.*, xix, 1918, pp. 347–9.

—— Lost Apocrypha of the Old Testament, 1920, London.

——, see also H. E. Ryle.

A. JAUBERT, "La Date de la dernière Cène", in *Revue de l'Histoire des Religions*, cxlvi, 1954, pp. 140–73, Paris.

—— La Date de la Cène, 1957, Paris.

—— "Le Calendrier des Jubilés et les jours liturgiques de la semaine", in *Vetus Testamentum*, vii, 1957, pp. 35–61, Leiden.

A. R. JOHNSON, Sacral Kingship in Ancient Israel, 1955, Cardiff.

M. DE JONGE, The Testaments of the Twelve Patriarchs, 1953, Assen.

—— "Christian Influence in the Testaments of the Twelve Patriarchs", in *Novum Testamentum*, iv, 1960, pp. 182–235, Leiden.

—— "Once More: Christian Influence in the Testaments of the twelve Patriarchs", *ibid.*, v, 1961–2, pp. 311–19.

R. KABISCH, Das Vierte Buch Esra und seine Quellen untersucht, 1889, Göttingen.

—— "Die Quellen der Apokalypse Baruchs", in *Jahrbücher für protestantische Theologie*, xviii, 1892, pp. 66–107, Braunschweig.

A. S. KAMINETSKY, "'Aliyyath Mosheh" (= The Assumption of Moses) in *Hash-Shiloaḥ*, xv, 1905, pp. 38–50, Cracow.

A. S. KAPELRUD, Joel Studies, 1948, Uppsala.

C. KAPLAN, "Angels in the Book of Enoch", in *Anglican Theological Review*, xii, 1929–30, pp. 423–37, Evanston, Illinois.

—— "The Pharisaic Character and the Date of the Book of Enoch", *ibid.*, xii, 1929–30, pp. 531–7.

C. F. KEIL, Commentar über die Bücher der Makkabäer, 1875, Leipzig.

J. KEULERS, Die eschatologische Lehre des vierten Esrabuches (Biblische Studien, xx, Heft 2–3), 1922, Freiburg.

M. KIDDLE, The Revelation of St. John, 1940, London.

G. KITTEL, "Jesu Worte über sein Sterben", in Deutsche Theologie, viii, 1936, pp. 166–89, Göttingen.

K. KOHLER, "The Apocalypse of Abraham and its Kindred", in Jewish Quarterly Review, vii, 1894–5, pp. 581–606, London.

—— "Dositheus, The Samaritan Heresiarch, and his relations to Jewish and Christian Doctrines and Sects", in American Journal of Theology, xv, 1911, pp. 405–35, Chicago.

—— "The Essenes and the Apocalyptic Literature", in Jewish Quarterly Review, N.S. xi, 1920–1, pp. 145–68, Philadelphia.

C. KUHL, "Zum Stand der Hesekiel-Forschung", in Theologische Rundschau, N.F. xxiv, 1956–7, pp. 1–53, Tübingen.

G. KUHN, "Zur Assumptio Mosis", in Zeitschrift für die alttestamentliche Wissenschaft, N.F. ii, 1925, pp. 124–9, Giessen.

P. DE LAGARDE, Gesammelte Abhandlungen, 1896, Leipzig.

M.-J. LAGRANGE, "Notes sur le messianisme au temps de Jésus", in Revue Biblique, N.S. ii, 1905, pp. 481–514, Paris.

—— Review of R. H. Charles (ed.), The Apocrypha and Pseudepigrapha of the Old Testament, in Revue Biblique, N.S. xi, 1914, pp. 131–6, Paris.

—— Évangile selon S. Marc (Études Bibliques), rev. ed., 1947, Paris.

K. LAKE, "The Date of the Slavonic Enoch", in Harvard Theological Review, xvi, 1923, pp. 397 f., Cambridge, Mass.

E. LANGTON, Good and Evil Spirits, 1942, London.

C. LATTEY, "The Messianic Expectation in 'The Assumption of Moses' ", in The Catholic Biblical Quarterly, 1942, pp.

11–21, Washington. (I have had access only to an off-print of this paper.)

R. LAURENCE, The Book of Enoch the Prophet, 3rd ed., 1838, Oxford.

R. H. LIGHTFOOT, The Gospel Message of St. Mark, 1950, Oxford.

J. LINDBLOM, Die Jesaja Apokalypse (Jes. 24–27), 1938, Lund.

R. A. LIPSIUS, "Apocryphal Book of Enoch", in Smith and Wace's Dictionary of Christian Biography, ii, 1880, pp. 124–8, London.

E. LITTMANN, "Enoch, Books of", in Jewish Encyclopedia, v, 1903, pp. 179–82, New York and London.

—— "Isaiah, Ascension of", in Jewish Encyclopedia, vi, 1907, pp. 642 f., New York and London.

A. LODS, "La chute des anges", in Revue d'Histoire et de Philosophie Religieuses, vii, 1927, pp. 295–315, Strasbourg.

—— De quelques récits de voyage au pays des morts, 1940, Macon.

W. F. LOFTHOUSE, Ezekiel (Century Bible), 1907, Edinburgh.

E. LOHMEYER, Die Offenbarung des Johannes (Handbuch zum neuen Testament iv. 2) 1926, Tübingen.

A. LOISY, L'apocalypse de Jean, 1923, Paris.

—— L'Évangile selon Marc, 1912, Paris.

J. LOWE, Review of T. F. Glasson, The Second Advent, in Journal of Theological Studies, xlvii, 1946, pp. 80–4, Oxford.

C. C. MCCOWN, "Hebrew and Egyptian Apocalyptic Literature", in Harvard Theological Review, xviii, 1925, pp. 357–411, Cambridge, Mass.

J. E. MCFADYEN, "Ezekiel", in Peake's Commentary, 1919, pp. 501–21, London.

T. W. MANSON, "Miscellanea apocalpytica III", in Journal of Theological Studies, xlviii, 1947, pp. 59–61, Oxford.

—— "The Son of Man in Daniel, Enoch and the Gospels", in Bulletin of the John Rylands Library, xxxii, 1949–50, pp. 171–93, Manchester.

—— "Some Reflexions on Apocalyptic", in Aux Sources de

la tradition chrétienne (Goguel Festschrift), 1950, pp. 139–45, Neuchâtel and Paris.

W. MANSON, Jesus the Messiah, 1943, London.

F. MARTIN, Le livre d'Hénoch, 1906, Paris.

—— "Le livre des Jubilés", in *Revue Biblique*, N.S. viii, 1911, pp. 321–44, 502–33, Paris.

A. MERX, Die Prophetie des Joel und ihre Ausleger von den ältesten Zeiten bis zu den Reformatoren, 1879, Halle.

N. MESSEL, "Über die textkritisch begründete Ausscheidung vermeintlicher christlicher Interpolationen in der zwölf Patriarchen", in Abhandlungen zur semitischen Religionskunde und Sprachwissenschaft (Baudissin Festschrift), 1918, pp. 355–74, Giessen.

—— Der Menschensohn in der Bilderreden des Henoch (Beihefte zur *Zeitschrift für die alttestamentliche Wissenschaft*, Nr. 35), 1922, Giessen.

—— Ezechielfragen, 1945, Oslo.

J. H. MICHAEL, "Why don't we Preach the Apocalypse?", in *Expository Times*, xlix, 1937–8, pp. 438–41, Edinburgh.

J. T. MILIK, Review of M. de Jonge, The Testaments of the Twelve Patriarchs, in *Revue Biblique*, lxii, 1955, pp. 297 f., Paris.

—— "Le Testament de Lévi en araméen", in *Revue Biblique*, lxii, 1955, pp. 398–406, Paris.

L. H. MILLS, Avesta Eschatology compared with the Books of Daniel and Revelation, 1908, Chicago.

E. MIREAUX, La Reine Bérénice, 1951, Paris.

J. A. MONTGOMERY, Critical and Exegetical Commentary on the Book of Daniel, 1927, Edinburgh.

W. R. MORFILL and R. H. Charles, The Book of the Secrets of Enoch, 1896, Oxford.

J. MORGENSTERN, "The Calendar of the Book of Jubilees, its Origin and its Character", in *Vetus Testamentum*, v, 1955, pp. 34–76, Leiden.

S. MOWINCKEL, "Henokskikkelsen i senjødisk apokalyptikk", in *Norsk Teologisk Tidsskrift*, 1940, pp. 206–36, Oslo.

—— "The Hebrew Equivalent of Taxo in Ass. Mos. ix", in

Congress Volume, Copenhagen 1953 (Supplement to *Vetus Testamentum*, i), 1953, pp. 88–96, Leiden.

J. K. MOZLEY, "Eschatology and Ethics", in *Journal of Theological Studies*, xl, 1939, pp. 337–45, Oxford.

J. MUILENBURG, "The Son of Man in Daniel and the Ethiopic Apocalypse of Enoch", in *Journal of Biblical Literature*, lxxix, 1960, pp. 197–209, Philadelphia.

J. L. MYRES, "Gog and the Danger from the North in Ezekiel", in *Palestine Exploration Fund Quarterly Statement*, 1932, pp. 213–19, London.

B. NOACK, "Er Essæerne omtalt i De sibyllinske Orakler?", in *Dansk Teologisk Tidsskrift*, xxv, 1962, pp. 176–89, Copenhagen.

J. O'DELL, "The Religious Background of the Psalms of Solomon", in *Revue de Qumran*, iii, 1961, pp. 241–57, Paris.

W. O. E. OESTERLEY, II Esdras (Westminster Commentaries), 1933, London.

J. OMAN, "The Abiding Significance of Apocalyptic", in In Spirit and in Truth (ed. by G. A. Yates), 1934, pp. 276–93, London.

C. VON ORELLI, Das Buch Ezechiel (Kurzgefasster Kommentar zu den heiligen Schriften Alten und Neuen Testaments), 1888, Nördlingen; 2nd ed., 1896, Munich.

A. S. PEAKE, "The Roots of Hebrew Prophecy and Jewish Apocalyptic", in The Servant of Yahweh, 1931, pp. 75–110, Manchester (reprinted from *Bulletin of the John Rylands Library*, vii, 1923).

A. PIGANIOL, "Observations sur la date de l'apocalypse synoptique", in *Revue d'Histoire et de Philosophie Religieuses*, iv, 1924, pp. 245–9, Strasbourg.

C. V. PILCHER, The Hereafter in Jewish and Christian Thought, 1940, London.

A. PLUMMER, "The Relation of the Testaments of the Twelve Patriarchs to the Books of the New Testament", in *The Expositor*, 7th series, vi, 1908, pp. 480–91, London.

F. C. PORTER, "The Book of Revelation", in Hastings' Dictionary of the Bible, iv, 1902, pp. 239–66, Edinburgh.

J. R. PORTER, "The Messiah in the Testament of Levi xviii", in *Expository Times*, lxi, 1949–50, pp. 90 f.

E. J. PRICE, "Jewish Apocalyptic and the Mysteries", in *Hibbert Journal*, xviii, 1919–20, pp. 95–112, London.

L. R. RADERMACHER, *see* J. Flemming.

B. RIGAUX, L'Antéchrist et l'opposition au royaume messianique dans l'Ancien et le Nouveau Testament, 1932, Gembloux.

H. W. ROBINSON, "The Old Testament Approach to Life after Death", in *The Congregational Quarterly*, iii, 1925, pp. 138–51, London.

J. ARMITAGE ROBINSON, "Isaiah, Ascension of", in Hastings' Dictionary of the Bible, ii, 1899, pp. 499–501, Edinburgh.

H. H. ROWLEY, "The Interpretation and Date of Sibylline Oracles III. 388–400", in *Zeitschrift für die alttestamentliche Wissenschaft*, N. F. iii, 1926, pp. 324–7, Giessen.

—— "The Bilingual Problem of Daniel", in *Zeitschrift für die alttestamentliche Wissenschaft*, N. F. ix, 1932, pp. 256–68, Giessen.

—— Darius the Mede and the Four World Empires in the Book of Daniel, 1935 (reprinted 1959), Cardiff.

—— "Some Problems in the Book of Daniel", in *Expository Times*, xlvii, 1935–6, pp. 216–20, Edinburgh.

—— "The figure of 'Taxo' in the Assumption of Moses", in *Journal of Biblical Literature*, lxiv, 1945, pp. 141–4, Philadelphia.

—— "Criteria for the Dating of Jubilees", in *Jewish Quarterly Review*, xxxvi, 1945–6, pp. 184–7, Philadelphia.

—— "The Prophet Jeremiah and the Book of Deuteronomy", in Studies in Old Testament Prophecy (T. H. Robinson Festschrift), 1950, pp. 157–74, Edinburgh.

—— "The Unity of the Book of Daniel", in *Hebrew Union College Annual*, xxiii, Part 1, 1951, pp. 233–73, Cincinnati, and in The Servant of the Lord, 1952, pp. 237–68, London.

—— The Servant of the Lord and other Essays, 1952, London.

H. H. ROWLEY, "Menelaus and the Abomination of Desolation", in Studia Orientalia Ioanni Pedersen dicata, 1953, pp. 303–15, Copenhagen.

—— review of M. Testuz, Les Idées religieuses du livre des Jubilés, in Theologische Literaturzeitung, lxxxvi, 1961, cols. 423–5, Leipzig.

—— "The Early Prophecies of Jeremiah in their Setting" in Bulletin of the John Rylands Library, xliv, 1962–3, pp. 198–234, Manchester.

W. RUDOLPH, Jesaja 24–27 (Beiträge zur Wissenschaft vom Alten und Neuen Testament IV. 10), 1933, Stuttgart.

H. E. RYLE and M. R. James, ΨΑΛΜΟΙ ΣΟΛΟΜΩΝΤΟΣ: Psalms of the Pharisees, commonly called the Psalms of Solomon, 1891, Cambridge.

J. SCHEFTELOWITZ, Die altpersischen Religion und das Judentum, 1920, Giessen.

N. SCHMIDT, "The Son of Man in the Book of Daniel", in Journal of Biblical Literature, xix, 1900, pp. 22–8, Boston.

—— "Scythians", in Encyclopaedia Biblica, iv, 1907, cols. 4330–9, London.

—— "The Two Rescensions of Slavonic Enoch", in Journal of the American Oriental Society, xli, 1921, pp. 307–12, New Haven.

—— "The Origin of Jewish Eschatology", in Journal of Biblical Literature, xli, 1922, pp. 102–14, New Haven.

—— "Recent Study of the term, Son of Man", ibid., xlv, 1926, pp. 326–49, New Haven.

D. SCHOTZ, Erstes und zweites Buch der Makkabäer (Echter Bibel), 1948, Würzburg.

K. SCHUBERT, "Die Entwicklung der Auferstehungslehre von der nachexilischen bis zur frührabbinischen Zeit", in Biblische Zeitschrift, N.F. vi, 1962, pp. 177–214, Paderborn.

M. SCHUMPP, Das Buch Ezechiel (Herders Bibelkommentar), 1942, Freiburg im Breisgau.

E. F. SCOTT, "The Place of Apocalyptical Conceptions in the Mind of Jesus", in Journal of Biblical Literature, xli, 1922, pp. 137–42, New Haven.

E. F. SCOTT The Book of Revelation, 4th ed., 1941, London.

R. SINKER, "Testamenta XII Patriarcharum", in Smith and Wace, Dictionary of Christian Biography, iv, 1887, pp. 865–74, London.

E. SJÖBERG, Der Menschensohn im äthiopischen Henochbuch, 1946, Lund.

C. R. SMITH, "The Three 'Woes' of the Apocalypse", in *The London Quarterly and Holborn Review*, January 1942, pp. 16–33, London.

H. F. D. SPARKS, Review of M. de Jonge, Testaments of the Twelve Patriarchs, in *Journal of Theological Studies*, N.S. vi, 1955, pp. 287–90, Oxford.

G. T. STOKES, "Isaiah, Ascension of", in Smith and Wace, Dictionary of Christian Biography, iii, 1882, pp. 295–301, London.

V. TAYLOR, The Gospel according to St. Mark, 1952, London.

M. TESTUZ, Les Idées religieuses du livre des Jubilés, 1960, Geneva and Paris.

D. WINTON THOMAS (ed. by), Documents from Old Testament Times, 1958, Edinburgh.

J. P. THORNDIKE, "The Apocalypse of Weeks and the Qumran Sect", in *Revue de Qumran*, iii, 1961, pp. 163–184, Paris.

E. TISSERANT, Ascension d'Isaïe, 1909, Paris.

C. C. TORREY, Pseudo-Ezekiel and the Original Prophecy, 1931, New Haven.

—— "Notes on the Greek Texts of Enoch", in *Journal of the American Oriental Society*, lxii, 1942, pp. 52–60, Baltimore.

—— " 'Taxo' in the Assumption of Moses", in *Journal of Biblical Literature*, lxii, 1943, pp. 1–7, Philadelphia.

—— " 'Taxo' Once More", *ibid.*, lxiv, 1945, pp. 395–7.

—— "The Messiah Son of Ephraim", in *Journal of Biblical Literature*, lxvi, 1947, pp. 253–77, Philadelphia.

C. H. TOY, The Book of the Prophet Ezekiel (Sacred Books of the Old Testament), 1899, Leipzig.

—— "Ezekiel", in Encyclopaedia Biblica, ii, 1901, cols. 1456–72, London.

L. VAGANAY, Le problème eschatologique dans le iv⁰ livre d'Esdras, 1906, Paris.

A. VAILLANT, Le livre des Secrets d'Hénoch, 1952, Paris.

B. VIOLET, Die Esra-Apokalypse (Die griechischen Christlichen Schriftsteller der ersten drei Jahrhunderte), 1910, Leipzig.

—— Die Apokalypsen des Esra und des Baruch (Die gr. Chr. Schriftst.), 1924, Leipzig.

J. VITEAU, Les Psaumes de Salomon, 1911, Paris.

D. VÖLTER, Die Menschensohn-Frage neu untersucht, 1916, Leiden.

J. M. VORSTMAN, Disquisitio de Testamentorum XII Patriarcharum origine et pretio, 1857, Rotterdam.

D. H. WALLACE, "The Semitic Origin of the Assumption of Moses", in *Theologische Zeitschrift*, xi, 1955, pp. 321–8, Basel.

A. C. WELCH, "A Zealot Pamphlet", in *The Expositor*, 8th series, xxv, 1923, pp. 273–87, London.

H. WINCKLER, Altorientalische Forschungen, 2 series, 1893–1900, Leipzig.

S. ZEITLIN, "The Book of Jubilees, its Character and Significance", in *Jewish Quarterly Review*, xxx, 1939–40, pp. 1–31, Philadelphia.

—— "The Book of Jubilees", *ibid.*, xxxv, 1944–5, pp. 12–16.

—— "Criteria for the Dating of Jubilees", *ibid.*, xxxvi, 1945–6, pp. 187–9.

—— "The Assumption of Moses and the Revolt of Bar Kokba", in *Jewish Quarterly Review*, xxxviii, 1947–8, pp. 1–45, Philadelphia.

F. ZIMMERMANN, "The Bilingual Character of 1 Enoch", in *Journal of Biblical Literature*, lx, 1941, pp. 159–72, Philadelphia.

(6) *The Qumran Scrolls and the Zadokite Work*

J. M. ALLEGRO, "Further Messianic References in Qumran Literature", in *Journal of Biblical Literature*, lxxv, 1956, pp. 174–87, Philadelphia.

—— The Dead Sea Scrolls, rev. ed., 1958, Harmondsworth.

N. AVIGAD and Y. Yadin, A Genesis Apocryphon, 1956, Jerusalem.

M. BAILLET, "Fragments araméens de Qumrân 2: Description de la Jérusalem Nouvelle", in *Revue Biblique*, lxii, 1955, pp. 222–45, Paris.

—— in "Le Travail d'édition des fragments manuscrits de Qumrân", *ibid.*, lxiii, 1956, pp. 54 f., Paris.

——, J. T. Milik, and R. de Vaux, Les "petites grottes" de Qumran (Discoveries in the Judaean Desert, iii), 1962, Oxford.

M. BARDTKE, Die Handschriftenfunde am Toten Meer, 1952, Berlin.

D. BARTHÉLEMY, "Notes en marge de publications récentes sur les manuscrits de Qumran", in *Revue Biblique*, lix, 1952, pp. 186–218, Paris.

—— and J. T. Milik, Qumran Cave I (Discoveries in the Judaean Desert, i), 1955, Oxford.

P. BENOIT, "Qumrân et le Nouveau Testament", in *New Testament Studies*, vii, 1960–1, pp. 276–96, Cambridge.

A. BERTHOLET, "Zur Datierung der Damaskus-Schrift", in Beiträge zur alttestamentlichen Wissenschaft (Budde Festschrift, Beihefte zur *Zeitschrift für die alttestamentliche Wissenschaft*, Nr. 34), 1920, pp. 31–7, Giessen.

M. BLACK, "Theological Conceptions in the Dead Sea Scrolls", in *Svensk exegetisk Årsbok*, xviii–xix, 1955, pp. 72–97, Lund.

—— The Scrolls and Christian Origins, 1961, Edinburgh.

W. H. BROWNLEE, "John the Baptist in the New Light of Ancient Scrolls", in K. Stendahl (ed.), The Scrolls and the New Testament, 1958, London.

F. F. BRUCE, Second Thoughts on the Dead Sea Scrolls, 2nd ed., 1961, London.

A. BÜCHLER, "Schechter's Jewish Sectaries", in *Jewish Quarterly Review*, N.S. iii, 1912–13, pp. 429–95, Philadelphia.

C. BURCHARD, Bibliographie zu den Handschriften vom Toten Meer, 1952, Berlin.

M. BURROWS, The Dead Sea Scrolls of St. Mark's Monastery, i, 1950; ii, 2. 1951, New Haven.

M. BURROWS, The Dead Sea Scrolls, 1955, New York.

—— More Light on the Dead Sea Scrolls, 1958, New York.

J. CARMIGNAC, "Les Rapports entre l'Ecclésiastique et Qumran", in *Revue de Qumran*, iii, 1961, pp. 209–18, Paris.

F. M. CROSS, The Ancient Library of Qumrân and Modern Biblical Studies, 1958, London.

M. DELCOR, "Le Midrash d'Habacuc", in *Revue Biblique*, lviii, 1951, pp. 521–48, Paris.

—— Essai sur le Midrash d'Habacuc, 1951, Paris.

—— Contribution à l'étude de la législation des sectaires de Damas et de Qumrân, in *Revue Biblique*, lxi, 1954, pp. 533–53, lxii, 1955, pp. 60–75, Paris.

—— "Dix ans de travaux sur les manuscrits de Qumrân", in *Revue Thomiste*, lviii, 1958, pp. 734–79, lix, 1959, pp. 131–53, Paris.

H. E. DEL MEDICO, The Riddle of the Scrolls, Eng. trans. by H. Garner, 1958, London.

A. DUPONT-SOMMER, "Le Testament de Lévi (xvii–xviii) et la secte juive de l'Alliance", in *Semitica*, iv 1951–2, pp. 33–53, Paris.

—— The Dead Sea Scrolls, Eng. trans. by E. M. Rowley, 1952, Oxford.

—— The Jewish Sect of Qumran and the Essenes, Eng. trans. by R. D. Barnett, 1954, London.

—— The Essene Writings from Qumran, Eng. trans. by G. Vermes, 1961, Oxford.

O. EISSFELDT, "Der Anlass zur Entdeckung der Höhle und ihr ähnliche Vorgänge aus älterer Zeit", in *Theologische Literaturzeitung*, lxxiv, 1949, cols. 597–600, Berlin.

K. ELLIGER, Studien zum Habakuk-Kommentar vom Toten Meer, 1953, Tübingen.

E. E. ETTISCH, "Die Gemeinderegel und der Qumrankalender", in *Revue de Qumran*, iii, 1961, pp. 125–33, Paris.

C. T. FRITSCH, The Qumrān Community, 1956, New York.

T. H. GASTER, The Scriptures of the Dead Sea Sect, 1957, London.

H. GRESSMANN, Review of Schechter's Documents of Jewish Sectaries, in *Zeitschrift der deutschen morgenländischen Gesellschaft*, lvi, 1912, pp. 491–503, Leipzig.

W. GROSSOUW, "The Dead Sea Scrolls and the New Testament", in *Studia Catholica*, xxvi, 1951, pp. 289–99, xxvii, 1952, pp. 1–8, Nijmegen.

F. F. HVIDBERG, Menigheden af den Nye Pagt i Damascus, 1928, Copenhagen.

—— "Die 390 Jahre der sogenannte Damaskusschrift", in *Zeitschrift für die alttestamentliche Wissenschaft*, N.F. x, 1933, pp. 309–11, Giessen.

A. JAUBERT, "Le Calendrier des Jubilés et de la secte de Qumrân", in *Vetus Testamentum*, iii, 1953, pp. 250–64, Leiden.

—— "Jesus et le calendrier de Qumran", in *New Testament Studies*, vii, 1960–1, pp. 1–30, Cambridge.

K. G. KUHN, "The two Messiahs of Aaron and Israel", in K. Stendahl (ed.), The Scrolls and the New Testament, 1958, pp. 54–64, London.

M.-J. LAGRANGE, "La secte juive de la Nouvelle Alliance au pays de Damas", *Revue Biblique*, xxi (N.S. ix), 1912, pp. 213–40, 321–60.

W. S. LASOR, "The Messiahs of Aaron and Israel", in *Vetus Testamentum*, vi, 1956, pp. 425–9, Leiden.

—— Bibliography of the Dead Sea Scrolls, 1948–1957, 1958, Pasadena.

M. R. LEHMANN, "Ben Sira and the Qumran Literature", in *Revue de Qumran*, iii, 1961, pp. 102–16, Paris.

J. LIVER, "The Doctrine of the two Messiahs in Sectarian Literature in the time of the Second Commonwealth", in *Harvard Theological Review*, lii, 1959, pp. 149–85, Cambridge, Mass.

J. MAIER, Die Texte vom Toten Meer, 1960, Munich and Basel.

G. MARGOLIOUTH, "The two Zadokite Messiahs", in *Journal of Theological Studies*, xii, 1910–11, pp. 446–50, Oxford.

A. MARMORSTEIN, "Eine unbekannte jüdische Sekte", in *Theologisch Tijdschrift*, lii, 1918, pp. 92–122, Leiden.

E. MEYER, Die Gemeinde des Neuen Bundes im Lande Damaskus: eine jüdische Schrift aus der Seleukidenzeit, 1919, Berlin.

A. MICHEL, Le Maître de Justice, 1954, Avignon.

J. T. MILIK, "Elenchus textuum ex caverna Maris Mortui", in *Verbum Domini*, xxx, 1952, pp. 34–45, 101–9, Rome.

—— in "Le Travail d'édition des fragments manuscrits de Qumrân", in *Revue Biblique*, lxiii, 1956, pp. 60–2, Paris.

—— Ten Years of Discovery in the Wilderness of Judaea, Eng. trans. by J. Strugnell, 1958, London.

——, see also M. Baillet and D. Barthélemy.

G. F. MOORE, "The Covenanters of Damascus", in *Harvard Theological Review*, iv, 1911, pp. 330–77, Cambridge, Mass.

B. NOACK, "Qumran and The Book of Jubilees", in *Svensk exegetisk Årsbok*, xxii–xxiii, 1957–8, pp. 191–207, Lund.

F. NÖTSCHER, Zur theologischen Terminologie der Qumrantexte (Bonner Biblische Beiträge, x), 1956, Bonn.

—— Gotteswege und Menschenwege in der Bibel und in Qumran (Bonner Biblische Beiträge, xv), 1958, Bonn.

J. OBERMANN, "Calendaric Elements in the Dead Sea Scrolls", in *Journal of Biblical Literature*, lxxv, 1956, pp. 285–97, Philadelphia.

B. OTZEN, "Die neugefundenen hebräischen Sektenschriften und die Testamente der zwölf Patriarchen", in *Studia Theologica*, vii, 1953 (1954), pp. 125–44, Lund.

M. PHILONENKO, Les Interpolations chrétiennes des Testaments des douze Patriarches et les manuscrits de Qumrân, 1960, Paris.

J. F. PRIEST, "Mebaqqer, Paqid, and the Messiah", in *Journal of Biblical Literature*, lxxxi, 1962, pp. 55–61, Philadelphia.

C. RABIN, "The 'Teacher of Righteousness' in the 'Testaments of the Twelve Patriarchs'?", in *Journal of Jewish Studies*, iii, 1952, pp. 127 f., London.

—— The Zadokite Documents, 2nd ed., 1958, Oxford.

I. RABINOWITZ, "The Authorship, Audience and date of the de Vaux Fragment of an Unknown Work", in *Journal of Biblical Literature*, lxxi, 1952, pp. 19–32, Philadelphia.

—— "A Reconsideration of 'Damascus' and '390 years' in the 'Damascus' ('Zadokite') Fragments", in *Journal of Biblical Literature*, lxxiii, 1954, pp. 11–35, Philadelphia.

P. RABINOWITZ, "Sequence and Dates of the extra-Biblical Dead Sea Scroll Texts and 'Damascus' Fragments", in *Vetus Testamentum*, iii, 1953, pp. 175–85, Leiden.

L. ROST, Die Damaskusschrift, 1933, Berlin.

C. ROTH, The Historical Background of the Dead Sea Scrolls, 1958, Oxford.

H. H. ROWLEY, "The Internal Dating of the Dead Sea Scrolls", in *Ephemerides Theologicae Lovanienses*, xxviii, 1952, pp. 257–76, Louvain.

—— "The Covenanters of Damascus and the Dead Sea Scrolls," in *Bulletin of the John Rylands Library*, xxxv, 1952–3, pp. 111–54, Manchester.

—— The Zadokite Fragments and the Dead Sea Scrolls, 1952, Oxford.

—— "The Kittim and the Dead Sea Scrolls", in *Palestine Exploration Quarterly*, lxxxviii, 1956, pp. 92–109, London.

—— Jewish Apocalyptic and the Dead Sea Scrolls, 1957, London.

—— "Some Traces of the History of the Qumran Sect", in *Theologische Zeitschrift*, xiii, 1957, pp. 530–40, Basel.

—— "The 390 Years of the Zadokite Work", in Mélanges Bibliques (Robert Festschrift), 1957, pp. 341–7, Paris.

—— "The Teacher of Righteousness and the Dead Sea Scrolls", in *Bulletin of the John Rylands Library*, xl, 1957–8, pp. 114–46, Manchester.

—— The Dead Sea Scrolls from Qumran, 1958, Southampton.

—— "The Qumran Sect and Christian Origins", in *Bulletin of the John Rylands Library*, xliv, 1961–2, pp. 119–56, Manchester, and in From Moses to Qumran, 1963, pp. 239–79, London.

H. J. SCHOEPS, "Der Habakuk-Kommentar von 'Ain Feshkha —ein Dokument der Hasmonäischen Spätzeit", in *Zeitschrift für die alttestamentliche Wissenschaft*, lxiii, 1951, pp. 249–58, Berlin.

—— "Handelt es sich wirklich um ebionitische Dokumente?", in *Zeitschrift für Religions- und Geistesgeschichte*, iii, 1951, pp. 322–36, Erlangen.

J. SCHOUSBOE, La Secte juive de l'Alliance Nouvelle au pays de Damas et le Christianisme naissant, 1942, Copenhagen.

K. SCHUBERT, "Der Sektenkanon von En Feshcha und die Anfänge der jüdischen Gnosis", in *Theologische Literaturzeitung*, lxxviii, 1953, cols. 495–506, Berlin.

M. H. SEGAL, "The Habakkuk 'Commentary' and the Damascus Fragments", in *Journal of Biblical Literature*, lxx, 1951, pp. 131–47, Philadelphia.

E. STAUFFER, "Zur Fruhdatierung des Habakukmidrasch", in *Theologische Literaturzeitung*, lxxvi, 1951, cols. 667–74, Berlin.

A. STROBEL, "Zur Funktionsfähigkeit des essenischen Kalenders", in *Revue de Qumran*, iii, 1961, pp. 395–412, Paris.

J. STRUGNELL, "The Angelic Liturgy at Qumran—4 Q Serek šîrôt 'ôlat haššabbāt", in Congress Volume, Oxford, 1959 (Supplements to *Vetus Testamentum*, vii), 1960, pp. 318–45, Leiden.

E. L. SUKENIK, The Dead Sea Scrolls of the Hebrew University, 1955, Jerusalem.

E. F. SUTCLIFFE, The Monks of Qumran, 1960, London.

S. TALMON, "The Calendar Reckoning of the Sect from the Judaean Desert", in Aspects of the Dead Sea Scrolls (Scripta Hierosolymitana, iv), 1958, pp. 162–99, Jerusalem.

J. L. TEICHER, "The Damascus Fragments and the Origin of the Jewish Christian Sect", in *Journal of Jewish Studies*, ii, 1950–1, pp. 115–43, London.

—— "The Teaching of the pre-Pauline Church in the Dead Sea Scrolls", *ibid.*, iii, 1952, pp. 111–18, 139–50, iv, 1953, pp. 1–13, 49–58, 93–103, 153.

M. TREVES, "The Two Spirits in the Rule of the Community", in *Revue de Qumran*, iii, 1961, pp. 449–52, Paris.

R. DE VAUX, "À propos des manuscrits de la Mer Morte", in *Revue Biblique*, lvii, 1950, pp. 417–29, Paris.

—— L'Archéologie et les manuscrits de la Mer Morte (Schweich Lectures), 1961, London.

—— see also M Baillet.

G. VERMES, The Dead Sea Scrolls in English, 1962, Harmonds-worth.

W. H. WARD, "The Zadokite Document", in *Bibliotheca Sacra*, lxviii, 1911, pp. 429–56, Oberlin.

P. WERNBERG-MØLLER, "A Reconsideration of the Two Spirits in the Rule of the Community", in *Revue de Qumran*, iii, 1961, pp. 412–41, Paris.

E. WIESENBERG, "Chronological Data in the Zadokite Fragments", in *Vetus Testamentum*, v, 1955, pp. 284–308, Leiden.

A. S. VAN DER WOUDE, Die messianischen Vorstellungen der Gemeinde von Qumrân, 1957, Assen.

Y. YADIN, The Message of the Scrolls, 1957, London.

—— The Scroll of the War of the Sons of Light against the Sons of Darkness, Eng. trans. by B. and C. Rabin, 1962, Oxford.

——, *see also* N. Avigad.

INDEX

(a) Subjects

AARON and Israel, Messiah from, 82 f., 91 f.

Abed-nego, 183

Abel, enthroned, 128; murdered, 97

Abomination of desolation, 52, 131 ff.

Abraham, death of, 128 f.; resurrection of, 73

Abraham: Apocalypse of, 126 ff.; contents of, 126 f.; date of, 126; imminence of end of age in, 128; Jaoel and Azazel in, 127; judgement in, 127; Messiah in, 128

Abraham: Testament of, 128 f.; date and character of, 128; judgement in, 128 f.; no background of crisis in, 129; no Messiah in, 129; Second Advent in, 129; seven world ages in, 129

Adam and Eve: life of, 113 f., 122; date of, 113; Golden Age in, 114; judgement in, 114; Messiah in, 114; two forms of, 113

Advent, Second, 129, 133 f., 135 ff., 163 ff.

Ahab, 17, 43

Ahaz, 17

Ahura Mazda, 43

Alexander the Great, 45; and Gog, 36

Alexander Jannaeus, 59, 95

Alexandria, 45 f.

Allat, 49

Amesha Spentas, 43

Angelic Liturgy, 92

Angelology: of Daniel, 56 f.; of Jubilees, 67 f.; of Qumran Scrolls, 92; of Testaments, 73; Persian influence on, 43, 57

Angels, Fallen, 57 f., 63, 97, 112, 171 f.; and Antiochus IV, 97

Angra Mainyu, 43, 73

Antichrist, 35 n., 171 f.; and Antiochus IV, 33 f.; and Persian thought, 43; collective roots of concept, 34 f.; Dan and, 73; development of idea of, 33 ff.; duration of reign of, in Ascension of Isaiah, 159 f.; in Ascension of Isaiah, 124 f.; in 2 Baruch, 121; in Ezekiel, 35 ff.; in

4 Ezra, 115; in Revelation, 144 f., 146 f.; in Sibylline Oracles, 77; in Testaments, 72 f.; meaning of, 174

Antiochus III, 44

Antiochus IV (Epiphanes), 30, 59, 73, 95, 146, 154, 172 f.; and abomination of desolation, 52, 130 f.; and Antichrist, 37 f.; and calendar, 102; and circumcision, 104; and Gog, 36; and Rome, 47 f.; and stories of Daniel, 50 f.; and sabbath, 104; Daniel and, 55; hellenizing policy of, 47 ff.; mixed roots of revolt against, 18 f.; persecution of, 96 f.; seized throne, 45

Antiochus V (Eupator), 36

Antipater, 82

Apocalypse of Abraham, see Abraham, Apocalypse of

Apocalypse of Baruch, see 2 Baruch

Apocalypse of Gospels, Little, 129 ff., 160 ff.; abomination of desolation in, 131 ff.; and Little Apocalypse theory, 130 n.; authenticity of, 160 ff.; date of, 133 n.; in circulation separately?, 131; pseudonymous?, 130 f., 134 n.; Second Advent in, 133 f., 135 ff.; source of, 160 ff.; unity of, 162 f.

Apocalypse of Isaiah, 25 f.

Apocalypse of Moses, 65

Apocalypse of Weeks, see Weeks, Apocalypse of

Apocalypse of Zephaniah, see Zephaniah, Apocalypse of

Apocalyptic, passim; addressed to loyal, 23; and eschatology, 25, 26 n., 54; and prophecy, 15 f.; and pseudonymity, 38 ff.; canonical works not puzzles for ingenious, 13 f.; child of prophecy, 15; contemporary message of, 16; Daniel first great work of, 43 f.; difference from prophecy of form of, 39; Egyptian, 162; enduring message of, 166 ff.; esoteric character of, 16, 42, 119, 131; Greek influence on, 15 n.; influence of foreign thought

(b) Authors

(c) Texts